UNITED NATIONS CONFERENCE ON TRADE A

REVIEW OF MARITIME TRANSPORT

2019

UNITED NATIONS

Geneva, 2019

United Nations Publications

300 East 42nd Street

New York, New York 10017

United States of America

Email: publications@un.org

Website: un.org/publications

The designations employed and the presentation of material on any map in this work do not imply the expression of any opinion whatsoever on the part of the United Nations concerning the legal status of any country, territory, city or area or of its authorities, or concerning the delimitation of its frontiers or boundaries.

Mention of any firm or licensed process does not imply the endorsement of the United Nations.

United Nations publication issued by the United Nations Conference on Trade and Development

UNCTAD/RMT/2019

ISBN 978-92-1-112958-8

eISBN 978-92-1-004302-1

ISSN 0566-7682

eISSN 2225-3459

Sales No. E.19.II.D.20

ACKNOWLEDGEMENTS

The *Review of Maritime Transport 2019* was prepared by UNCTAD under the overall guidance of Shamika N. Sirimanne, Director of the Division on Technology and Logistics of UNCTAD, and under the coordination of Jan Hoffmann, Chief of the Trade Logistics Branch. Administrative support and formatting were provided by Wendy Juan. Regina Asariotis, Mark Assaf, Gonzalo Ayala, Hassiba Benamara, Dominique Chantrel, Jan Hoffmann, Anila Premti, Luisa Rodríguez and Frida Youssef were contributing authors.

The publication was edited by the Intergovernmental Support Service of UNCTAD. Magali Studer designed the cover and prepared the layout.

Comments and input provided by the following reviewers are gratefully acknowledged: Hashim Abbas, Niklas Bengtsson, Johannah Christensen, Trevor Crowe, Neil Davidson, Mahin Faghfouri, Beatriz García, Frederik Haag, Max Johns, Mikael Lind, John Mangan, Carlos Daniel Martner Peyrelongue, James Milne, Yasmina Rauber, Jean-Paul Rodrigue, Satya Sahoo, Ruvarashe Samkange, Antonella Teodoro and Richard Watts.

Comments received from other UNCTAD divisions as part of the internal peer review process, as well as comments from the Office of the Secretary-General, are also acknowledged with appreciation.

Thanks are also due to Vladislav Shuvalov for reviewing the publication in full.

TABLE OF CONTENTS

Tables

Figures

Boxes

ABBREVIATIONS

ASEAN	Association of Southeast Asian Nations
BIMCO	Baltic and International Maritime Council
COSCO	China Ocean Shipping Company
dwt	dead-weight ton(s)
e-commerce	electronic commerce
FEU	40-foot equivalent unit
GDP	gross domestic product
IBM	International Business Machines
IMO	International Maritime Organization
MARPOL	International Convention for the Prevention of Pollution from Ships
ONE	Ocean Network Express
TEU	20-foot equivalent unit
UNEP	United Nations Environment Programme

NOTE

The *Review of Maritime Transport* is a recurrent publication prepared by the UNCTAD secretariat since 1968 with the aim of fostering the transparency of maritime markets and analysing relevant developments. Any factual or editorial corrections that may prove necessary, based on comments made by Governments, will be reflected in a corrigendum to be issued subsequently.

This edition of the Review covers data and events from January 2018 until June 2019. Where possible, every effort has been made to reflect more recent developments.

All references to dollars ($) are to United States dollars, unless otherwise stated.

"Ton" means metric ton (1,000 kg) and "mile" means nautical mile, unless otherwise stated.

Because of rounding, details and percentages presented in tables do not necessarily add up to the totals.

Two dots (..) in a statistical table indicate that data are not available or are not reported separately.

All websites were accessed in September 2019.

The terms "countries" and "economies" refer to countries, territories or areas.

Since 2014, the *Review of Maritime Transport* does not include printed statistical annexes. Instead, UNCTAD has expanded the coverage of statistical data online via the following links:

Overview: http://stats.unctad.org/maritime

Seaborne trade: http://stats.unctad.org/seabornetrade

Merchant fleet by flag of registration: http://stats.unctad.org/fleet

Merchant fleet by country of ownership: http://stats.unctad.org/fleetownership

National maritime country profiles: http://unctadstat.unctad.org/CountryProfile/en-GB/index.html

Shipbuilding by country in which built: http://stats.unctad.org/shipbuilding

Ship scrapping by country of demolition: http://stats.unctad.org/shipscrapping

Liner shipping connectivity index: http://stats.unctad.org/lsci

Liner shipping bilateral connectivity index: http://stats.unctad.org/lsbci

Container port throughput: http://stats.unctad.org/teu

Vessel groupings used in the *Review of Maritime Transport*

Group	Constituent ship types
Oil tankers	Oil tankers
Bulk carriers	Bulk carriers, combination carriers
General cargo ships	Multi-purpose and project vessels, roll-on roll-off (ro-ro) cargo, general cargo
Container ships	Fully cellular container ships
Other ships	Liquefied petroleum gas carriers, liquefied natural gas carriers, parcel (chemical) tankers, specialized tankers, reefers, offshore supply vessels, tugboats, dredgers, cruise, ferries, other non-cargo ships
Total all ships	Includes all the above-mentioned vessel types

Approximate vessel-size groups according to commonly used shipping terminology

Crude oil tankers	
Very large crude carrier	200,000 dead-weight tons (dwt) and above
Suezmax crude tanker	120,000–200,000 dwt
Aframax crude tanker	80,000–119,999 dwt
Panamax crude tanker	60,000–79,999 dwt
Dry bulk and ore carriers	
Capesize bulk carrier	100,000 dwt and above
Panamax bulk carrier	65,000–99,999 dwt
Handymax bulk carrier	40,000–64,999 dwt
Handysize bulk carrier	10,000–39,999 dwt
Container ships	
Neo-Panamax	Ships that can transit the expanded locks of the Panama Canal with up to a maximum 49m beam and 366 m length overall
Panamax	Container ships above 3,000 20-foot equivalent units (TEUs) with a beam below 33.2 m, i.e. the largest size vessels that can transit the old locks of the Panama Canal

Source: Clarksons Research.

Note: Unless otherwise indicated, the ships mentioned in the Review of Maritime Transport include all propelled seagoing merchant vessels of 100 gross tons and above, excluding inland waterway vessels, fishing vessels, military vessels, yachts, and fixed and mobile offshore platforms and barges (with the exception of floating production storage and offloading units and drill-ships).

EXECUTIVE SUMMARY

Global maritime trade expanded at a slower pace in 2018, while volumes reached 11 billion tons

Reflecting developments in the world economy and trade activity, international maritime trade lost momentum in 2018. Volumes expanded at 2.7 per cent in 2018, down from 4.1 per cent in 2017. The slowdown was broad-based and affected nearly all maritime cargo segments. It undermined global port cargo-handling activities, and growth in containerized global port throughput decelerated to 4.7 per cent, down from 6.7 per cent in 2017.

A range of downside risks that had intensified in 2018 contributed to the slowdown in maritime trade growth. Trade tensions and protectionism topped the list, followed by the decision by the United Kingdom of Great Britain and Northern Ireland to leave the European Union ("Brexit"); the economic transition in China; geopolitical turmoil; and supply-side disruptions, such as those occurring in the oil sector. Country-specific developments, including recessions in some emerging economies, weakness in industrial sectors across many regions, a slowdown in China and weaker import demand in both developed and developing countries, also hindered growth. Despite the setbacks, a milestone was reached in 2018, with total volumes amounting to 11 billion tons.

Further growth is projected amid heightened uncertainty and varied downside risks

UNCTAD expects international maritime trade to expand at an average annual growth rate of 3.5 per cent over the 2019–2024 period, driven in particular by growth in containerized, dry bulk and gas cargoes. However, uncertainty remains an overriding theme in the current maritime transport environment, with risks tilted to the downside.

In addition to heightened trade tensions between China and the United States of America, growth in maritime trade is also being affected by developments in market segments that suffered some setbacks earlier in 2019. These include disruptions to iron-ore trade caused by *Cyclone Veronica* in Australia and the severe repercussions of the Vale dam incident in Brazil. Crude oil shipments from the Atlantic basin to Asia are expected to support tanker trade volumes, while sanctions affecting the Islamic Republic of Iran and the Bolivarian Republic of Venezuela, as well as effective compliance with production cuts imposed by the Organization of the Petroleum Exporting Countries, are likely to put further pressure on tanker trade.

Some positive developments in the offing may help offset current pressure on maritime trade. These include the Belt and Road Initiative of China, new bilateral and regional trade agreements, and potential opportunities stemming from the global energy transition, such as the growing gas trade.

Trade tension: A major risk to maritime trade causing disruption to supply chains

Tariff escalation between China and the United States dominated the headlines in 2018 and early 2019. Nearly 2 per cent of world maritime trade volume is estimated to be affected by tariff hikes applied in September 2018 and May and June 2019. Exposure varies by cargo type and market segment. Grain, containerized trade and steel products stand to be affected the most, reflecting the structure of trade between China and the United States. In addition to reducing trade flows, tariffs are generating winners and losers, given product and supplier substitution and trade diversion effects.

For example, soybean exports from Brazil to China, which surged in 2018, displaced shipments from the United States and brought about additional ton-mile shipping demand. Supply chain disruptions have also been observed and could deepen if trade tensions and tariffs are prolonged. Some China-based manufacturing activity is reported to have already moved to new locations in East Asia.

Overreliance on import demand in China: Another downside risk for maritime trade

As the world's factory, China is a key player in dry bulk and containerized trade, accounting for nearly half of global maritime trade growth in the past decade. In 2018, maritime imports from China were estimated at one fourth of maritime trade worldwide. In this context, the outlook for such trade is highly dependent on developments in the Chinese economy. A reduction in iron ore and coal imports into China have had an adverse effect on trade in dry bulk, the mainstay of global maritime trade for about two decades. A tapering in the country's dry bulk import demand reflects its recent reform agenda, promoting a shift from investment-led growth and manufacturing towards consumer spending and services.

A "new normal" in maritime trade: Reshaping the future of the sector

A new normal in the sector appears to be taking hold, reflecting moderated growth in the global economy and trade. It is characterized by the following trends: a supply chain restructuring in favour of more regionalized trade flows, a continued rebalancing in the economy of China, a larger role played by technology and services in value chains and logistics, intensified and more frequent natural disasters and climate-related disruptions, and an accelerated environmental sustainability agenda with an increased awareness of the impact of global warming.

The new landscape is also being defined by recent supply-side trends. Carriers are increasingly eying growth prospects associated with a wider range of services, including landside operations. Ports and shipping interests are focusing attention on inland logistics with additional revenue-generation potential. In addition, efforts by carriers to become freight integrators and action by some major global container lines to acquire regional carriers could be indicative of the industry's endeavours to adapt to changing conditions.

Sustained consolidation and vertical integration in container shipping and port performance

Owing to further consolidation in the container shipping segment, the combined market share of the top 10 container shipping lines increased from 68 per cent in 2014 to 90 per cent in 2019. In addition, deployed capacity rose during the same period from about 55 million to 96 million 20-foot equivalent units (TEUs) on the three major East–West container routes. In other markets, too, such as islands in the Caribbean Sea, the Indian Ocean and the Pacific Ocean, fewer operators were carrying higher volumes.

In 2018 and 2019, several alliances and joint ventures were established between terminal operators, as well as between liner companies and terminal operators, to engage in the joint operation of berths. Vertical integration and the further expansion of shipping lines into terminal operations can affect competition and choices for shippers. National competition authorities, regulators and port authorities should carefully monitor markets and evaluate alternative options when granting container terminal concessions to private operators, taking into account vertical and horizontal market integration.

Oversupply of vessels despite decline in fleet growth

Oversupply remained a prominent characteristic of most shipping segments. In early 2019, total world fleet capacity stood at 1.97 billion dead-weight tons (dwt), equivalent to 2.61 per cent growth – the slowest growth of the decade. Gas carriers experienced the highest growth (7.25 per cent during the 12 months to January 2019), mainly due to significant expansion in the liquefied natural gas sector. This trend can be expected to continue in view of mounting environmental concerns and pressure on the maritime sector to switch to cleaner fuels. The world container fleet also continued to increase (5 per cent). In comparison, the chemical-tanker and dry-bulk-carrier segments registered stable growth, and the oil tanker segment underwent a downward trend.

Bulk carriers recorded the highest level of ship deliveries, representing 26.7 per cent of total gross tonnage built in 2018, followed by oil tankers (25 per cent), container ships (23.5 per cent) and gas carriers (13 per cent). Since 2014, there has been a trend towards an increased number of container-ship and gas-carrier newbuildings, compared with the number of newbuildings of oil tankers and dry bulk carriers, which has decreased. This can be attributed to greater demand for container ships of large capacity (above 15,000 TEUs) and less demand for oil tankers and bulk carriers as a result of the existing oversupply in those segments. In 2018, China, Japan and the Republic of Korea maintained their traditional leadership in global shipbuilding, representing together 90 per cent of all shipbuilding activity. China alone accounted for 40 per cent of the activity, while Japan and the Republic of Korea boasted shares of 25 per cent each. To cope with declining orders, the shipbuilding sector has been undergoing reforms and has witnessed consolidation and increased government support.

In 2018, most of the tonnage sold for demolition were oil tankers from Bangladesh, India, Pakistan and Turkey. Traditionally, China, India and Turkey have headed the list but their market shares decreased in 2018. Recent regulatory developments and voluntary initiatives of industry to make ship recycling safer and more environmentally friendly may explain these trends.

Container shipping: Market imbalances and pressures on rates from trade tensions and new air-emission control regulations

The year 2018 witnessed a mixed performance in container freight rates. Weak trade growth and the sustained delivery of mega container ships exerted further pressure on freight rates in the first half of the year. There was a temporary surge in late 2018, triggered by an increase in shipments from China to the United States, before the potential application of higher tariffs on Chinese imports. Overall, container fleet supply capacity rose by 6 per cent in 2018, surpassing 2.6 per cent growth in containerized seaborne trade.

In 2019, the temporary withdrawal of ships to allow the installation of scrubbers on board somewhat reduced the oversupply of capacity. In the medium term, however, intensified trade tensions, combined with the challenges and additional costs of complying with the new 2020 regulation of the International Maritime Organization (IMO) on sulphur fuel limits, will have an impact on market fundamentals.

Environmental sustainability and the maritime industry

In recent years, environmental sustainability has become a major policy concern in global maritime transport. Environmentally driven regulations are increasingly affecting shipping market dynamics. In 2018, fuel economy and environmental sustainability were burning issues, and this trend will continue in 2019 and beyond.

The new IMO 2020 regulation, bringing the sulphur cap in fuel oil for ships down from 3.50 per cent to 0.50 per cent, is expected to bring significant benefits for human health and the environment. The regulation will enter into force on 1 January 2020. Enforcement, compliance with and monitoring of the new sulphur limit is the responsibility of States party to the International Convention for the Prevention of Pollution from Ships (MARPOL), 1973, as modified by the Protocol of 1978 (MARPOL 73/78), annex VI. Ships found to be not in compliance may be detained by port State control inspectors, and/or sanctions may be imposed for violations. An additional amendment to MARPOL 73/78 will enter into force on 1 March 2020. The amendment will prohibit not only the use, but also the carriage of non-compliant fuel oil for combustion purposes for propulsion or operation on board a ship, unless it is fitted with a scrubber, which is an exhaust-gas cleaning system.

The entry into force of the IMO 2020 regulation raises fresh challenges for the shipping industry. Potential issues may include an increase in operating fuel costs and price volatility, and a reduction in supply capacity and vessel availability. Any additional costs may have an impact on the price to be paid by end users, as carriers will seek to pass on increased costs to shippers through various forms, including new bunker surcharge formulas.

With regard to combating ship-source pollution and the proliferation of invasive alien species, an important development was the entry into force in 2017 of the International Convention for the Control and Management of Ships' Ballast Water and Sediments, 2004. In this respect, the current focus of international efforts is on the effective and uniform implementation of the Convention, and on an associated experience-building phase, during which data on its application will be gathered. Another potentially important international legal instrument which, however, has not yet entered into force, is the International Convention on Liability and Compensation for Damage in Connection with the Carriage of Hazardous and Noxious Substances by Sea, 1996, as amended by the 2010 Protocol thereto. Entry into force of the 2010 Convention would address an important regulatory gap, complementing the international regime for liability and compensation for ship-source oil pollution, and could provide significant benefits to coastal States that are exposed to potential accidents and pollution incidents. However, as of July 2019, the 2010 Convention had been ratified by only five States. With the number of ships carrying hazardous and noxious substances growing steadily, and more than 200 million tons of chemicals traded annually, other countries, including developing countries, are encouraged to consider becoming parties to the Convention.

The entry into force of several global environmental instruments and voluntary standards being adopted in the sector has also had an impact on shipbuilding and shipyards, as they are responsible for incorporating new standards into the design and construction of ships. Pressure on the industry to develop cleaner and energy-efficient vessels is increasing. Certification schemes are being introduced, and considerable investment is going into the development of better hydrodynamics, more energy-efficient engines and low-carbon fuels for ships.

Greater interlinkages between oceans, climate change and sustainable development

A number of international developments continued to contribute to the implementation of the 2030 Agenda for Sustainable Development, the Paris Agreement under the United Nations Framework Convention on Climate Change and the Sendai Framework for Disaster Risk Reduction 2015–2030. Together, these instruments provide the foundation for sustainable, low-carbon and resilient development in a changing climate.

Of note are the following developments: the Katowice climate package, adopted by the twenty-fourth session of the Conference of the Parties to the United Nations Framework Convention on Climate Change in Katowice, Poland, in December 2018, which aims to promote international cooperation and encourage greater ambition for implementing the Paris Agreement; the United Nations Climate Action Summit, held in New York, United States in September 2019 with a view to boosting political and economic efforts to strengthen climate action and ambition on a global scale; ongoing work at IMO towards setting emissions-reduction targets in line with the Paris Agreement; and the initiation of the fourth IMO greenhouse gas study.

The call to global climate action by civil society and industry leaders at the Global Climate Action Summit held in San Francisco, United States in September 2018 further highlights the interlinkages between oceans, sustainable development and climate change mitigation and adaptation. Further, there is a growing recognition – implicit in General Assembly resolution 72/73 of 5 December 2017 proclaiming the United Nations Decade of Ocean Science for Sustainable Development, 2021–2030 – that ocean science will be key in developing effective measures for coastal protection and coastal zone management, as well as climate-risk assessment, adaptation and resilience-building for seaports and other coastal transport infrastructure.

Port indicators: Analysing the linkages between port performance and maritime trade

More and more, ports are expected to align their performance with sustainability considerations. As a result, they must rethink their strategies and operations in an environment of increased scrutiny of action taken to reduce externalities. At the same time, protecting ports from the impact of climate change and variability is crucial. The implementation of activities and measures that can support the shift to greener and more sustainable ports will have cost implications and will require further funding, the development of new capabilities and the promotion of new technologies and their transfer, especially to developing countries.

In 2018, ships spent a median time of 23.5 hours in port. In particular, dry bulk carriers spent 2.05 days in port, while container ships spent 0.7 days. A typical ship call had a turnaround time of 0.97 days. A shorter time in port is a positive indicator of the level of port efficiency and trade competitiveness. The countries with longer turnaround times are mostly developing countries or least developed countries. By contrast, the economies with the shortest turnaround times are mostly advanced economies with large port traffic volumes (for example, Singapore, dry bulk vessels) or very small economies that handle low cargo volumes at each port call (for example, the Faroe Islands and Saint Vincent and the Grenadines, container ships). Other examples include a few developing countries such as China (container ships) and Peru (liquid bulk carriers).

To minimize ship time in ports – for a given volume of cargo handled – ports, maritime authorities and policymakers may wish to adopt a multipronged approach featuring the following measures: port call optimization (ships should only arrive when they need to arrive, as arriving too early implies additional costs in port, as well as extra expenditures and more pollution, including air emissions); trade and transport facilitation (once a ship arrives at the pier, operations should start immediately, without having to wait for authorities to clear paperwork or carry out other procedures); and port operations (fast and reliable loading and unloading operations require investment in infrastructure and superstructures, as well as technological and human capacities).

Train for Trade Port Management Programme: Experiences and lessons learned

Experiences from the UNCTAD Train for Trade Port Management Programme offer further insights into the financial performance of ports. Traditional revenue profiles in ports have relied heavily on the dues charged to ship and cargo owners, usually through agents. This revenue stream is required to build and maintain port infrastructure for vessels and for cargo handling. Other revenue streams would consist of rent on storage sites and the provision of services such as tugboats and pilot boats. Data from the members of the Programme suggest that port dues are the largest generator of revenue. However, the trend towards privatization, which began in the 1980s, introduced a new category and growing source of revenue – concession fees. The level of concessions is higher in large ports with significant container operations.

Environmental reporting is becoming increasingly important for ports in the face of growing environmental concerns and stakeholder pressure from market players, public bodies and social interest groups. Ports account for environmental spending in different ways. Some record specific costs, while for many, the environmental portion of a project is embedded in the overall costs. This applies to both capital and operating costs. Data from the Train for Trade Port Management Programme indicate that large ports in Europe record such performance indicators. Feedback received from ports suggests the need to establish a common basis for recording and a basis for comparison against a benchmark value of appropriate spending.

UNCTAD liner shipping connectivity index: Measuring the positions of countries and ports in global liner shipping networks

According to the liner shipping connectivity index developed by UNCTAD, 5 of the top 10 most connected economies are in Asia, 4 are in Europe and 1 is in North America. Since 2006, the most connected country – China – has improved its index by 51 per cent. The average index has gone up by 24 per cent, and the lowest index of 2019 was below the lowest index of 2006. A comparison of the most and least connected countries shows a growing connectivity divide. In 2006, the least connected countries, which included several small island developing States, saw very little improvement during the period – trade in shipped goods remains problematic in those countries, with economic knock-on effects.

The Pacific Island economies are among those with the lowest container shipping connectivity. Port Vila, Vanuatu, for example, receives about one container ship every three days. Only four companies provide regular shipping services to the country. On Kiribati, only one operator offers regular liner shipping services, with one ship arriving about every 10 days, connecting the island to only four other ports. While most other regions in the world have experienced improved connectivity, Pacific small island developing States have not undergone any fundamental improvements. They are confronted with a vicious cycle wherein low trade volumes discourage shipping companies and ports from investing in better maritime transport connectivity; faced with low shipping connectivity, trade in goods becomes costly and uncompetitive.

The most connected ports in Africa are in Egypt, Morocco and South Africa, on the edges of the continent, connecting North–South and East–West shipping routes. Western Africa has relatively low connectivity, as its geographical position does not link it to any major North–South or East–West shipping routes. In Eastern Africa, the most connected port is Port Louis, Mauritius, providing trans-shipment services to other Eastern and Southern African ports. Mombasa, Kenya and Dar es Salaam, the United Republic of Tanzania have witnessed relatively stagnant connectivity. Both ports are important gateways to overseas trade in Eastern Africa, including the landlocked countries of Burundi, Rwanda and Uganda. Yet they are highly congested, limiting their potential for improved connectivity.

A country's geographical position is a given but maritime connectivity can be improved

Liner shipping connectivity can be improved at the port level. Port and shipping operations can tap into the opportunities offered by digitalization, artificial intelligence, the Internet of things and blockchain. Many technological advances are applicable in ports and terminals and represent an opportunity for port stakeholders to improve efficiency and enhance productivity, two important factors that influence port call selection. Several leading regional ports – for example, Rotterdam in Northern Europe, Cartagena in the wider Caribbean and Lomé in Western Africa – have also invested heavily in port community systems, port call optimization, automation and other technologies.

Easing restrictions that affect regional or domestic cabotage markets and limit the ability of shipping lines to expand the hinterland and consolidate cargo can also help improve connectivity. Ports should also aim to attract cargo from neighbouring countries. There is a common interest between many seaports and importers and exporters in neighbouring countries, in particular in landlocked countries. Transit facilitation and investment in corridors, regional trucking markets and cross-border trade can help in this respect.

Digitalization and automation: Transforming skills requirements in shipping

Further, digitalization and automation are transforming the shipping sector and requiring new skills. The latest technologies provide new opportunities to achieve greater sustainability in shipping and ports, as well as enhanced performance and efficiency. Digitalization and joint collaborative platforms and solutions enabled by new technologies and innovations, including blockchain, are being increasingly used by the shipping industry, transforming business and partnership models. The aim is to promote efficient and secure trade, including by offering greater supply-chain visibility and use of electronic documents, ultimately benefitting customers who rely on shipping industry services.

Importantly, autonomous ships, also known as maritime autonomous surface ships, may soon become a reality, holding out the promise of enhanced safety and cost savings by removing the human element from certain operations. However, before autonomous ships start to be fully used in commercial operations, the technology needs to be proven, and appropriate institutional and regulatory safeguards and frameworks should be developed.

Currently applicable maritime laws and regulations operate on the assumption of having a master and crew on board the ship. In autonomous shipping, the traditional roles of the master and crew on board, as well as the role of artificial intelligence and of remote-control crew working ashore, will need to be assessed and (re)defined. Important international regulatory developments include an ongoing scoping exercise, initiated at IMO in 2017, for the review of relevant legal instruments, to ensure the safe design, construction and operation of autonomous ships, and to make certain that the legal framework provides autonomous ships with the same levels of protection as conventional ships.

With the spread of digitalization and automation in the shipping industry, the requirements and skills needed for individual jobs will change. In particular, an increase in shore-based jobs and reductions in the number of crew on board vessels might be expected. New and different skills and knowledge, especially in relation to information technology, will be required from seafarers if they are to assume the redefined roles on board and ashore that will be necessary to ensure the safety of vessels and efficiency of operations. In addition, women may enjoy increased opportunities to pursue a maritime career, given that less physically strenuous tasks, combined with the need for more information technology skills and knowledge, are being required in the maritime sector.

1

INTERNATIONAL MARITIME TRADE AND PORT TRAFFIC

World maritime trade lost momentum in 2018, with volumes expanding at 2.7 per cent, below the historical averages of 3.0 per cent and 4.1 per cent recorded in 2017. Total volumes are estimated to have reached 11 billion tons, an all-time high, according to UNCTAD records. UNCTAD is projecting 2.6 per cent growth in 2019 and an annual average growth rate of 3.4 per cent for the period 2019–2024. However, the outlook remains challenging, given the heightened uncertainty regarding trade policy and wide-ranging downside risks clouding the horizon.

In 2018, world merchandise trade growth decelerated at an unexpected rate, and tariffs on trade between China and the United States of America escalated amid mounting trade tensions and a proliferation of national trade-restrictive measures. Apart from trade policy crosscurrents, geopolitics and sanctions, environmental concerns, fuel economics and tensions involving the Strait of Hormuz – a strategic maritime chokepoint – were in the headlines.

Other forces at work continued to slowly reshape the maritime transport landscape. A new normal, contrasting with the historical perspective, appears to be taking hold. This trend is characterized by overall moderate growth in the global economy and trade, a supply chain restructuring in favour of more regionalized trade flows, a continued rebalancing of the Chinese economy, a larger role of technology and services in value chains and logistics, intensified and more frequent natural disasters and climate-related disruptions, and an accelerated environmental sustainability agenda with an increased awareness of the impact of global warming.

A transition to the new normal calls for an improved understanding of the main issues at stake, better planning, and flexible and forward-looking-policies that can effectively anticipate change and enable appropriate response measures that take into account the heterogenous nature of developing countries as a group and their varied local conditions and needs.

WORLD MARITIME TRADE AND PORT TRAFFIC

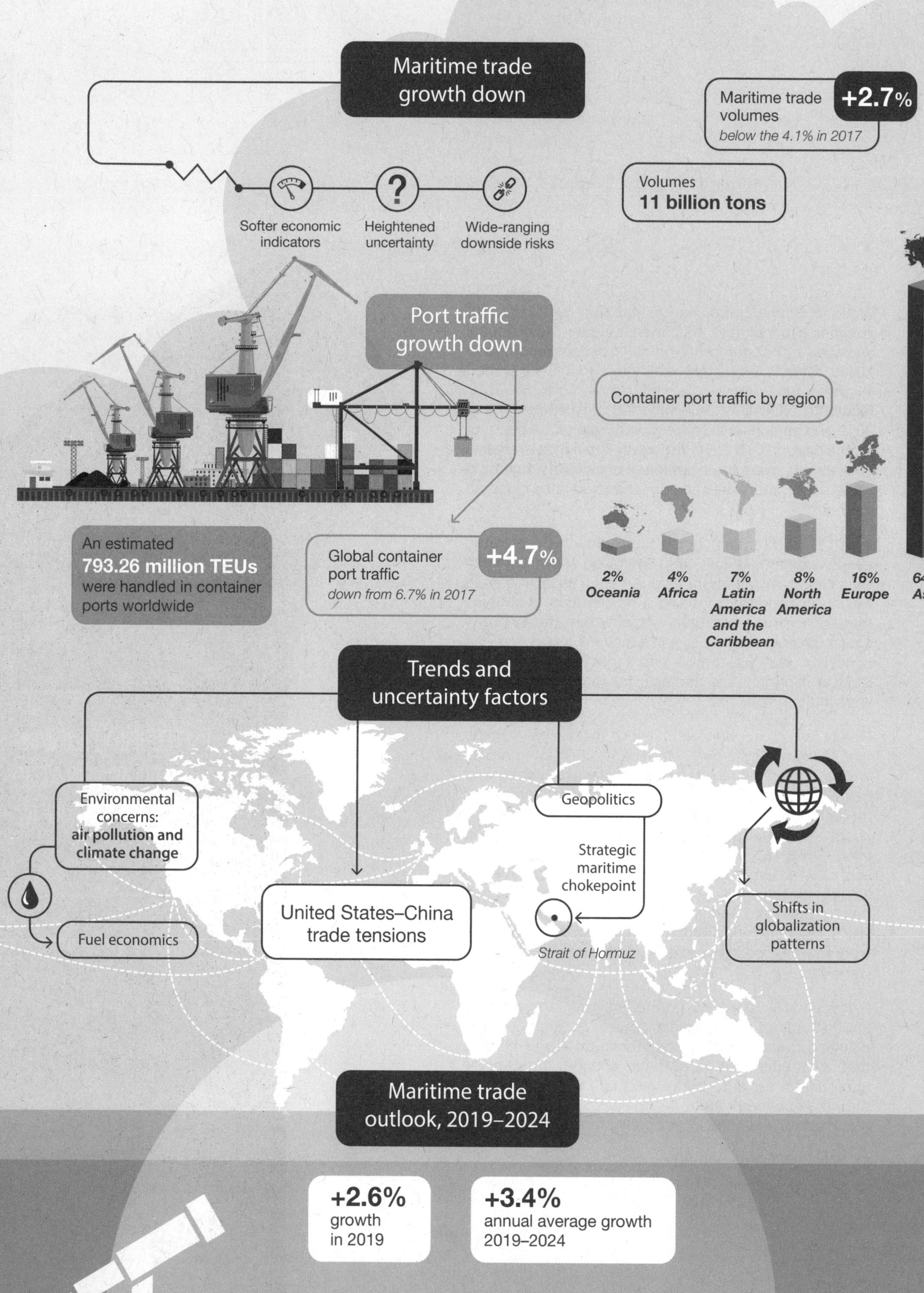

A. TRENDS IN MARITIME TRADE FLOWS

The present chapter considers developments shaping global demand for maritime transport and services. More specifically, sections A and B review trends in the global economy, merchandise trade, maritime cargo flows and container port cargo-handling activity. Section C discusses the outlook for maritime trade, puts forward some considerations and highlights potential action areas for policymakers and stakeholders in maritime transport.

1. Global economic growth in 2018 and 2019

Global economic growth dipped in 2018 and is expected to decline further in 2019. After reaching 3.1 per cent in 2017, growth in world gross domestic product (GDP) remained steady but edged down to 3.0 per cent in 2018, below the historical average recorded between 1994 and 2008 (table 1.1). Fiscally induced growth in the United States helped to somewhat offset weak performance in Argentina, China, the Islamic Republic of Iran, Japan, Turkey and the European Union.

Global growth slowed down abruptly during the fourth quarter of 2018, reflecting in part recessions in some emerging economies and weakness in industrial sectors across many regions. Global industrial production – a leading indicator of demand for maritime transport services – decelerated to 3.1 per cent, down from 3.6 per cent in 2017.[1] In addition to country- and sector-specific factors, high policy uncertainty arising from trade tensions between China and the United States generated strong downward pressure on global growth.

In developing economies, GDP growth slowed to an estimated 4.2 per cent in 2018, while growth in the least developed countries fell short of meeting the targets set under the Sustainable Development Goals. In the developed countries, except for the United States, GDP growth decelerated from 2.3 per cent in 2017 to 2.2 per cent in 2018. Elsewhere, in countries with economies in transition, GDP growth improved from 2.1 per cent in 2017 to 2.8 per cent in 2018.

Industrial production figures and surveys of purchasing managers suggest that the slower momentum is likely to continue in 2019. UNCTAD projects global GDP growth to further decline in 2019.

[1] J Osterhaus, Director, Oxford Economics, "GDP and merchandise trade forecasts and models", personal communication (email and discussion) with the UNCTAD secretariat, 26 and 27 June and 1 July 2019.

Table 1.1 World economic growth, 2017–2019
(Annual percentage change)

Region or country	1994–2008	2017	2018[a]	2019[b]
World	**3.3**	**3.1**	**3.0**	**2.3**
Developed countries	**2.6**	**2.3**	**2.2**	**1.6**
of which:				
United States	3.2	2.2	2.9	2.2
European Union (28)	2.5	2.5	2.0	1.3
Japan	1.1	1.9	0.8	0.8
Developing countries	**5.1**	**4.4**	**4.2**	**3.5**
of which:				
Africa	4.6	2.6	2.8	2.8
East Asia	8.1	6.2	5.9	5.4
of which:				
China	9.7	6.9	6.6	6.1
South Asia	5.7	6.3	6.0	4.1
of which:				
India	6.6	6.9	7.4	6.0
South-East Asia	4.2	5.2	5.0	4.5
Western Asia	4.3	2.8	2.3	0.7
Latin American and the Caribbean	**2.9**	**1.0**	**0.8**	**0.2**
of which:				
Brazil	2.9	1.1	1.1	0.6
Transition economies	**4.1**	**2.1**	**2.8**	**1.4**
of which:				
Russian Federation	3.9	1.6	2.3	0.5
Least developed countries	**6.0**	**4.3**	**4.4**	**4.6**

Source: UNCTAD secretariat calculations, based on data from UNCTAD, 2019a, the *Trade and Development Report 2019: Financing a Global Green New Deal.*

[a] Partly estimated.

[b] Forecast.

2. Disappointing growth in global merchandise trade

In tandem with developments in global output, global merchandise trade growth (imports and exports) fell to 2.8 per cent in 2018, an unexpected performance contrasting with an increase of 4.5 per cent in 2017 (table 1.2). World merchandise exports increased by 2.5 per cent, while imports expanded by 3.1 per cent. Trade between China and the United States is estimated to have declined by over 15.0 per cent since September 2018, following the second round of tariff hikes. This has also had an impact on global value chains in East Asia and other trading partners (United Nations, 2019a).

The slowdown was broad-based, reflecting weaker import demand in both developed and developing countries, although some regions were more strongly affected than others. The reduced pace reflects the downside pressure on export orders and global manufacturing activity. Global capital goods production, which is highly trade-intensive, slowed in Europe and developing Asia. While also trending downward, growth in import demand outpaced that of exports.

Aside from the United States–China tariffs, trade restrictions introduced by other countries have also weighed heavily on international trade. In 2018, import restrictions and tariff increases were also put in place as retaliatory actions, or as measures aimed at reducing current account vulnerabilities, for example those relating to Egypt, Indonesia, the Islamic Republic of Iran, Pakistan, Sri Lanka and Turkey. The growing use of anti-dumping and countervailing duties and safeguards hindered trade even further (World Bank, 2019).

With the exception of the United States, developed countries recorded a slowdown in their export and import demand. Export growth in developing countries waned as volumes expanded at 2.9 per cent, down from 5.2 per cent in 2017. Their import demand decreased to 4.0 per cent, down from 6.8 per cent in 2017, reflecting a slowdown in China and East Asia, as well as negative growth in Western Asia, where a weaker oil price environment, geopolitical tensions and political unrest contributed to constrain trade. Overall, slower trade growth in Asia and Europe has been a major drag on global trade due to their large share in world imports, 36.3 per cent and 38 per cent, respectively (UNCTAD, 2019b).

Table 1.2 Growth in volume of merchandise trade, 2016–2018 (Annual percentage change)

Volume of exports			Countries or regions	Volume of imports		
2016	2017	2018		2016	2017	2018
1.3	**4.1**	**2.5**	**World**	**1.2**	**4.8**	**3.1**
1.0	**3.3**	**2.1**	**Developed countries** *of which:*	**2.2**	**3.1**	**2.5**
2.3	6.0	2.7	Japan	0.8	2.8	2.0
-0.2	4.0	4.1	United States	0.5	4.0	5.3
1.1	3.6	1.6	European Union	**3.1**	2.6	**1.5**
0.0	**4.5**	**4.1**	**Transition economies** *of which:*	**5.8**	**13.0**	**3.9**
-0.3	4.2	4.3	Commonwealth of Independent States	5.1	14.1	3.3
2.0	**5.2**	**2.9**	**Developing countries**	**-0.4**	**6.8**	**4.0**
0.5	3.7	-0.6	Africa	-5.4	-0.4	4.5
0.1	6.1	6.3	Sub-Saharan Africa	-10.4	1.1	2.1
2.5	3.0	2.5	Latin America and the Caribbean	-6.0	5.2	**5.9**
1.3	**6.5**	**3.3**	East Asia *of which:*	**1.7**	**6.9**	**4.6**
1.4	7.1	4.1	China	3.7	8.9	6.4
5.7	**5.8**	**2.5**	South Asia *of which:*	**1.3**	**11.5**	**2.8**
2.7	6.6	4.3	India	-1.8	11.7	3.1
2.6	8.9	4.6	South-East Asia	2.4	9.5	6.8
2.5	-1.2	2.0	Western Asia	-1.7	2.5	-4.1

Source: UNCTAD secretariat calculations, based on data from UNCTAD, 2019a, *Trade and Development Report 2019: Financing a Global Green New Deal.*

3. International maritime trade

Maritime transport remains the backbone of globalized trade and the manufacturing supply chain, as more than four fifths of world merchandise trade by volume is carried by sea. However, growth in international maritime trade fell slightly in 2018, owing to softer economic indicators amid heightened uncertainty and the build-up of wide-ranging downside risks. This decline reflects developments in the world economy and trade activity. Volumes increased at 2.7 per cent, below the historical average of 3.0 per cent from 1970–2017 and 4.1 per cent in 2017. Nonetheless, total volumes reached a milestone in 2018, when they achieved an all-time high of 11 billion tons – the first time on UNCTAD record (tables 1.3 and 1.4). Dry bulk commodities, followed by containerized cargo, other dry bulk, oil, gas and chemicals, contributed the most to this growth.

Figure 1.1 shows the structure of international maritime trade over the years. In 2018, major dry bulk commodities – iron ore, grain and coal – accounted for more than 40.0 per cent of total dry cargo shipments, while containerized trade and minor bulks accounted for 24.0 per cent and 25.8 per cent, respectively. Remaining volumes were made of other dry cargo, including break bulks.

Tanker trade shipments (oil, gas and chemicals), accounted for 29.0 per cent of total maritime trade volume, down from 55 per cent nearly five decades earlier. This is consistent with the ongoing shift in the maritime trade structure that is largely rooted in the 1980s. The decade saw a decrease in tanker trade of 6.2 per cent, reflecting the constrained petroleum consumption in main consumer countries that followed the oil shocks of the 1970s. Over the same period, major bulks, including iron ore, grain and coal, increased by more than half. Containerized cargo expanded at the fastest rate, with volumes rising at an annual average rate of 8.0 per cent between 1980 and 2018. The compositional shift in world maritime trade was further emphasized by the development of pipeline trade and the rise of manufactures trade, propelled by fragmentated global production processes and international division of labour since the mid-1990s.

While UNCTAD carries no data on cargo ton-miles, estimates by Clarksons Research indicate that, once adjusted for distance travelled, maritime trade expanded at a slightly faster pace than tons alone. Volumes grew by about 3.3 per cent, and total cargo ton-miles were estimated at 58,812 billion (figure 1.2). Growing Asian import demand from the Atlantic (i.e. United States and West Africa), in particular, crude oil and gas exports from the United States, underpinned this performance. The shale revolution and the removal of the ban on crude oil exports propelled the United States to the position of a world exporter of oil and gas and changed the global tanker and gas trade landscape.

Table 1.3 Development in international maritime trade, selected years
(Million tons loaded)

Year	Tanker trade[a]	Main bulks[b]	Other dry cargo[c]	Total (all cargoes)
1970	1 440	448	717	2 605
1980	1 871	608	1 225	3 704
1990	1 755	988	1 265	4 008
2000	2 163	1 186	2 635	5 984
2005	2 422	1 579	3 108	7 109
2006	2 698	1 676	3 328	7 702
2007	2 747	1 811	3 478	8 036
2008	2 742	1 911	3 578	8 231
2009	2 641	1 998	3 218	7 857
2010	2 752	2 232	3 423	8 408
2011	2 785	2 364	3 626	8 775
2012	2 840	2 564	3 791	9 195
2013	2 828	2 734	3 951	9 513
2014	2 825	2 964	4 054	9 842
2015	2 932	2 930	4 161	10 023
2016	3 058	3 009	4 228	10 295
2017	3 146	3 151	4 419	10 716
2018	3 194	3 210	4 601	11 005

Sources: Compiled by the UNCTAD secretariat based on data supplied by reporting countries, as posted on government and port industry websites, and data provided by specialist sources. Dry cargo data for 2006 onwards were revised and updated to reflect improved reporting, including more recent figures and a better breakdown by cargo type. Since 2006, the breakdown of dry cargo into main bulks and dry cargo other than main bulks is based on various issues of *Shipping Review and Outlook*, produced by Clarksons Research. Total maritime trade figures for 2018 are estimated based on preliminary data or on the last year for which data were available.

[a] Crude oil, refined petroleum products, gas and chemicals.

[b] Iron ore, grain, coal, bauxite/alumina and phosphate. Since 2006, main bulks include iron ore, grain and coal only. Data relating to bauxite/alumina and phosphate are included under other dry cargo.

[c] Minor bulks, containerized trade and residual general cargo.

Figure 1.1 International maritime trade, by cargo type, selected years
(Million tons loaded)

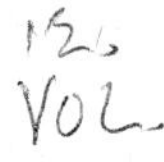

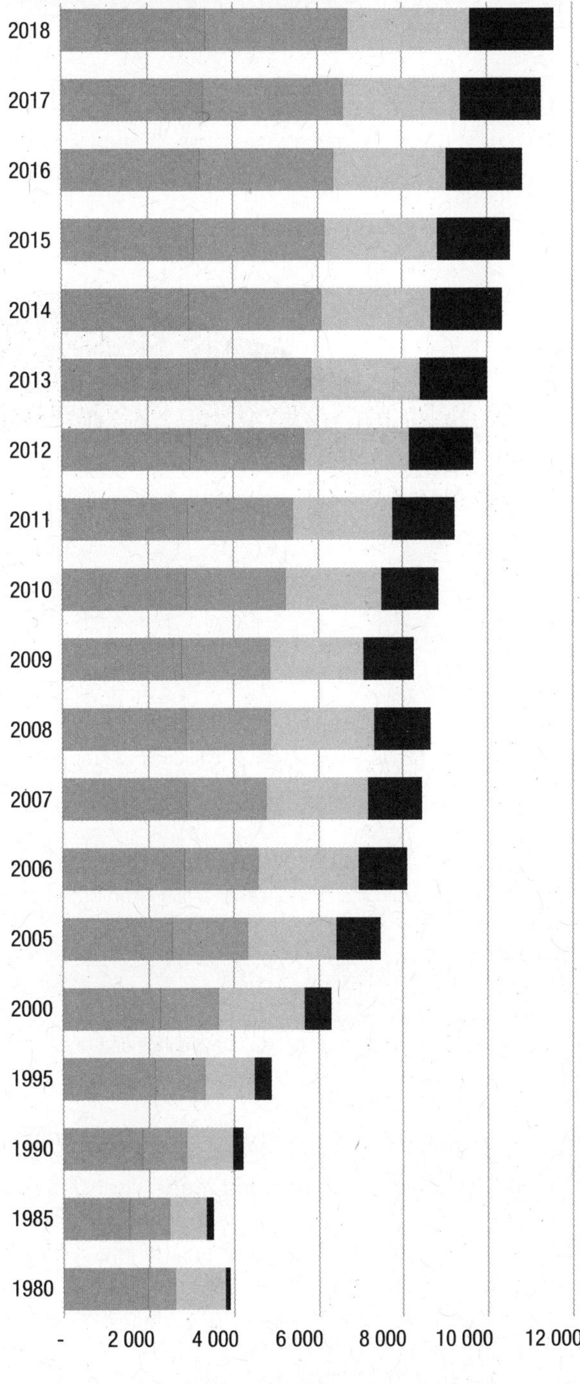

Sources: Review of Maritime Transport, various issues. From 2006 to 2018, the breakdown by cargo type is based on data from Clarksons Research, 2019a, *Shipping Review and Outlook*, spring.

Note: From 1980 to 2005, figures for main bulks include iron ore, grain, coal, bauxite/alumina and phosphate. In 2006, the category was modified to include iron ore, grain and coal only. Data relating to bauxite/alumina and phosphate are included under other dry cargo.

[a] Iron ore, grain, coal, bauxite/alumina and phosphate. In 2006, the category was modified to include iron ore, grain and coal only. Data relating to bauxite/alumina and phosphate are included under other dry cargo.

[b] Crude oil, refined petroleum products, gas and chemicals.

Figure 1.2 International maritime trade in cargo ton-miles, 2000–2019
(Estimated billion ton-miles)

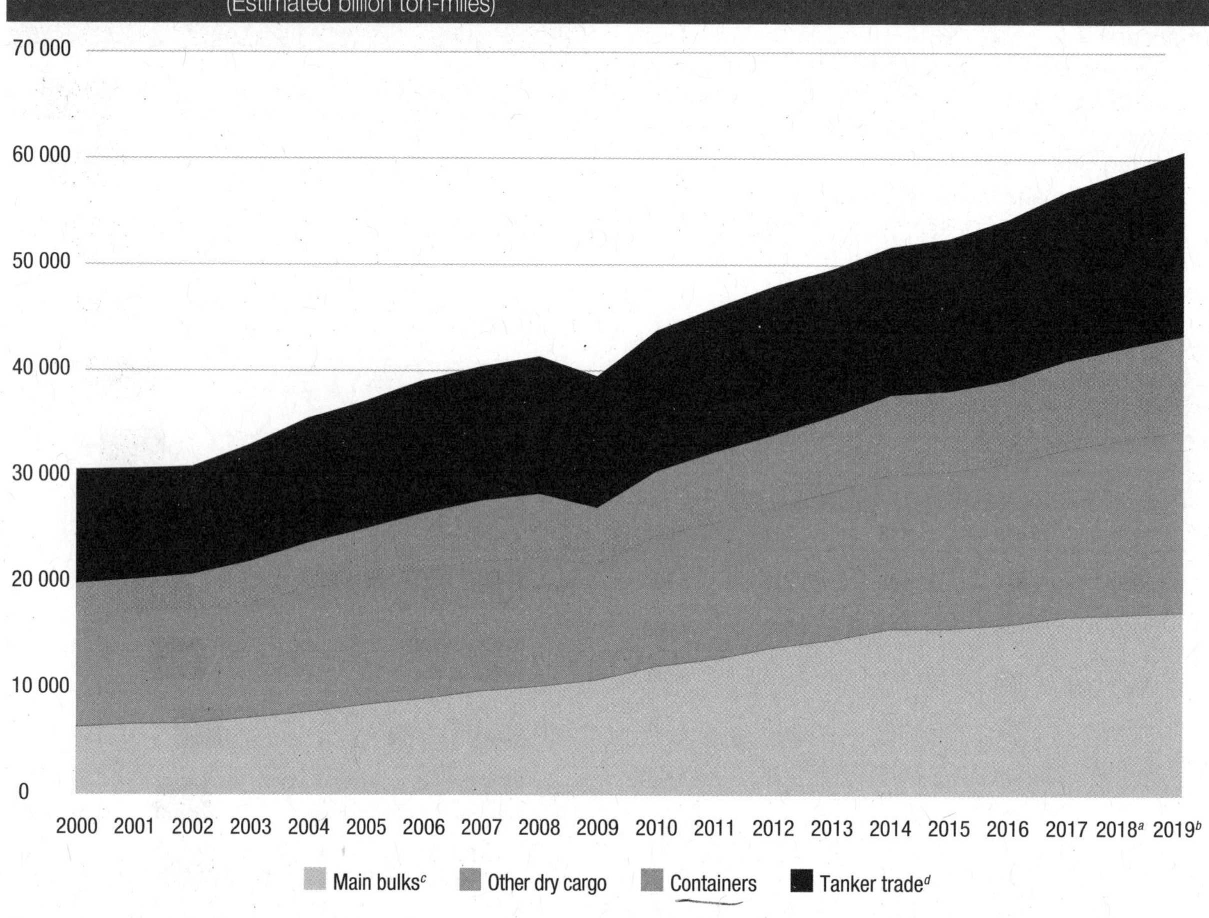

Source: UNCTAD secretariat calculations, based on data from Clarksons Research, 2019a, *Shipping Review and Outlook*, spring.

Note: Given methodological differences, containerized trade data in tons sourced from Clarksons Research are not comparable with data in TEUs sourced from MDS Transmodal.

[a] Estimated.

[b] Forecast.

[c] Iron ore, grain, coal, bauxite/alumina and phosphate. In 2006, the category was modified to include iron ore, grain and coal only. Data relating to bauxite/alumina and phosphate are included under other dry cargo.

[d] Crude oil, refined petroleum products, gas and chemicals.

UNCTAD pays particular attention to developing countries' participation in world trade, consistently checking where the cargo is loaded and unloaded, that is, who generates the trade and where it goes. Figure 1.3 (a) features the share of developing countries in international maritime trade in terms of goods loaded and unloaded between 1970 and 2018. Developing countries have been the main exporting countries, with nearly two thirds of maritime trade originating in their territories. The 1980s showed a decline in this trend, reflecting oil trade developments that followed the oil shocks of the 1970s. Developing countries did not figure prominently in view of the colonial trade patterns whereby as marginal players, they exported raw materials and imported mainly consumer goods.

In 2018, developing countries continued to account for most global maritime trade flows, both in terms of exports (goods loaded) and imports (goods unloaded). These countries loaded an estimated 58.8 per cent in 2018 and unloaded 64.5 per cent of this total (figure 1.3 (a)). Since 2000, the contribution of developing countries to maritime trade has shifted, reflecting their growing role as major exporters of raw materials, as well as major exporters and importers of finished and semi-finished goods. Participation in containerized trade, however, has been concentrated in Asia, notably in China and neighbouring countries. Other developing regions did not contribute equally, a reflection of their varying degrees of integration into global value chains and manufacturing networks. Figure 1.3 (b) paints an entirely different picture when China is not included in the grouping.

By contrast, developed countries saw their share of both types of traffic decline over time, hovering at around one third in terms of goods loaded and unloaded, respectively. The share of transition economies remained relatively smaller. A total of 6.5 per cent of world maritime trade volumes were loaded in these economies' ports and less than 1.0 per cent was unloaded in their territory.

Table 1.4 International maritime trade, 2017–2018
(Type of cargo, country group and region)

Country group	Year	Goods loaded: Total	Goods loaded: Crude oil	Goods loaded: Other tanker trade[a]	Goods loaded: Dry cargo	Goods unloaded: Total	Goods unloaded: Crude oil	Goods unloaded: Other tanker trade[a]	Goods unloaded: Dry cargo
Millions of tons									
World	2017	10 716.2	1 874.6	1 271.6	7 570.1	10 702.3	2 033.7	1 289.4	7 379.2
	2018	11 005	1 886.2	1 308.1	7 810.7	11 002.2	2 048.5	1 321.8	7 631.9
Developed economies	2017	3 709	152.7	491.2	3 065.1	3 795	979.1	494.7	2 321.2
	2018	3 821.7	157.7	511.2	3 152.7	3 822.9	946.5	495.8	2 380.5
Transition economies	2017	694.4	206.8	41.6	445.9	81.4	0.3	4.6	76.4
	2018	713.3	203.8	39.6	469.9	86.5	0.3	4.8	81.3
Developing economies	2017	6 312.8	1 515	738.8	4 059	6 825.9	1 054.3	790	4 981.6
	2018	6 469.9	1 524.7	757.3	4 188	7 092.8	1 101.6	821.2	5 170
Africa	2017	740.9	291.3	70.4	379.1	496.8	40.5	93.8	362.6
	2018	767.2	289.3	73.8	404	516.3	42.5	93.9	380
America	2017	1 371.8	225.2	71.9	1 074.7	617.2	47.5	141.4	428.2
	2018	1 403.7	219.3	78.3	1 106.1	652.5	51.8	149	451.8
Asia	2017	4 192	996.9	595.6	2 599.5	5 696.9	965.4	549.4	4 182.1
	2018	4 290.7	1 014.4	604.1	2 672.1	5 908.3	1 006.5	572.5	4 329.3
Oceania	2017	8.1	1.6	0.8	5.7	14.9	0.8	5.4	8.7
	2018	8.4	1.6	1.0	5.8	15.6	0.8	5.8	9

Country group	Year	Goods loaded: Total	Goods loaded: Crude oil	Goods loaded: Other tanker trade[a]	Goods loaded: Dry cargo	Goods unloaded: Total	Goods unloaded: Crude oil	Goods unloaded: Other tanker trade[a]	Goods unloaded: Dry cargo
Percentage share									
World	2017	100	17.5	11.9	70.6	100	19	12.1	69
	2018	100	17.1	11.9	71	100	15.5	11.6	72.9
Developed economies	2017	34.6	8.1	38.6	40.5	35.5	48.1	38.4	31.5
	2018	34.7	8.4	39.1	40.4	34.7	46.2	37.5	31.2
Transition economies	2017	6.5	11	3.3	5.9	0.8	0	0.4	1
	2018	6.5	10.8	3	6	0.8	0	0.4	1.1
Developing economies	2017	58.9	80.8	58.1	53.6	63.8	51.8	61.3	67.5
	2018	58.8	80.8	57.9	53.6	64.5	53.8	62.1	67.7
Africa	2017	6.9	15.5	5.5	5	4.6	2	7.3	4.9
	2018	7	15.3	5.6	5.2	4.7	2.1	7.1	5
America	2017	12.8	12	5.7	14.2	5.8	2.3	11	5.8
	2018	12.8	11.6	6	14.2	5.9	2.5	11.3	5.9
Asia	2017	39.1	53.2	46.8	34.3	53.2	47.5	42.6	56.7
	2018	39	53.8	46.2	34.2	53.7	49.1	43.3	56.7
Oceania	2017	0.1	0.1	0.1	0.1	0.1	0	0.4	0.1
	2018	0.1	0.1	0.1	0.1	0.1	0	0.4	0.1

Source: Compiled by the UNCTAD secretariat based on data supplied by reporting countries, as posted on government and port industry websites, and data provided by specialist sources. Dry cargo data for 2006 onwards were revised and updated to reflect improved reporting, including more recent figures and a better breakdown by cargo type. Total maritime trade figures for 2018 are estimated based on preliminary data or on the last year for which data were available.

Note: For longer time series and data prior to 2017, see UNCTADstat Data Centre at http://unctadstat.unctad.org/wds/TableViewer/tableView.aspx?ReportId=32363.

[a] Refined petroleum products, gas and chemicals.

Figure 1.3 (a) Participation of developing countries in international maritime trade, selected years
(Percentage share in total tonnage)

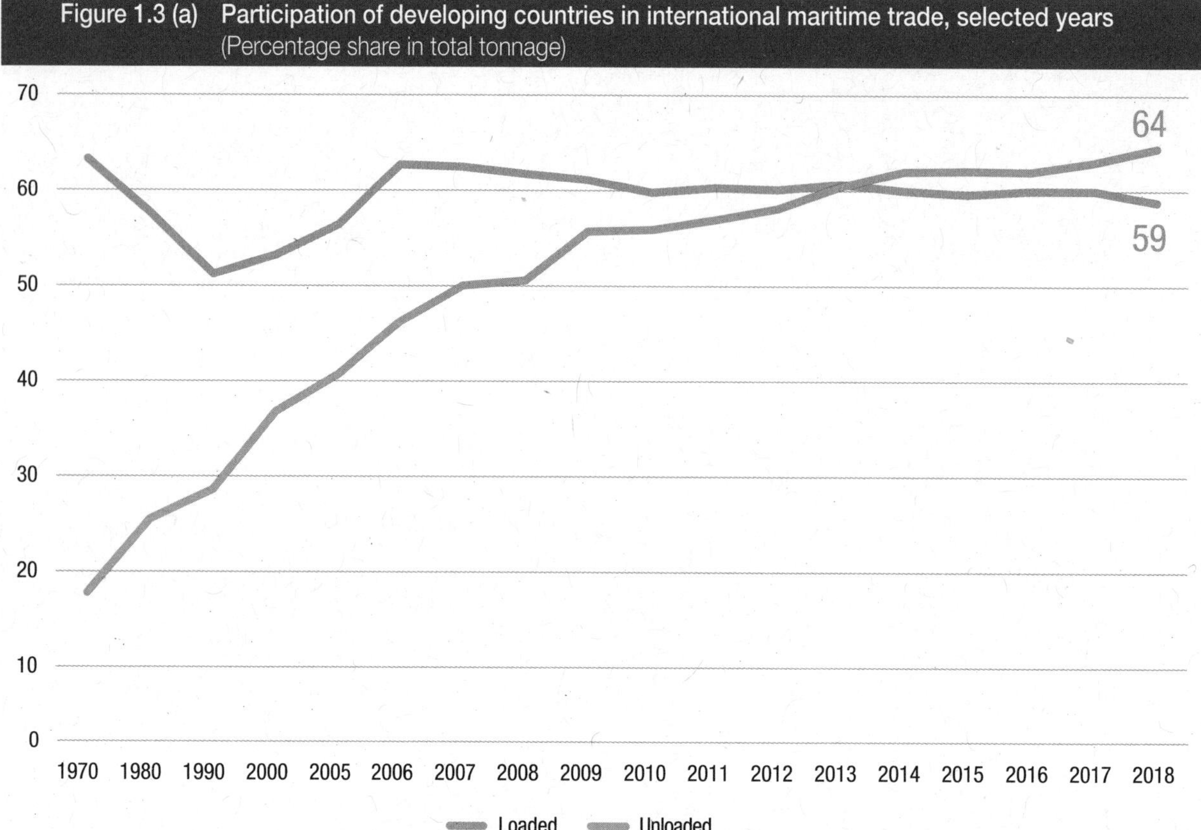

Sources: UNCTAD secretariat calculations, based on data from the *Review of Maritime Transport*, various issues, and table 1.4 of this report.

Figure 1.3 (b) Participation in international maritime trade of developing countries other than China, selected years
(Percentage share in total tonnage)

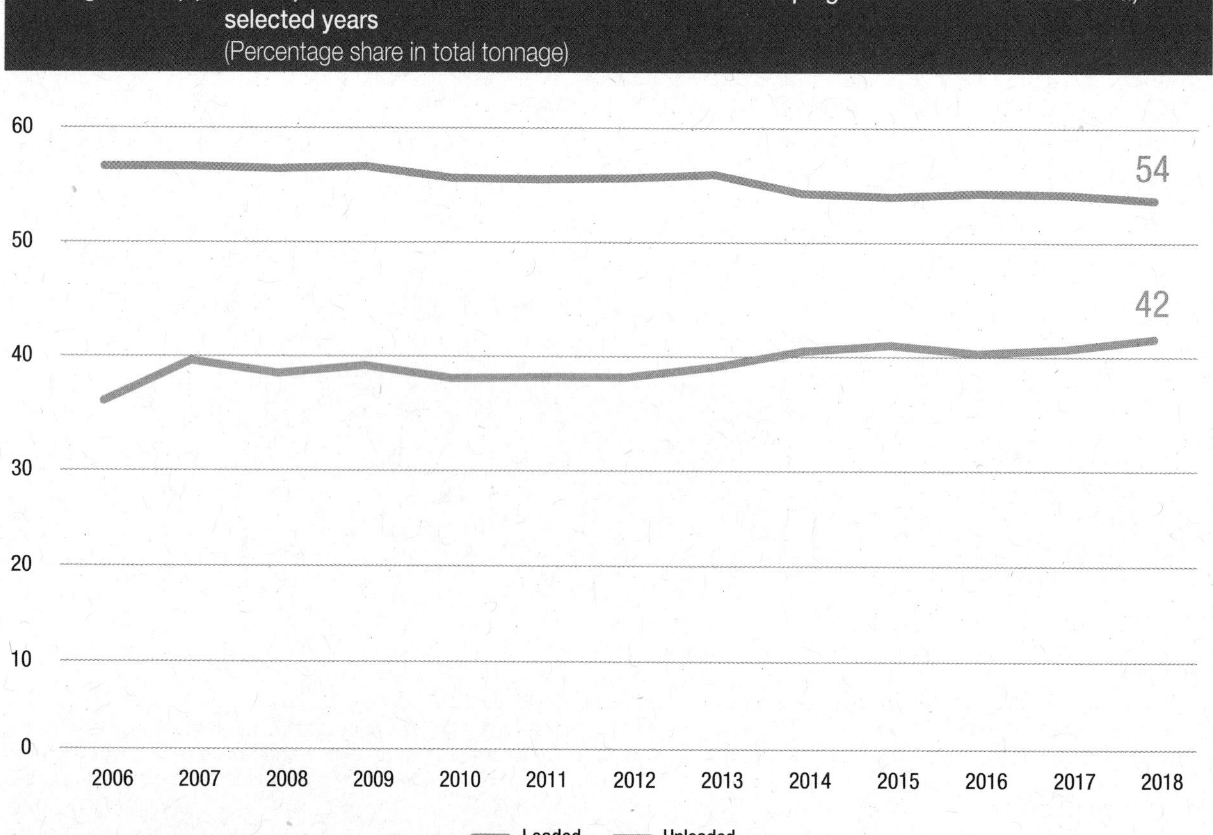

Sources: UNCTAD secretariat calculations, based on data from the *Review of Maritime Transport*, various issues, and table 1.4 of this report.

Figure 1.4 International maritime trade by region, 2018
(Percentage share in world tonnage)

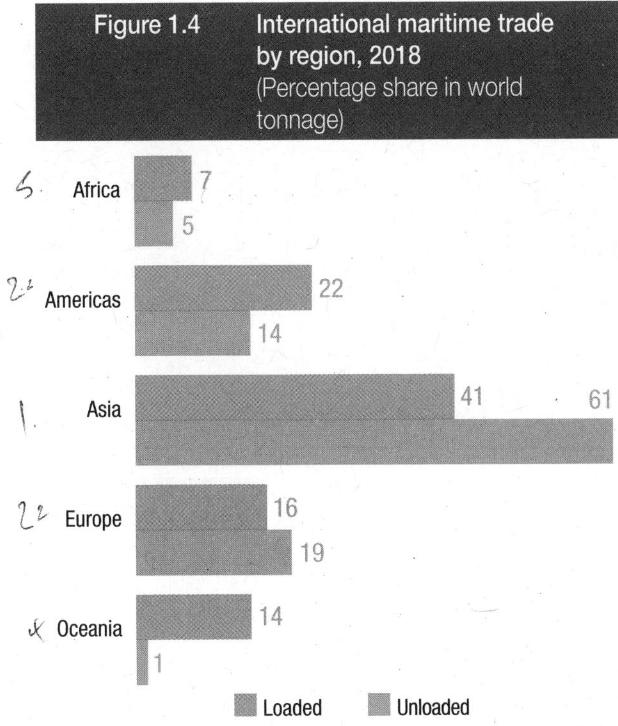

Sources: Compiled by the UNCTAD secretariat based on data supplied by reporting countries, as posted on government and port industry websites, and data provided by specialist sources.

Note: Estimated figures are based on preliminary data or on the last year for which data were available.

Figure 1.4 highlights the regional distribution of global maritime trade. In 2018, 41 per cent of the total goods loaded in 2018 originated in Asia and 61 per cent of total goods unloaded were received in this same region. Over the years, the participation of Africa declined, particularly in terms of goods loaded, reflecting the reduced importance of traditional African exporters of liquid and dry bulk cargoes. This was only partly compensated for by alternative raw material sources from Africa, not by Africa becoming more active in exporting goods with more value added and goods that are generally carried in containers, including manufactured goods and processed food or industrial products. The relative decline of Latin American countries as a source of trade volumes is equally notable. In contrast, Asian countries have experienced a large increase in intraregional trade mostly based on manufactures trades and reflecting fragmented production processes. Parts are generally manufactured in multiple locations across Asia and assembled in another location. This was not observed in Africa and only to a limited extent in Latin America, due to in part to the similarities in factor endowments in the region and to limitations in infrastructure and shipping services (UNCTAD, 2018).

4. Slowdown in key market segments of maritime trade

In tandem with the world economy and trade, and further shaped by country-specific trends, most notably in China, growth slowed down across nearly all cargo segments except for minor bulks, gas and refined petroleum product trades.

After strong growth in 2017, tanker trade dwindled in 2018. The geographical dispersion of trade in oil in East Asia continued in 2018. Exports were concentrated less on traditional exporters from Western Asia and included suppliers from the Atlantic basin (Angola, Brazil, Canada, Nigeria and the United States). As shown in table 1.5, global tanker trade increased by 1.5 per cent in 2018, hampered by fewer crude oil shipments. A sharp decline in oil trade growth was partly offset by rapidly expanding gas trade (liquefied natural gas and liquefied petroleum gas).

Table 1.5 Tanker trade, 2017–2018
(Million tons and annual percentage change)

	2017	2018	Percentage change 2017–2018
Crude oil	1 874.6	1 886.2	0.6
Other tanker trade *of which:*	1 271.6	1 308.1	2.9
Liquefied natural gas	292	318	8.9
Liquefied petroleum gas	90	97	7.8
Total tanker trade	**3 146.2**	**3 194.3**	**1.5**

Sources: UNCTAD secretariat calculations, derived from table 1.4 of this report. Figures for liquefied natural gas and liquefied petroleum gas are derived from Clarksons Research, 2019b, *Seaborne Trade Monitor*, Volume 6, No. 6, June 2019.

Note: Tanker trade includes crude oil, refined petroleum products, gas and chemicals.

UNCTAD estimates that world trade in crude oil was 1.9 billion tons in 2018, following an increase of less than 1.0 per cent. Growth was partly limited by declining imports into Europe and the United States and a slowdown in import demand in China, owing to refinery capacity constraints suffered earlier during the year. To put things in perspective, in China, crude oil imports increased by about 15.6 per cent in 2016, 9.2 per cent in 2017 and 7.3 per cent in 2018 (Clarksons Research, 2019c). Disruptions on the supply side involving the Islamic Republic of Iran and the Bolivarian Republic of Venezuela, as well as supply cuts led by the Organization of the Petroleum Exporting Countries, weighed on crude oil shipments. However, trade in ton-miles recorded stronger growth.

Trade in refined petroleum products was held up by falling imports from Brazil and South-East Asia and the drawing on stocks in some regions. However, firm import demand in Mexico and expanding shipments from Western Asia and the United States helped offset the negative trend somewhat (Clarksons Research, 2018a). An overview of global players in the oil and natural gas sector is presented in table 1.6.

Table 1.6 Major producers and consumers of oil and natural gas, 2018
(World market share in percentage)

World oil production		World oil consumption	
Western Asia	33	Asia and the Pacific	36
North America	22	North America	23
Transition economies	15	Europe	15
Developing America	9	Western Asia	9
Africa	9	Developing America	9
Asia and the Pacific	8	Transition economies	4
Europe	4	Africa	4
Oil refinery capacities		**Oil refinery throughput**	
Asia and the Pacific	35	Asia and the Pacific	36
North America	21	North America	22
Europe	15	Europe	15
Western Asia	11	Western Asia	11
Transition economies	8	Transition economies	8
Developing America	8	Developing America	5
Africa	2	Africa	3
World natural gas production		**World natural gas consumption**	
North America	26	North America	24
Transition economies	22	Asia and the Pacific	21
Western Asia	18	Transition economies	16
Asia and the Pacific	16	Western Asia	16
Europe	6	Europe	12
Developing America	6	Developing America	7
Africa	6	Africa	4

Source: UNCTAD secretariat calculations, based on data published in *British Petroleum (BP) Statistical Review of World Energy 2019*, June 2019.

Note: Oil includes crude oil, shale oil, oil sands and natural gas liquids (the liquid content of natural gas where this is recovered separately). The term does not include liquid fuels from other sources such as biomass and coal derivatives.

Gas trade continued its bullish growth, supported by growing supply capacity and ongoing environmental and energy policy shifts. Liquified natural gas shipments totalled 318 million tons in 2018, reflecting an increase of 8.9 per cent (table 1.5) (Clarksons Research, 2019b). Demand growth originated mostly in Asia, bolstered by ongoing energy policy shifts and rising export capacity in Australia and the United States. In China, liquefied natural gas imports increased by over 40.0 per cent in 2018, partly supported by the growing importance of its environmental agenda (Clarksons Research, 2019c). Key exporters included Qatar, the largest liquefied natural gas supplier, Australia, Malaysia and the United States.

Liquified petroleum gas shipments picked up speed and increased by 7.8 per cent, up from 2.2 per cent in 2017 (Clarksons Research, 2019b). Strong import demand in India and Europe and expanding supply from the United States and Western Asia underpinned this performance. On the export side, shipments from the United States to Asia expanded, benefiting from growing production and pricing dynamics. Additional support was provided by growing supply in Western Asia as a result of petrochemical capacity expansion in the region (Clarksons Research, 2019a).

Major bulks

Trade in dry bulks supported maritime shipments in 2018 but trends varied by commodity, and some underlying risks became more apparent. Growth in dry bulks (major and minor bulks) trade expanded by 2.6 per cent in 2018, down from 4.0 per cent in 2017. Backed by robust growth in coal, trade in major dry bulks (iron ore, coal and grain) grew at 1.9 per cent in 2018 (table 1.7), down from 4.7 per cent in 2017. Risks to trade in dry bulks began materializing in 2018 as major bulks[2] – the mainstay of maritime trade in volume for more than two decades – came under pressure. Trade in major dry bulks increased steadily for almost two decades at an average annual rate of 5.9 per cent. The one exception was in 2015, characterized by weak growth.

Table 1.7 Dry bulk trade, 2017–2018
(Million tons and annual percentage change)

	2017	2018	Percentage change 2017–2018
Major bulks[a] *of which:*	3 151	3 210	1.9
Iron ore	1 473	1 476	0.2
Coal	1 202	1 263	5.1
Grain	476	471	-1.1
Minor bulks *of which:*	1 947	2 020	3.7
Steel products	392	390	-0.5
Forest products	365	378	3.6
Total dry bulks	**5 098**	**5 230**	**2.6**

Source: UNCTAD secretariat calculations, based on Clarksons Research, 2019d, *Dry Bulk Trade Outlook,* Volume 25, No. 6, June.

[a] Iron ore, coal (steam and coking) and grains (wheat, coarse grain and soybean).

Some negative trends unfolded in 2018. Growth in iron ore shipments nearly came to a halt as import demand in China contracted. Coal trade expanded at 5.1 per cent but remained, nevertheless, under pressure due to the growing concerns about coal's environmental footprint and the emphasis on diversifying the energy mix in major importing countries such those of the European Union, where coal imports contracted by about 5.8 per cent in 2018. As trade in iron ore and coal represents

2 Detailed figures on dry bulk commodities are derived from Clarksons Research, 2019d, *Dry Bulk Trade Outlook*, Volume 25, No. 6, June.

28.2 per cent and 24.1 per cent, respectively, of global dry bulk trade, which in turn accounts for nearly half of global maritime trade, any pressure on these sectors does not bode well for shipping or demand for maritime transport services in general. These developments underscore the issue of overreliance on a limited number of commodities and trade markets to support maritime trade. Risks associated with the overreliance of maritime transport on China, as well as iron ore and coal, have been building for the past few years.

In China, maritime imports of major bulk commodities were estimated at 1.4 billion tons, or 43.5 per cent of global maritime major bulk trade in 2018. After two decades of consistent growth, maritime iron ore imports in that country – 71.0 per cent of global iron ore trade – contracted by close to 1.0 per cent in 2018. Supply-side constraints in Australia and Brazil – which together accounted for some 83.0 per cent of the global market in 2018 – rising scrap use for steel industry in China and the use of existing iron ore inventories have limited the demand for iron ore imports in China. Other exporters, in order of magnitude are South Africa, Canada, Sweden and India, which contribute only smaller shares to global iron ore trade. An overview of global players in the dry bulk commodities trade sector is presented in table 1.8.

With regard to trade in coal, growth was supported by import demand into China, which accounted for an estimated 19.0 per cent of world coal maritime imports in 2018. Growing emphasis on environmental and safety policies and a supply-side reform programme in China resulted in limiting domestic production and favouring imports, factors that affected the country's appetite for foreign coal. In 2018, robust import demand in China (+8.8 per cent) was further supported by large volumes shipped into India (+12.8 per cent). Indonesia and Australia remained the leading global coal exporters, with a combined market share of 63.0 per cent in 2018. Indonesia increased shipments by 9.3 per cent, while exports from Australia increased at less than half this rate.

Negative trends, for example, tariffs and limited shipments from suppliers such as Argentina, weighed on trade in global grains in 2018. In China, it is estimated that imports of soybeans declined by 8.3 per cent in 2018, despite record shipments from Brazil. Brazil increased its total grain exports by approximately 10.0 per cent. At the same time, total maritime grain exports from the United States fell by 1.4 per cent in 2018, reflecting the rapid drop in soybean exports to China.

The performance of the global dry bulk trade sector underscored the central role of China and the challenges associated with an overreliance on it as the main market. Consequently, any shift however small, in the demand for imports in China, including as a result of trade tensions with the United States, can have a marked impact on global maritime trade patterns (see C. Outlook and policy considerations).

Minor bulks

Reflecting trends in the steel production sector and a slowdown in the global economy, minor bulk trade grew at an accelerated rate of 3.7 per cent in 2018, up from 2.8 per cent in 2017 (table 1.7). China is an important import market, representing roughly 20 per cent of the market in 2018. Much of the expansion resulted from growth in metals and minerals, including nickel ore, manganese ore, cement and bauxite trade, which in recent years has seen growing shipments from Guinea to China. In 2018, Guinea consolidated its position as the leading world exporter of bauxite.

Table 1.8 Major dry bulks and steel: Producers, users, exporters and importers, 2018
(World market shares in percentage)

Steel producers		Steel users	
China	51	China	49
India	6	United States	6
Japan	6	India	6
United States	5	Japan	4
Republic of Korea	4	Republic of Korea	3
Russian Federation	4	Germany	2
Germany	2	Russian Federation	2
Turkey	2	Turkey	2
Brazil	2	Italy	2
Other	18	Mexico	1
		Other	23
Iron ore exporters		**Iron ore importers**	
Australia	57	China	71
Brazil	26	Japan	8
South Africa	4	Europe	7
Canada	3	Republic of Korea	5
Sweden	2	Other	9
India	1		
Other	7		
Coal exporters		**Coal importers**	
Indonesia	33	China	19
Australia	30	India	18
Russian Federation	11	Japan	15
United States	8	Europen Union	11
Colombia	6	Republic of Korea	11
South Africa	6	Taiwan Province of China	5
Canada	2	Malaysia	3
Other	4	Other	18
Grain exporters		**Grain importers**	
United States	26	East and South Asia	45
Brazil	23	Africa	14
Russian Federation	11	Western Asia	14
Ukraine	9	South and Central America	12
Argentina	9	European Union	10
European Union	7	Other	3
Canada	6		
Australia	4		
Other	5		

Sources: UNCTAD secretariat calculations, based on data from the World Steel Association (2019a), Global crude steel output increases by 4.6% in 2018, 25 January; World Steel Association (2019b), *World Steel Short-range Outlook April 2019*, 16 April; Clarksons Research, 2019d, *Dry Bulk Trade Outlook*, Volume 25, No. 6, June.

Other dry cargo: Containerized trade

In 2018, global containerized trade unfolded amid great uncertainty, ranging from the implications of the new IMO 2020 regulation imposing a sulphur cap on bunker fuels (see chapters 2 and 4), trade frictions, trends in China, weakness in consumer markets and unfavourable developments in the world economy. Together, these factors put a brake on containerized trade, with volumes expanding at a relatively much slower rate than in 2017.

Volumes as measured in 20-foot equivalent units (TEUs) increased at 2.6 per cent in 2018, down from 6 per cent in 2017, bringing the total to 152 million TEUs (figure 1.5). This range of growth is a dramatic change compared with the double-digit growth rates of the 2000s and less than half the 5.8 per cent average annual growth rate recorded over the past two decades.

A large share of globalized containerized trade continues to be carried across the major East–West containerized trade arteries, namely Asia–Europe, the Trans-Pacific and the Transatlantic (figure 1.6). However, with 60 per cent of global containerized trade occurring on non-mainlane trade routes (other routes), secondary routes involving developing countries' trade are increasingly important. Of these other routes, intraregional flows, dominated by intra-Asian movements, account for the largest proportion, followed, in descending order, by the non-mainlane or secondary East–West trade routes (for example, the Eastern Asia–South Asia–Western Asia routes), South–South and North–South trade routes.

The year 2018 was a mixed year for container shipping. Trade continued to grow on the major East–West trade lanes, with volumes expanding by 4.8 per cent, down from 5.7 per cent in 2017 (tables 1.9 and 1.10; figure 1.7). Trans-Pacific trade remained the busiest trade route, accounting for 28.2 million TEUs, followed by the Asia–Europe route (24.4 million TEUs) and the Transatlantic route (8.0 million TEUs).

The rapid 5.4 per cent growth observed on the Trans-Pacific route is supported by a 7.0 per cent surge in volumes on the peak leg, reflecting the frontloading by importers in the United States ahead of the potential introduction of additional tariffs on Chinese goods. By April 2019, shipments from China to the United States had dropped by 6.0 per cent year over year (JOC.com, 2019a), a significant contraction, given the share of Chinese exports in Trans-Pacific trade. By contrast, exports to the United States from neighbouring South-East Asian countries increased by nearly one third, compared with the same period in 2018.

Preparing for the slowdown and due to high inventory levels built up during the frontloading phase, operators on the Trans-Pacific route have started implementing blank sailings (JOC.com, 2019a). Another wave of frontloading cannot be excluded. Several shippers are

Figure 1.5 Global containerized trade, 1996–2018
(Million 20-foot equivalent units and annual percentage change)

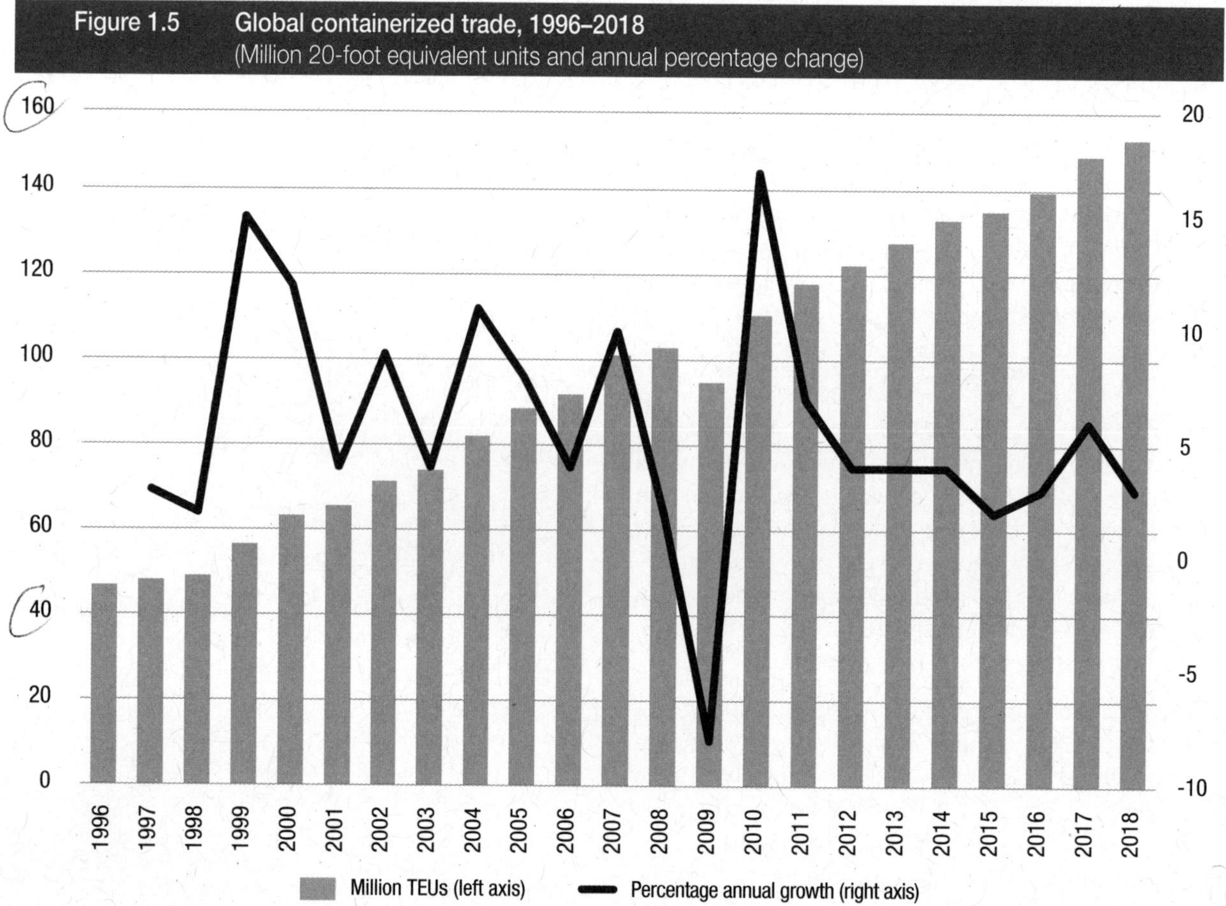

Source: UNCTAD secretariat calculations, based on data from MDS Transmodal, World Cargo Database, May 2019.

Figure 1.6 Global containerized trade by route, 2018
(Market shares, in percentage)

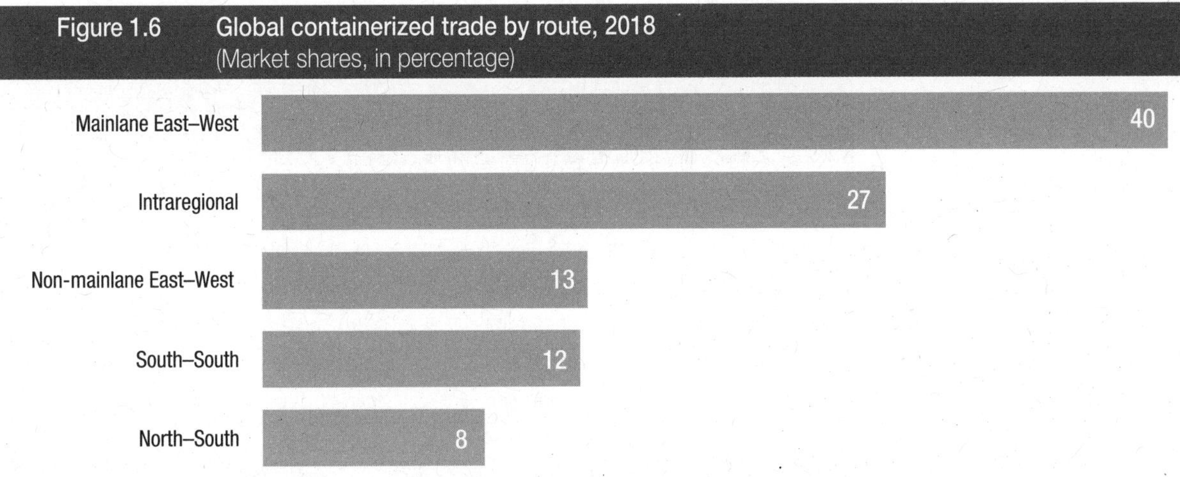

Source: UNCTAD secretariat calculations, based on data from MDS Transmodal, World Cargo Database, May 2019.

rushing again to speed up shipments before tariffs are applied to the remaining $300 billion in United States imports of Chinese goods.

Eastbound and westbound Asia–Europe trade increased by 3.6 per cent, reflecting weaker European import demand and other developments affecting the route. Backhaul eastbound volumes from Europe and westbound volumes on the Trans-Pacific routes were affected by the ban on waste imports into China (Clarksons Research, 2018b). While waste products have been shipped to alternative destinations in neighbouring countries, a growing number of these countries, including Malaysia and the Philippines, are taking a stand and demanding that nations take back their waste (BBC News, 2019). Concerns include the limited processing capacity and the sustainability aspects of waste recycling. This development will likely undermine volumes on the return trip on Asia–Europe and Trans-Pacific containerized trade routes. Elsewhere on the Transatlantic route, growth reached 6.4 per cent, reflecting firm import demand in the United States.

Containerized trade volumes on other routes increased at 1.3 per cent in 2018, down from 6.2 per cent in 2017 (table 1.10). Negative growth on the non-mainlane East–West trade routes (i.e. Western Asia and Indian subcontinent trades with Europe, North America and East Asia), reflect to a large extent contractions across the Western Asia–East Asia route, as well as the Western Asia–North America route. Limited growth on North–South routes – Oceania, sub-Saharan Africa and Latin American trade with Europe and North America – exposed the weakened import demand in Latin American countries.

Intraregional trade growth fell sharply, caused by negative growth on both the Western Asia–South Asia and intra-Latin America trade routes. Growth on the South–South trade routes (Oceania, Western Asia, East Asia, sub-Saharan Africa and Latin America) was constrained by negative growth in Western Asia and Latin America.

Table 1.9 Containerized trade on major East-West trade routes, 2014–2018
(Million 20-foot equivalent units and annual percentage change)

	Trans-Pacific			Asia–Europe			Transatlantic		
	Eastbound	Westbound		Eastbound	Westbound		Eastbound	Westbound	
	East Asia–North America	North America–East Asia	Trans-Pacific	Northern Europe and Mediterranean to East Asia	East Asia to Northern Europe and Mediterranean	Asia–Europe	North America to Northern Europe and Mediterranean	Northern Europe and Mediterranean to North America	Transatlantic
2014	16.2	7.0	**23.2**	6.3	15.4	**21.8**	2.8	3.9	**6.7**
2015	17.5	6.9	**24.4**	6.4	15.0	**21.5**	2.7	4.1	**6.9**
2016	18.3	7.3	**25.6**	6.8	15.4	**22.2**	2.7	4.2	**7.0**
2017	19.5	7.3	**26.8**	7.1	16.5	**23.6**	3.0	4.6	**7.6**
2018	20.9	7.4	**28.2**	7.0	17.4	**24.4**	3.1	4.9	**8.0**
Annual percentage change									
2014–2015	7.9	-2.0	**4.9**	1.4	-2.6	**-1.4**	-2.4	5.6	**2.2**
2015–2016	4.4	6.6	**5.1**	6.3	2.5	**3.6**	0.4	2.9	**1.9**
2016–2017	6.7	-0.5	**4.7**	4.1	6.9	**6.0**	7.9	8.3	**8.1**
2017–2018	7.0	0.9	**5.4**	-1.3	5.7	**3.6**	5.8	6.8	**6.4**

Source: UNCTAD secretariat calculations, based on data from MDS Transmodal, World Cargo Database, May 2019.

Table 1.10 Containerized trade on mainlane East–West routes and other routes, 2016–2019
(Million 20-foot equivalent units and annual percentage change)

	2016	2017	2018	2019[a]
	TEUs			
Mainlane East–West routes	54 845 031	57 950 975	60 721 427	63 710 784
Other routes *of which:*	84 802 064	90 097 054	91 236 532	96 744 144
Non-mainlane East–West	18 530 451	19 609 905	19 463 013	20 517 827
North–South	11 396 198	11 995 463	12 131 139	12 691 808
South–South	17 178 486	18 475 650	18 927 033	21 191 690
Intraregional	37 696 928	40 016 036	40 715 347	42 342 819
World total	**139 647 095**	**148.048 029**	**151 957 959**	**160 454 928**
	Percentage change			
	2016	2017	2018	2019[a]
Mainlane East–West routes	4.07	5.7	4.8	4.9
Other routes (non-mainlane) *of which:*	3.05	6.2	1.3	6.0
Non-mainlane East–West	3.43	5.8	-0.8	5.4
North–South	-0.05	5.3	1.1	4.6
South–South	0.25	7.6	2.4	12.0
Intraregional	5.19	6.2	1.8	4.0

Source: UNCTAD secretariat calculations, based on data from MDS Transmodal, World Cargo Database, May 2019.
Notes: Non-mainlane East-West: Trade involving East Asia, Europe, North America and Western Asia and the Indian subcontinent.
North–South: Trade involving Europe, Latin America, North America, Oceania and sub-Saharan Africa.
South–South: Trade involving East Asia, Latin America, Oceania, sub-Saharan Africa and Western Asia.
[a] Forecast.

In 2018, containerized trade patterns emerged against other trends shaping the liner shipping market. These ranged, among others, from intensified efforts by the shipping industry to embrace digitization as a means of promoting efficiencies and generating greater value across global supply chains (Lloyd's Loading List, 2019a; Lloyd's Loading List, 2019b), to consolidation and vertical integration. While consolidation among major operators remains a key theme in the sector, consolidation activity has involved smaller, regional operators (Clarksons Research, 2019e). There are also signs that carriers are considering vertical integration by taking greater control of inland logistics and aiming to provide integrated service offerings and generate more value. This marks a shift from the approach adopted in the 2000s, when shipping interests were outsourcing such operations to focus on their core business. Some of the largest carriers, including Maersk (Lloyd's Loading List, 2019c) and China COSCO Shipping, are planning to expand their presence to inland terminals, warehouses, customs brokerage and logistics to tap additional business opportunities. They aim to reposition themselves as wider solution providers with strong, long-lasting relationships with customers (Christensen et al., 2019). It was reported that up to 80 per cent of Maersk's earnings currently comes from container shipping and the plan is to achieve a 50:50 split between ocean and non-ocean services in the next few years (Lloyd's Loading List, 2019d).

B. CONTAINER PORT-CARGO HANDLING

1. Global port container throughput slows in 2018

As shown in table 1.11, global container port throughput increased by 4.7 per cent in 2018, down from 6.7 per cent in 2017. In 2018, 793.26 million TEUs were handled in container ports worldwide, reflecting an additional 35.3 million TEUs over 2017, an amount equivalent to the port cargo-handling activity of Singapore, the second leading global container hub in 2018. Growth was supported by traffic on the intra-Asian trade routes, firm consumer demand in the United States and frontloading on the Trans-Pacific route.

The central role of Asia in global trade and shipping is also emphasized by trends in global container port-handling activity. In 2018, the region continued to account for nearly two thirds (figure 1.8) of such activity. Volumes handled increased by 4.4 per cent. With a total of 260.8 million TEUs recorded in 2018, China, including Hong Kong, China and Taiwan Province of China, accounted for over half of the regional total. The maintenance of the Government's ban of waste material imports is likely to increase the incidence of empties in the overall traffic handled by ports.

Figure 1.7 Containerized cargo flows on major East-West container trade routes, 1995–2019
(Million 20-foot equivalent units)

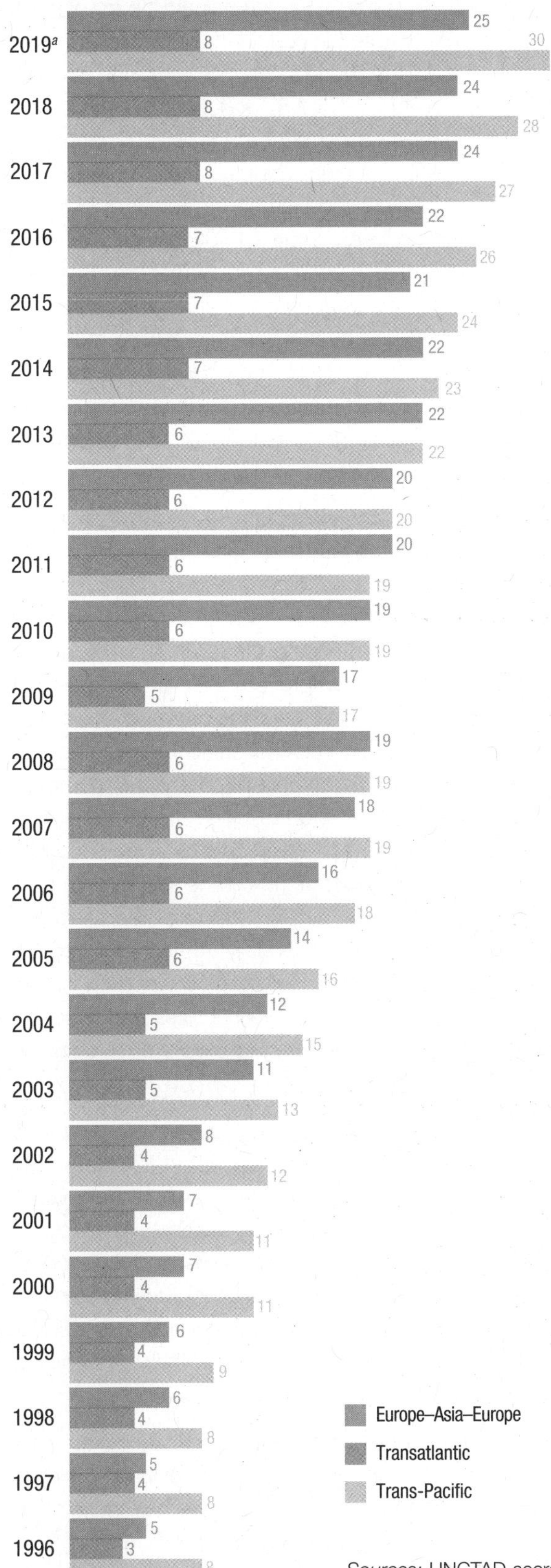

Sources: UNCTAD secretariat calculations, based on Economic Commission for Latin America and the Caribbean, 2010, International maritime transport in Latin America and the Caribbean in 2009 and projections for 2010. Figures from 2009 onward are derived from data provided by MDS Transmodal and Clarksons Research.

[a] Forecast.

Table 1.11 World container port throughput by region, 2017–2018
(20-foot equivalent units and annual percentage change)

	2017	2018	Annual percentage change 2017–2018
Africa	30 398 569	30 940 898	1.8
Asia	488 852 650	510 513 120	4.4
Europe	119 359 397	125 888 633	5.5
Latin America and the Caribbean	48 863 196	51 669 025	5.7
North America	58 510 434	61 352 043	4.9
Oceania	12 003 344	12 896 887	7.4
World total	**757 987 590**	**793 260 606**	**4.7**

Sources: UNCTAD secretariat calculations, based on data collected by various sources, including Lloyd's List Intelligence, Dynamar B.V., Drewry Maritime Research, as well as information posted on the websites of port authorities and container port terminals.

Note: Data are reported in the format available. In some cases, country volumes were estimated based on secondary source information and reported growth rates. Country totals may conceal the fact that minor ports may not be included. Therefore, in some cases, data in the table may differ from actual figures.

Other regions accounted for 16 per cent (Europe), 8 per cent (North America), 6 per cent (Latin America and the Caribbean), 4 per cent (Africa) and 2 per cent (Oceania) of container port-handling activity. These shares reflect to a large extent countries' participation levels in global manufacturing networks and supply chains.

2. Global container port-handling and trade tensions

Asian container ports expanded at a rate of 4.4 per cent, falling short of performance in 2017, where throughput had risen by 7.6 per cent. Ports in China reported 4.2 per cent growth in 2018 (table 1.11). Rapid growth in South-East Asian ports continued, reflecting positive economic performance in countries of the Association of Southeast Asian Nations (ASEAN). Joint ventures of PSA International with the shipping lines seem to have benefited the port of Singapore, as its volumes increased by 8.7 per cent, more than double that of 2017 (3.1 per cent; table 1.12). In 2018, Ocean Network Express (ONE) followed the Mediterranean Shipping Company, CMA CGM, Pacific International Lines and China COSCO Shipping in establishing joint venture terminals in Singapore. Overall, however, Asian container

Figure 1.8 **World container port throughput by region, 2017–2018**
(Percentage share in total 20-foot equivalent units)

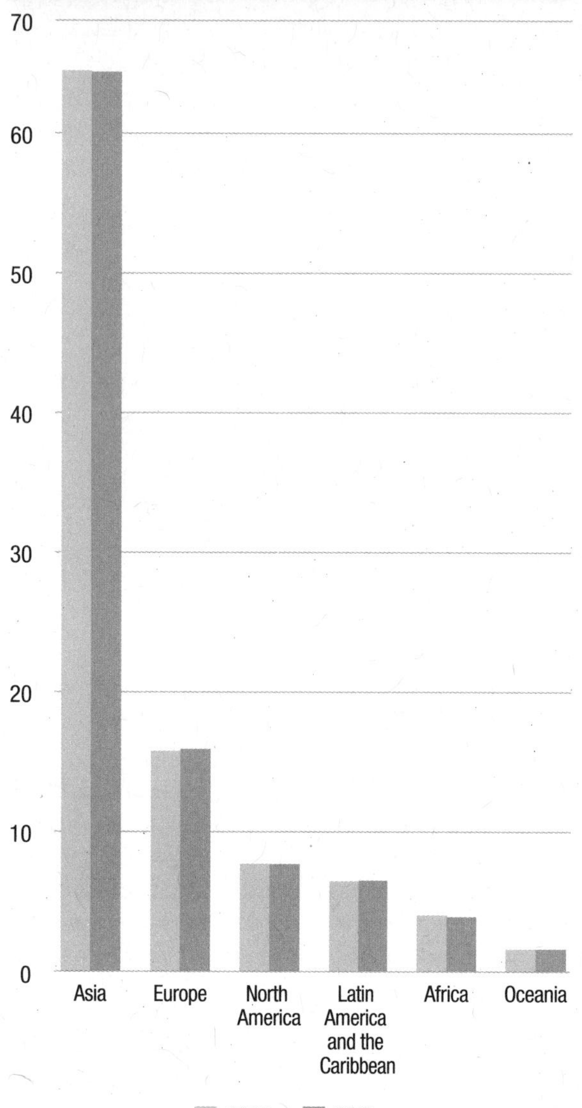

Source: UNCTAD secretariat calculations, based on table 1.11 of this report.

port handling has been affected by constrained growth in Western Asia, a region hampered by sanctions, political tensions and disruptions caused by weather events such as *Cyclone Mekunu* in May 2018.

Supported by trade between China and the European Union, container port throughput in Europe grew steadily at 5.5 per cent, down from 7.2 per cent in 2017. Volumes handled at Rotterdam and Antwerp ports increased rapidly, benefiting from increased imports and trans-shipments, respectively, and route adjustments made by shipping alliances in Antwerp (Shanghai International Shipping Institute, 2019). Container cargo-handling in ports in North America increased by 4.9 per cent, up from 3.9 per cent in 2017. This rate also reflects the distortion caused by frontloading in late 2018. In Africa, container port throughput improved over that of 2017, expanding at a rate of 1.8 per cent in 2018. However, activity was limited by negative developments in the three largest economies of sub-Saharan Africa: South Africa, Nigeria and Angola.

As shown in table 1.12, container cargo handling remains concentrated in certain major ports. Combined throughput at the world's top 20 container terminals increased reached 347.8 million TEUs in 2018, accounting for 43.8 per cent of the world's total. Apart from the contraction in volumes suffered by Dubai, Hong Kong, China and Hamburg, growth at individual ports varied between a low of 0.4 per cent in Klang and a high of 8.7 per cent in Singapore. Shanghai remained the busiest container port worldwide, with volumes expanding by 4.4 per cent, adding more than 2 million TEUs to container port traffic in Shanghai in 2018. Only five ports outside Asia are featured among the 20 leading container ports, namely, Antwerp, Hamburg, Los Angeles, Long Beach and Rotterdam.

With regard to megaships and their implications for container port cargo handling, some observers maintain that the challenges are "past their worst", although there are still some hurdles to be cleared by ports and their customers (Lloyd's Loading List, 2019e). It is argued that terminals have improved their management of ultra large container ship handling but problems remain when ships arrive in port off schedule. Pressure on port-handling capacity is compounded by the combined effects of volume peaks resulting from mega-sized ships and reduced service frequency. This is causing disruption to liner operations on the landside at ports (Lloyd's Loading List, 2019f). That said, the cascading of larger vessels to secondary routes and regional trades with smaller ports will continue to bring its own share of challenges. Larger vessel sizes and fewer but longer ship calls put increasing pressure on container terminals.

According to some observers, however, growth in container ship sizes is not a concern at this stage. This trend appeared to be reinforced, as noted above, by the growing interest of leading carriers in deepening their involvement in inland operations and logistics. By expanding activities beyond the port gate into the wider supply chain, carriers and ports alike aim to diversify sources of revenue and increase their proximity to shippers and the cargo (JOC.com, 2019b).

Another key development with implications for port-cargo handling relates to the impact of trade tensions. Given that imports from China are becoming more expensive, carriers expect volumes and demand to fall on the Trans-Pacific route. As a result, carriers have already started to decrease capacity on this major shipping route with blank sailings by skipping ports (see discussion below on the impact of tariff escalation).

Table 1.12 Leading 20 global container ports, 2018
(20-foot equivalent units, annual percentage change)

	Throughput 2018	Annual percentage change 2017–2018
Shanghai	42 010 000	4.4
Singapore	36 600 000	8.7
Ningbo-Zhoushan	26 350 000	6.9
Shenzhen	25 740 000	2.1
Guangzhou	21 920 000	7.6
Busan	21 660 000	5.5
Hong Kong, China	19 600 000	-5.6
Qingdao	19 320 000	5.5
Tianjin	16 000 000	6.2
Dubai	14 950 000	-2.9
Rotterdam	14 510 000	5.7
Klang	12 030 000	0.4
Antwerp	11 100 000	6.2
Xiamen	10 700 000	3.1
Kaohsiung	10 450 000	1.8
Dalian	9 770 000	0.6
Los Angeles	9 460 000	1.3
Tanjung Pelepas	8 790 000	6.4
Hamburg	8 780 000	-0.2
Long Beach	8 070 000	3.7

Source: Shanghai International Shipping Institute, 2019, *Global Port Development 2018*, April.

C. OUTLOOK AND POLICY CONSIDERATIONS

1. Prospects of world maritime trade, 2019–2024

According to UNCTAD projections, international maritime trade will increase by 2.6 per cent in 2019 and will continue rising at a compound annual growth rate of 3.4 per cent over the 2019–2024 period. These figures are based on the estimated income elasticity of maritime trade over the 2006–2018 period and the latest growth in GDP forecast by the International Monetary Fund for 2019–2024.

Projected growth falls within the range of some existing forecasts (table 1.13) and is consistent with historical trends whereby maritime trade increased at an annual average growth rate of 3.4 per cent between 2006 and 2018. Containerized and dry bulk trades are expected to grow at a compound annual growth rate of 4.5 per cent and 3.9 per cent, respectively, over the 2019–2024 period. Tanker trade (combined crude oil, refined petroleum products, gas and chemicals) is projected to grow by 2.2 per cent during the same period.

Uncertainty remains an overriding theme in the current maritime transport environment, and estimated growth is subject to the realization of forecasted GDP growth and its underlying assumptions. Growth will also be affected by trends in some market segments that had suffered some setbacks in early 2019. These include disruptions to iron ore trade caused by *Cyclone Veronica* in Australia and the severe disruption caused by the Vale dam incident in Brazil. Grain and containerized trades will remain at the forefront of current trade tensions. Crude oil shipments from the Atlantic basin to Asia are expected to support tanker volumes, while sanctions affecting the Islamic Republic of Iran and the Bolivarian Republic of Venezuela, as well as effective compliance with production cuts by the Organization of the Petroleum Exporting Countries, are likely to put pressure on tanker trade. Overall, the outlook for global maritime trade growth will be affected by the degree and speed at which some of these trends unfold.

2. Downside risks and uncertainty

Although not entirely new, a range of existing downside risks intensified and became apparent in 2018. Trade tensions and growth in protectionism topped the list, followed by the decision of the United Kingdom of Great Britain and Northern Ireland to leave the European Union (Brexit). Its impact is more likely to be political – and the impact on global maritime trade is likely to be relatively small. Other risks were the economic transition in China, geopolitical turmoil, natural disasters and disruptions to shipping routes and supply chains, as well as the transition to lower sulphur bunker fuels and low-carbon shipping. These forces were influential in 2018 and can be expected to exert further pressure on maritime transport and trade in the near and longer terms.

Trade tensions and tariff escalation

Escalating tariffs and heighted trade tensions in 2018 and 2019 contrast sharply with past trends, whereby trade liberalization and multilateralism had been mainstreamed into the global trading framework. United States tariffs are matched by retaliatory tariff increases on United States exports by Canada, China and the European Union and by other countries bringing disputes to the World Trade Organization (see table 1.14).

While trade tensions have had an impact on some sectors, overall business sentiment and consumer confidence, as well as support measures (stimulus spending and direct subsidies), may have helped offset much of the direct negative impacts on China and the United States. The moderated impact may also reflect the share of bilateral trade between the two countries. Although these are the two biggest traders in the world, their bilateral trade accounted for only 3.2 per cent of

Table 1.13 International maritime trade development forecasts, 2017–2026

	Growth	Years	Seaborne trade flows	Source
	Compound annual growth (Percentage)			
UNCTAD	3.4	2019–2024	Seaborne trade	*Review of Maritime Transport 2019*
	4.5	2019–2024	Containerized trade	
	3.9	2019–2024	Dry bulk	
	2.2	2019–2024	Tanker trade	
Lloyd's List Intelligence	3.1	2019–2026	Seaborne trade	Lloyd's List Intelligence research, 2017
	4.6	2017–2026	Containerized trade	
	3.6	2017–2026	Dry bulk	
	2.5	2017–2026	Liquid bulk	
	Annual growth			
UNCTAD	2.6	2019	Seaborne trade	*Review of Maritime Transport 2019*
Clarksons Research	2.3	2019	Seaborne trade	*Seaborne Trade Monitor*, June 2019
UNCTAD	1.5	2019	Tanker trade	*Review of Maritime Transport 2019*
Clarksons Research	2.6	2019	Liquid bulk	*Seaborne Trade Monitor*, June 2019
UNCTAD	3.2	2019	Containerized trade	*Review of Maritime Transport 2019*
Lloyd's List	3.0–4.0	2019	Containerized trade	*DynaLiners Monthly*, March 2019
Maersk Line	2.5–3.5	2019	Containerized trade	*DynaLiners Monthly*, April 2019
COSCO	4.5	2019	Containerized trade	*DynaLiners Monthly*, May 2019
Hapag-Lloyd	4.0	2019	Containerized trade	*DynaLiners Monthly*, May 2019
IHS Markit	4.8	2019	Containerized trade	*DynaLiners Monthly*, May 2019
Dynamar	3.5	2019	Containerized trade	*DynaLiners Monthly*, April 2019
Clarksons Research	3.6	2019	Containerized trade	*Container Intelligence Monthly*, May 2019
UNCTAD	3.1	2019	Dry bulk	*Review of Maritime Transport 2019*
Clarksons Research	1.3	2019	Dry bulk	*Dry Bulk Trade Outlook*, June 2019

Source: UNCTAD secretariat calculations, based on forecasts published by the institutions and data providers indicated.

global merchandise trade in 2017. This is dwarfed by the size of intraregional trade, especially in Asia, Europe and North America (UNCTAD, 2019c).

However, the impact can be significant on all countries if tariffs and retaliatory measures are scaled up and prolonged. They will likely compress global volumes, divert trade flows and disrupt global value chains operations, while increasing costs to producers and consumers in China, the United States and other countries.

With regard to maritime trade volumes, gauging the precise actual impact is a complex exercise, given the uncertainty over the sensitivity of demand to tariff-impacted pricing and the potential for trade and volume substitution. Also, exposure varies by cargo type and market segment (table 1.14). Less than 2.0 per cent of global maritime trade by volume (metric tons) is estimated to be subject to tariffs, including when taking into account tariffs enacted in May and June 2019. The direct impact of tariffs through 2019 is estimated to be a reduction of 0.2 per cent in maritime trade in tons and 0.4 per cent lower in ton-miles (Clarksons Research, 2019f).

Trade in grain, notably soybean, and in steel products remain the most affected. Trade in dry bulks is expected to be marginally affected, although the January 2019 disruption in iron ore supply in Brazil is likely to have a greater impact. The impact on iron ore, crude oil, oil products, liquefied petroleum gas, liquefied natural gas and chemicals is expected to be limited. Following a temporary boost to Trans-Pacific container flows due to the rush to build inventories and ship cargoes ahead of the announced additional tariffs, the May 2019 tariffs are expected to affect containerized trade on the Trans-Pacific route the most. However, a knock-on effect on intra-Asian volumes is also likely. In terms of distance-adjusted maritime trade, the impact is also expected to be negative but marginal, as some United States exports are directed towards Europe (e.g. liquefied petroleum gas) and as China increases its purchases from other exporters (liquefied natural gas and grain).

Table 1.14 Tariffs and their estimated impact on international maritime trade, 2018–2019
(Million tons)

	United States tariffs	Retaliatory action	Estimated impact
Round 1	United States introduces tariffs on imports of washing machines and solar panels	China applies tariffs to imports of United States sorghum Tariffs enforced between 17 April and 18 May 2018, then cancelled	Approximately 1 million tons Approximately 5 million tons of grain [now cancelled] Approximately 1 million tons of containers
Round 2	United States introduces tariffs on imports of steel and aluminum	Canada, China, India, Mexico and European Union introduce or propose tariffs	Approximately 33 million tons 22 million tons of steel products 3 million tons of containers 5 million tons of minor bulks 2 million tons of coal 1 million tons of grain
Round 3	United States introduces tariffs of 25 per cent on $34 billion of annual imports from China, followed by tariffs on a further $16 billion of imports from China	China introduces tariffs of 25 per cent on $34 billion of annual imports from the United States, followed by tariffs on a further $16 billion of imports from the United States	Approximately 72 million tons 40 million tons of grain 19 million tons of containers 4 million tons of minor bulks 3 million tons of coal 3 million tons of liquefied petroleum gas 1 million tons of oil products 1 million tons of chemicals 0.4 million tons of vehicles
Round 4	United States introduces 10 per cent import tariffs on $200 billion of imports from China Tariff increased to 25 per cent on 10 May 2019	China introduces 5–10 per cent import tariffs on $60 billion of annual imports from the United States Tariff increased to 5–25 per cent on 1 June 2019	Approximately 66 million tons 46 million tons of containers 15 million tons of minor bulks 2 million tons of liquefied natural gas 2 million tons of chemicals 1 million tons of oil products 1 million tons of iron ore
Round 5	United States threatens to introduce tariffs on the remaining $325 billion of imports from China	China expected to retaliate	Approximately 19 million tons
Round 6	United States considers the introduction of tariffs on imports of cars	European Union preparing a list of products to apply retaliatory tariffs; other countries could also retaliate	Approximately 5 million tons Approximately 5 million tons of vehicles Products affected by retaliatory action not yet announced

Source: UNCTAD secretariat calculations, based on Clarksons Research, 2019f, *Tariffs and the Shipping Context: Assessing the Impact*, Update No. 7, May.

Note: Proposed tariffs are based on official policy announcements, with affected products listed in detail. Possible tariffs are based on informal announcements. Estimated maritime trade affected is based on announcements as of 15 May 2019. The estimate of total trade that is affected by the tariffs is based on 2017 trade data, that is to say, 2017 data are used as the last year before any impacts from these tariffs were realized.

Some sectors are reported to have faced increases in cost of inputs and uncertainty in investment plans, thereby affecting production networks, which are based on vertical specialization and interconnected value chains (United Nations, 2019b). There are already some signs of relocation of manufacturing facilities. Whether these trends can be attributed entirely to the tariff hikes is yet to be confirmed, as increased labour costs in China and automation may have been contributing factors. A report by the European Chamber of Commerce in Beijing found that 25 per cent of European companies with activities in China were affected by the trade tensions and that some 10 per cent of European companies were moving or considering moving their factories away from China to destinations such as Eastern Europe and South-East Asia (Lloyd's Loading List, 2019g). A survey by the American Chamber of Commerce in China and Shanghai found that over 40 per cent of United States manufacturing businesses located in China are considering relocating facilities or have already done so. Of those which left, destinations of choice were South-East Asia (25 per cent) and Mexico (10.5 per cent). Only 6 per cent are reported to be considering shifting operations to the United States (JOC.com, 2019c). Together, these factors are putting pressure on trade volumes and demand for maritime transport services. This is especially relevant to East Asian countries such as Viet Nam that are more integrated into the supply chains of trade between China and the United States (United Nations, 2019b).

Supply chain restructuring implies a potential shift in routing, shipping networks and configuration, service levels and frequency, port call coverage and connectivity. For example, relocating production to other East Asian countries or diverting trade to these countries would result in changes to shipping schedules and port calls. In the foreseeable future, China will remain the main container export hub, as any alternative markets will not be able to readily and without additional cost replicate the scale of the factory experience in China.

Trade diversion and substitution could also occur. Drewry Maritime Research calculates that a 10 per cent increase in United States import prices of goods from China would result in a 6 per cent decline in TEU volume from China to the United States over time, assuming that all other factors are held constant. With tariffs of 25 per cent, the potential TEU contraction would be around 15 per cent for that leg alone (Drewry Maritime Research, 2019a). United States importers will probably consider rerouting products through Taiwan Province of China and Viet Nam, resulting in some trade substitution.

There will be potential winners and losers. Those countries standing to lose will be mainly those supplying raw materials and semi-finished goods to China. UNCTAD estimates that over 80 per cent of the trade affected by United States and Chinese tariffs will be picked up by other countries – with the European Union set to make the biggest gains through increased exports (UNCTAD, 2019c). The study estimates that of the $250 billion in Chinese exports subject to United States tariffs since September 2018, about 82 per cent will be captured by firms in other countries. About 12 per cent will be retained by Chinese firms, and only about 6 per cent will be captured by United States firms. Further, of the approximately $85 billion in United States exports subject to tariffs imposed by China, about85 per cent will be captured by firms in other countries. Canada, Japan and Mexico are expected to attract over $20 billion in trade. Other countries such as India, Pakistan, the Philippines and Viet Nam would capture less of this trade but would still benefit.

These findings are partially supported by the conclusions of another report (Bloomberg, 2018), which expects countries in Asia to be the biggest beneficiaries of product or sourcing substitution. Their findings are more bullish on Argentina, Chile, China, Malaysia, Taiwan Province of China and Viet Nam, than Europe (Lloyd's Loading List, 2019h). CMA CGM also argues that South-East Asian countries will improve their volumes and gain from the bilateral trade tensions (JOC.com, 2019a). Relocating manufacturing operations to South-East Asia could benefit maritime trade and the deployment of smaller vessels. Countries in Eastern Asia do not have the same capabilities as China and will, therefore, require increased trade in intermediate inputs and result in further fragmentation of production. Benefits to shipping from increased intra-Asian trade will depend on the configuration of the new networks.

There remain other concerns, including the possibility that the United States may introduce a global tariff of 25 per cent on cars and automotive parts, which would affect automotive imports from major trading partners. Another concern is the potential imposition of additional tariffs on the aircraft and food industries by the United States on the European Union. Any tariffs will have an impact on key East–West containerized trade routes, including the Trans-Pacific and the Transatlantic routes. In terms of ports, Baltimore, Los Angeles/Long Beach and the Port of New York/New Jersey would be exposed the most. With regard to sourcing countries, China, Germany and Japan will be affected, given their important role in the automotive parts and finished vehicles manufacturing and trade (Drewry Maritime Research, 2019b).

On the upside, however, some developments may help offset some of the pressure. Together, the Belt and Road Initiative of China, continued growth in developing economies and opportunities that may arise from changes in the world energy mix, and other factors could help support continued expansion in global maritime flows. Shipping could also benefit from further trade liberalization deals. The recent entry into force of the Comprehensive and Progressive Agreement for Trans-Pacific Partnership, the Agreement between the European Union and Japan for an Economic Partnership and the Agreement Establishing the African Continental Free Trade provide some support (Economist Intelligence Unit, 2019). The conclusion of the Agreement between the United States of America, the United Mexican States and Canada as a replacement of the North American Free Trade Agreement and efforts to revitalize the multilateral trading system are also expected to diffuse some of the uncertainty about trade policy and to underpin trade growth. An example in this respect is the 13-group member initiative led by Canada and launched in October 2018 with a view to reforming the World Trade Organization and safeguarding its dispute-settlement mechanism. The members include Australia, Brazil, the European Union, Japan and the Republic of Korea.

Accelerating environmental and regulatory agenda

In recent years, environmental sustainability has become a priority on the global policy agenda. Accordingly, a wave of environmentally driven regulation is affecting shipping market dynamics and putting pressure on the maritime transport industry to deliver on the environmental and social responsibility imperative. In this context, a main issue of concern to industry in 2018 was the pending entry into force on 1 January 2020 of the IMO regulation calling for a new 0.5 per cent global sulphur cap on fuel content (see chapters 2 and 4). Therefore, fuel economics and environmental sustainability moved to the centre stage of the debate in 2018. Compliance with the new regulation has implications for shipping in the form of adjustment costs. Approaches to compliance include investing in

environmental equipment, particularly scrubbers, low-sulphur fuels and vessels powered by liquefied natural gas.

Low sulphur and cleaner new fuels are expected to come at a premium, which shipping operators are likely to pass on to their customers through the supply chain. Some observers expect the new IMO regulation to raise the industry's fuel bill by some 50 per cent in 2020. In particular, container shipping is expecting a $10–$15 billion increase in fuel costs (Drewry Maritime Research, 2019a). Shippers are concerned about liner proposals to pass on costs to customers (Lloyd's Loading List, 2019i), although in principle they agree to be charged higher prices if the increase is justified with a credible and trusted mechanism, as well as transparency regarding the applied bunker adjustment factor formula.

For maritime trade, the global sulphur cap could initially have a positive impact on refined petroleum products and crude oil trade volumes as refineries increase their throughput to generate low sulphur-compliant fuels and as demand for different types of crude (sweet and heavy crude oil) changes. The new regulation is expected to increase demand for sweeter crudes that are produced in Brazil, the North Sea and the United States, and boost shipments of sour crudes from, among others, Western Asia to the United States, where refinery capabilities are more adequate for the processing of this grade of crude. One estimate puts the potential increase in tanker demand and trade at 1 per cent (Clarksons Research, 2019g).

Any discussion on fuel economics is also linked to the debate on carbon emission control. One approach being considered at IMO with a view to decarbonizing shipping relates to the setting of mandatory speed restrictions on ships. While supported by a group of stakeholders, including 120 shipping companies, none of which represent the container shipping market, the proposal was rejected by container carriers. The latter maintain that imposing mandatory speed limits would undermine technological advances necessary for decarbonizing shipping and could jeopardize the broader objective of climate change mitigation (JOC.com, 2019d). It is argued that, while there were some marginal gains to be had from further lowering ships' sailing speeds – in terms of fuel consumption and cost – a thorough analysis of the pros and cons of the proposal was still required (Lloyd's Loading List, 2019j). See chapters 2 and 4 for a detailed discussion.

Disruptions to maritime transport operations networks show need for resilience-building

The year 2018 underscored the growing importance of building resilience in supply chains, including maritime transport. Any shock to such systems, resulting in disruptions such as delays, congestion or closure of shipping routes and maritime nodes, including canals, chokepoints and ports, cause inefficiencies and increase the costs of logistics and trade.

In addition to trade protectionism, geopolitical flash points have major implications for maritime trade and shipping. Currently, Western Asia is a geopolitical hotspot affected by tensions involving the Islamic Republic of Iran and some Western Asian countries. The newly imposed sanctions on the Islamic Republic of Iran and incidents involving attacks on tankers (Ratner, 2018) sailing through the Strait of Hormuz in mid-2019 have heighted the concerns about disruptions to oil supply, as well as to containerized trade flows on the East–West containerized trade route linking Asia to Europe. With tensions still running high, container carrier costs are rising, and it is reported that container lines are applying surcharges for cargoes transiting through the region (Lloyd's Loading List, 2019k).

About one third of global oil trade by sea passes through the Strait of Hormoz. This is estimated to be about twice as much as the entire oil production of the United States today (CNN Business, 2019). About 28 per cent of global liquefied natural gas shipments transit through the Strait annually (Ratner, 2018). There are limited alternative oil pipeline routes that could be relied upon to bypass the Strait. Any disruption would entail serious implications for oil supply, maritime trade and oil prices, especially when global oil stocks are low.

Climate change and damage caused by extreme weather events, such as droughts, floods and changes in sea and water levels, undermine the functioning of shipping and port operations and disrupt supply chain operations (see chapter 4). The rising number of hurricanes and typhoons resulting in ports closures in recent years is a case in point. The top container gateway in Bangladesh closed for 72 hours due to a tropical cyclone, causing a backlog of containers at the port and at support inland facilities (JOC.com, 2019e). In addition, low rainfall caused drought in Panama, which required the authorities to impose draft restrictions on ships passing through the Canal. This, in turn, resulted in disruption to smooth passage (JOC.com, 2019f). Similarly, the Rhine river and other inland waterways in Europe experienced the negative effects of severe drought in 2018 (JOC.com, 2019f).

Structural shifts in globalization patterns

Overlapping with trade tensions, supply chain disruptions and an accelerated environmental agenda, some structural forces are unfolding in parallel with the potential to deeply influence the outlook. The following section highlights relevant developments that may signal a transition towards a new normal, whereby growth rates of the magnitude seen over a decade ago are more than likely a thing of the past and globalization as it is known today has undergone significant change since the 1970s.

The *Review of Maritime Transport 2016* questioned whether the slowdown observed in merchandise trade since the 2009 Great Recession had resulted mainly from cyclical factors (weaker GDP growth and macroeconomic cycles) or whether it could be an indication of deeper structural forces such as the ending of globalization. Three parallel drivers of change were noted, namely the limited growth in vertical specialization and the global fragmentation of production, reflecting maturing value chains in China and the United States; the change in the composition of global demand, with slow recovery in investment goods that are more trade intensive than government and consumer spending; and a shift in the composition of consumer demand away from tradeable goods to services. It was argued that these three forces were contributing to create a new normal, whereby the high levels of trade growth of the late 1990s and early 2000s, and the era of high trade-to-GDP ratios would be difficult to replicate and maintain under the new conditions.

Downward pressure on global economic and trade growth and uncertainty triggered by growing trade policy tensions may have exposed trends that support the argument of a structural shift in the nature of globalization with potentially important implications for, inter alia, merchandise trade, supply chains, shipping networks, ship sizes, maritime cargo flows and port-call patterns.

A recent study analysing the dynamics of global value chains in 23 industries reveals that subtle trends have been developing over time. These include falling trade intensity in goods-producing value chains and a growing importance of trade in services and its rapid expansion (McKinsey Global Institute, 2019). Increasingly, a smaller share of goods produced is traded across borders. Between 2007 and 2017, exports declined from 28.1 per cent to 22.5 per cent of gross output in goods-producing value chains. Further, global value chains are becoming more knowledge intensive, with low-skilled and low-cost labour becoming less important for production. It is estimated that less than 20 per cent of trade in global goods is now driven by labour cost arbitrage (McKinsey Global Institute, 2019). Finally, goods-producing value chains, in particular those relating to the automotive, computer and electronics industries, are becoming more regionally concentrated, reflecting efforts to locate closer to demand and consumption markets.

Underpinning these shifts is the rise of technological advances such as digital platforms, the Internet of things, automation and artificial intelligence; in some cases, they could compress trade in goods and promote trade in services.

At their core, the structural shifts that are redefining globalization patterns reflect the growing demand in developing countries as they increasingly consume their own products and tend to reduce their imports of intermediate goods and invest in improved and more comprehensive domestic supply chains. More specifically, these shifts are closely linked with the changing role of China as the engine that has propelled growth in maritime trade over the past two decades. China has experienced robust economic growth over the past 40 years, when annual GDP growth averaged close to 10 per cent, but since 2010, the growth rate has been decreasing. The country's spectacular performance has been instrumental in driving maritime trade volumes, and its heavy reliance on capital investment and infrastructure development for its growth has fuelled demand for maritime transport services for many years.

Relating the expansion of overall imports into China to the performance of world maritime trade is revealing. Annual imports of all types of cargo into China grew by 1,510 million tons (equivalent to 49 per cent of growth in world imports) between 2008 and 2018 (Clarksons Research, 2019c). Therefore, nearly half of global maritime trade expansion over the past decade was attributed to China. In 2018, maritime imports into China accounted for about a quarter of maritime trade and half of dry bulk commodity trade. China is also a key player in containerized trade, given its role as the factory of the world.

Because of the importance of China, the outlook for maritime trade is highly dependent on developments taking place in the Chinese economy. In recent years, China has embarked on a reform agenda that promotes a transition towards a more sustainable economic growth model. Shifting the economy away from investment and manufacturing towards consumer spending and services is indicative of an economy that is maturing. The concern, however, is that the central role of China in driving maritime trade exposes the vulnerability of this trade to developments in that country.

With China cutting excess capacity in the steel and coal industries, the implications for maritime trade and demand for shipping and ports are of strategic importance. Its import demand supporting heavy industries – iron ore, coal and minor bulks – can be expected to moderate. Although the Belt and Road initiative could generate some additional dry bulk cargo flows (Hellenic Shipping News, 2018) and support containerized cargoes in the medium to the long term, it is uncertain whether the added volumes would offset the reduced import demand from China. A related development is the diminishing role of China as the Asian export powerhouse of low-cost manufacturing. As previously noted, China has become more self-reliant and increasingly requires less imported inputs for production. This shift is altering the demand for intermediate goods and weighing on intra-East Asian containerized trade flows. More recently, trade policy risks have underscored this trend.

3. Conclusions

The face of maritime transport is changing, reflecting a shift to a new normal. This is characterized by a moderation in global economic and trade growth, the expanding regionalization of supply chains and trade patterns, a continued rebalancing of the Chinese economy, a larger role of technology and services in value chains and logistics, intensified and more frequent natural disasters and climate-related disruptions, and an accelerated environmental sustainability agenda with an increased awareness of the impact of global warming in particular. Such developments call for improved planning, adequate response measures, and flexible and forward-looking transport policies that anticipate change.

In addition to the demand side, the new normal also entails some new trends on the supply side. Carriers have seemingly abandoned the quest for ever bigger ships and are increasingly eyeing growth prospects associated with the landside of operations. Ports and shipping interests appear to be focusing more attention on expanding activities to inland logistics and tapping potential underlying sources of revenue. Efforts by carriers to emerge as freight integrators and recent moves by some major global container lines to acquire regional carriers (e.g. Maersk's acquisition of Hamburg Süd or CMA CGM's purchase of the logistics company Containerships) could be indicative of industry efforts to adapt to changing conditions. Given the regionalization of trade flows and the trend towards restructuring supply chains, the new normal – despite the potential challenges – could generate opportunities, especially for developing countries striving to integrate more effectively into global trading networks.

Bearing in mind the special needs of developing countries, in particular those of small islands developing States and landlocked developing countries, it is recommended that the following actions be taken:

- Closely monitor demand side risks and assess their implications for maritime transport and trade of developing countries, including vulnerable economies such as small island developing States and landlocked developing countries.
- Favour measures that help boost economic growth, support trade, strengthen resilience and foster environmental sustainability.
- Revitalize trade growth and promote the participation of developing countries in global value chains, bearing in mind changes in globalization patterns, including regionalization and the reduced importance of low-skilled and low-cost labour as a factor of production.
- Encourage product and market diversification to better cope with adverse trade shocks, including the impacts of heightened tariffs and trade tensions. This is particularly relevant for commodity-dependent economies, including small island developing States and landlocked developing countries.
- Adopt a coordinated and multilateral approach to resilience building, including by addressing the risks of natural disasters and the impacts of climate change, especially in vulnerable areas such as small island developing States and delta regions.
- Promote better planning methods and approaches to ensure more flexibility when dealing with uncertainties and rapid shifts in production, trade and shipping patterns. Improved planning may involve scenario planning to inform port investment decisions, among other priorities.
- Foster policies that anticipate potential disruptions and associated response measures that are tailored to countries' developmental challenges and needs.

REFERENCES

Bloomberg (2018). These are the Asian countries that benefit from the trade war. 20 November.

British Broadcasting Corporation (BBC) News (2019). Why some countries are shipping back plastic waste. 2 June.

British Petroleum (2019). *BP Statistical Review of World Energy 2019*. London. June.

Cable News Network (CNN) Business (2019). Why the Strait of Hormuz is so important. 13 June.

Christensen E, Blaeser J, Drake J, Koch G, Labovitz J, Nemeth B, and Pringle H (2019). Global container shipping outlook: IMO 2020 weighs on an industry struggling to generate sustained profitability. Alix Partners. 19 February.

Clarksons Research (2018a). *Shipping Review and Outlook*. Autumn.

Clarksons Research (2018b). China's changing approach to waste imports. Shipping Intelligence Network. 31 May.

Clarksons Research (2019a). *Shipping Review and Outlook*. Spring.

Clarksons Research (2019b). *Seaborne Trade Monitor*. Volume 6. No. 6. June.

Clarksons Research (2019c). *China Intelligence Monthly*. Volume 14. No. 6. June.

Clarksons Research (2019d). *Dry Bulk Trade Outlook*. Volume 25. No. 6. June.

Clarksons Research (2019e). *Containership Market Update*. Quarter 2. 10 May.

Clarksons Research (2019f). *Tariffs and the Shipping Context: Assessing the Impact*. Update No. 7. May.

Clarksons Research (2019g). *IMO 2020 Global Sulphur Cap: Shipping Market Impacts*. 4 February.

Drewry Maritime Research (2019a). *Container Forecaster*. Quarter 2. June.

Drewry Maritime Research (2019b). Trade impact analysis of proposed US [United States] auto tariffs. White Paper. April.

Economic Commission for Latin America and the Caribbean (2010). International maritime transport in Latin America and the Caribbean in 2009 and projections for 2010. Bulletin FAL (Facilitation of Transport and Trade in Latin America and the Caribbean). Issue No. 288. Number 8/2010.

Economist Intelligence Unit (2019). US [United States] protectionism incentivizes regional trade pacts in the rest of the world. 25 March.

Hellenic Shipping News (2018). China's seaborne trade: A spectacular upwards trend. 24 April.

JOC.com (2019a). Trans-Pacific carriers begin blanking sailings. 22 May.

JOC.com (2019b). Cosco accelerates logistics push beyond ocean, ports. 10 May.

JOC.com (2019c).The high cost of sourcing outside China. 30 May.

JOC.com (2019d). Container lines reject mandatory speed limit. 6 May.

JOC.com (2019e). Chittagong port grapples with post-cyclone congestion. 6 May.

JOC.com (2019f). Climate change already pummeling supply chains. 8 May.

Lloyd's Loading List (2019a). Digital initiative can "change course" of container shipping. 18 April.

Lloyd's Loading List (2019b). Digitalization momentum continues to build in container shipping. 4 June.

Lloyd's Loading List. (2019c). Maersk to take control of APM's inland terminals. 16 May.

Lloyd's Loading List (2019d). Maersk to switch focus to inland logistics. 1 July.

Lloyd's Loading List (2019e). Port-handling problems for megaships "past their worst". 15 January.

Lloyd's Loading List (2019f). Ocean freight facing major "disruption" this year. 19 June.

Lloyd's Loading List (2019g). Europe takes cover from US [United States]–China tariffs. 6 June.

Lloyd's Loading List (2019h). US [United States]–China trade war prompts major shifts in goods flows. 10 June.

Lloyd's Loading List (2019i). Shippers condemn carriers' approach to IMO 2020. 1 May.

Lloyd's Loading List (2019j). Pros and cons to slowing box ships further. 13 May.

Lloyd's Loading List (2019k). More leading carriers add war risk charges. 8 July.

McKinsey Global Institute (2019). Globalization in transition: The future of trade and value chains. McKinsey and Company.

MDS Transmodal (2019). World Cargo Database. May.

Ratner M (2018). Iran's [Islamic Republic of Iran's] threats, the Strait of Hormuz and oil markets: In brief. Congressional Research Service Report. 6 August.

Shanghai International Shipping Institute (2019). *Global Port Development 2018*. April.

UNCTAD (2018). *50 Years of Review of Maritime Transport, 1968–2018: Reflecting on the Past, Exploring the Future*. Transport and Trade Facilitation Series. No. 10. (United Nations publication. New York and Geneva).

UNCTAD (2019a). *Trade and Development Report 2019: Financing a Global Green New Deal* (United Nations publication. Sales No. E.19.II.D.15. Geneva).

UNCTAD (2019b). UNCTADstat database. International trade in goods and services. Available at https://unctadstat.unctad.org/wds/ReportFolders/reportFolders.aspx. Accessed 10 July 2019.

UNCTAD (2019c). *Key Statistics and Trends in Trade Policy 2018: Trade Tensions, Implications for Developing Countries* (United Nations publication. Geneva).

United Nations (2019a). *World Economic Situation and Prospects as of mid-2019* (New York).

United Nations (2019b). *World Economic Situation and Prospects 2019* (Sales No. E.19.II.C.1. New York).

World Bank (2019). *Global Economic Prospects, January 2019: Darkening Skies*. World Bank. Washington, D.C.

World Steel Association (2019a). Global crude steel output increases by 4.6% in 2018. 25 January.

World Steel Association (2019b). *World Steel Short-range Outlook* April 2019. 16 April.

2

MARITIME TRANSPORT SERVICES AND INFRASTRUCTURE SUPPLY

The present chapter focuses on development in the supply of shipping services, freight rates and transport costs, as well as port-related infrastructure, superstructure and services. It presents data and trends pertaining to developments observed in 2018 in three main areas: the world fleet, the container shipping segment and port businesses and operations.

Mainstreaming sustainability dimensions (economic, social and environmental), including through IMO regulations and voluntary measures by industry, has become a priority in maritime transport. This chapters focuses on selected issues related to the supply of maritime transport and sustainability, such as regulatory developments affecting the supply of maritime transport, notably the IMO 2020 regulation, scheduled to come into force on 1 January 2020, imposing a more stringent sulphur cap on bunker fuels. The new regulation entails important implications for the maritime sector, including transport costs and the broader sustainable shipping agenda, as IMO 2020 will help address air emissions in shipping and ports.

World fleet developments examine annual fleet growth, changes to the structure and age of the world fleet and highlights from selected segments of the maritime supply chain, such as shipbuilding, ship demolition, ship ownership and ship registration. A more sustainable shipping scenario, driven by an expanding regulatory agenda, could mean short-term disruptions to vessel supply and increased compliance costs, decisions to scrap or to upgrade vessels, as well as incentives to innovate and invest in a new generation of vessels.

The container shipping section identifies leading shipping companies, reviews the evolution of freight rates, earnings and revenues, as well as the increased consolidation and market concentration affecting this shipping segment. A more sustainable shipping scenario, particularly from the perspective of the entry into force of the IMO 2020 regulation, could mean higher costs and price volatility, as well as longer transit times.

The port-related infrastructure and services section presents market shares of global port operators, increased competitive pressures and sustainability expectations affecting port services and infrastructure, and factors underpinning port competitiveness. Faced with increased sustainability expectations, ports are confronted with greater investment needs.

Potential implications for developing countries as providers and users of maritime transport infrastructure and services are also considered.

MARITIME TRANSPORT SERVICES AND INFRASTRUCTURE SUPPLY

In 2019

95,402 ships

1,976,491 thousand dwt

+2.6% carrying capacity

Average age of ships when scrapped **21 years**

In 2018, China, Japan and the Republic of Korea retained their traditional leadership in global ship production, representing 90% of shipbuilding activity.

China 40%

Japan 25%

Republic of Korea 25%

Bangladesh 47.2%

Bangladesh is now the main country of demolition.

Oil tankers = 59% of tonnage sold for demolition

Growth in container fleet capacity **+6%**

2018

2017

2016

2015

2014

2013

2012

Compliance with IMO 2020

will bring new challenges in the shipping industry, particularly in container shipping. Key issues for consideration may include higher costs and price volatility, as well as reduced capacity and increased transit time.

global delivery

China

60% *of bulk carriers*

47% *of general cargo ships*

49% *of container ships*

45% *of offshore vessels*

Republic of Korea

64% *of gas carriers*

42% *of oil tankers*

Japan

45% *of chemical tankers*

Container freight rates

2011

2012

2014

2016

2017

2018

6.4%

3.8%

6% *Supply growth*

2.6% *Demand growth*

Weak trade growth and the sustained delivery of mega container ships in an overly supplied market exerted further pressure on fundamental market balance, resulting in lower freight rates in general.

Recent regulatory developments and voluntary initiatives of industry are aimed at making ship recycling safer and more environmentally friendly.

A. WORLD FLEET

1. Declining growth amid overcapacity

In early 2019, the total world fleet stood at 95,402 ships, accounting for 1.97 billion dead-weight tons (dwt) of capacity. Bulk carriers and oil tankers maintained the largest market shares of vessels in the world fleet (dwt), at 42.6 per cent and 28.7 per cent, respectively (table 2.1). Carrying capacity grew by 2.6 per cent, compared with the beginning of 2018. The growth rate has been declining since 2011, except for a slight increase in 2017, and remains below the trend for the past decade (figure 2.1).[3]

Developments in the world fleet unfolded against a background of continued oversupply in ship-carrying capacity. Oversupply has remained a structural feature in most shipping segments, causing downward pressure on freight rates in 2018. This is particularly the case in the container ship segment (see D.1. Freight rates: Mixed results). Depressed market conditions and poor financial returns of recent years have been driving container shipping companies to adopt coping strategies, such as mergers and acquisitions, consolidation, vertical integration and change in deployment patterns (see D.3. Increasing consolidation and market concentration in container shipping). These strategies may affect developing countries' connectivity and transport costs (UNCTAD, 2018a).

Gas carriers were the most dynamic segment of the world fleet, experiencing the highest growth rate in the 12 months to 1 January 2019 (7.25 per cent of dwt) (figure 2.2). One of the reasons behind this trend is the liquefied natural gas sector, which has witnessed significant growth in recent years. This is likely to continue in the future, given heightening environmental concerns and the pressure of the maritime sector to switch to cleaner fuels (see chapter 1). Growth in the world container fleet also continued (5 per cent), although at more moderate rates compared with gas carriers. Two segments – chemical tankers and bulk carriers – have shown stable growth, unlike the oil tanker segment, which has undergone declining growth.

Table 2.1 World fleet by principal vessel type, 2018–2019
(Thousand dead-weight tons and percentage)

Principal types	2018	2019	Percentage change 2019/2018
Oil tankers	562 035	567 533	0.98
	29.2	*28.7*	
Bulk carriers	818 921	842 438	2.87
	42.5	*42.6*	
General cargo ships	73 951	74 000	0.07
	3.8	*3.7*	
Container ships	253 275	265 668	4.89
	13.1	*13.4*	
Other types	218 002	226 854	4.06
	11.3	*11.5*	
Gas carriers	64 407	69 078	7.25
	3.3	*3.5*	
Chemical tankers	44 457	46 297	4.14
	2.3	*2.3*	
Offshore vessels	78 269	80 453	2.79
	4.1	*4.1*	
Ferries and passenger ships	6 922	7 097	2.53
	0.4	*0.4*	
Other/ not available	23 946	23 929	-0.07
	1.2	*1.2*	
World total	**1 926 183**	**1 976 491**	**2.61**

Source: UNCTAD secretariat calculations, based on data from Clarksons Research.

Notes: Propelled seagoing merchant vessels of 100 tons and above; beginning-of-year figures.

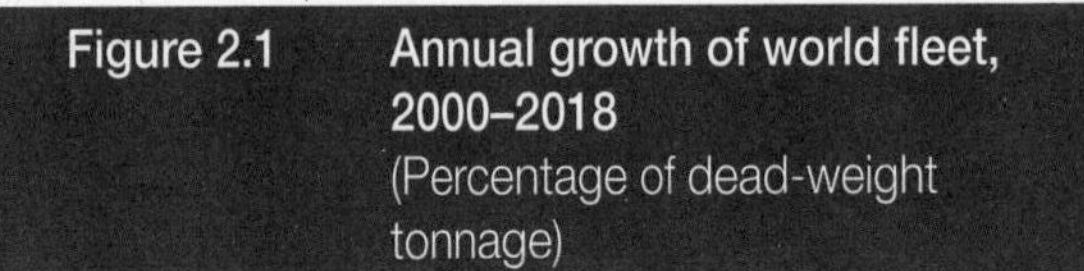

Figure 2.1 Annual growth of world fleet, 2000–2018
(Percentage of dead-weight tonnage)

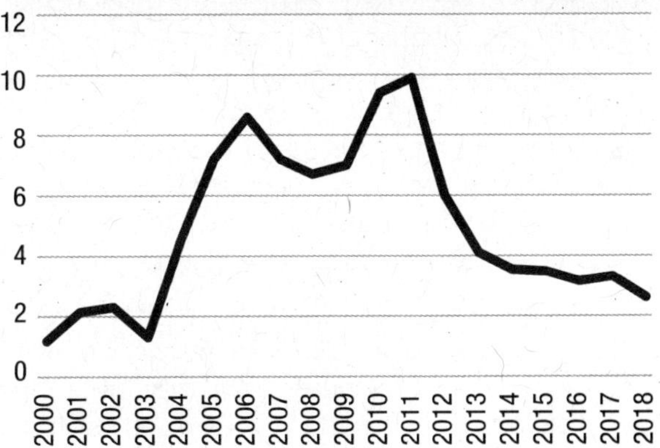

Source: UNCTAD, *Review of Maritime Transport*, various issues.

[3] Data in this chapter concerning tonnage and number of ships in the world fleet were provided by Clarksons Research. Unless stated otherwise, the vessels covered in the UNCTAD analysis include all propelled seagoing merchant vessels of 100 gross tons and above, including offshore drillships and floating production, storage and offloading units. Military vessels, yachts, waterway vessels, fishing vessels and offshore fixed and mobile platforms and barges are not included. Data on fleet ownership only cover ships of 1,000 gross tons and above, as information on the true ownership of smaller ships is often not available. For more detailed data on the world fleet, including registration, ownership, building and demolition, as well as other maritime statistics, see http://stats.unctad.org/maritime.

Figure 2.2 Growth of the world fleet in dead-weight tonnage, selected vessel types, 2013–2019 (Annual percentage change)

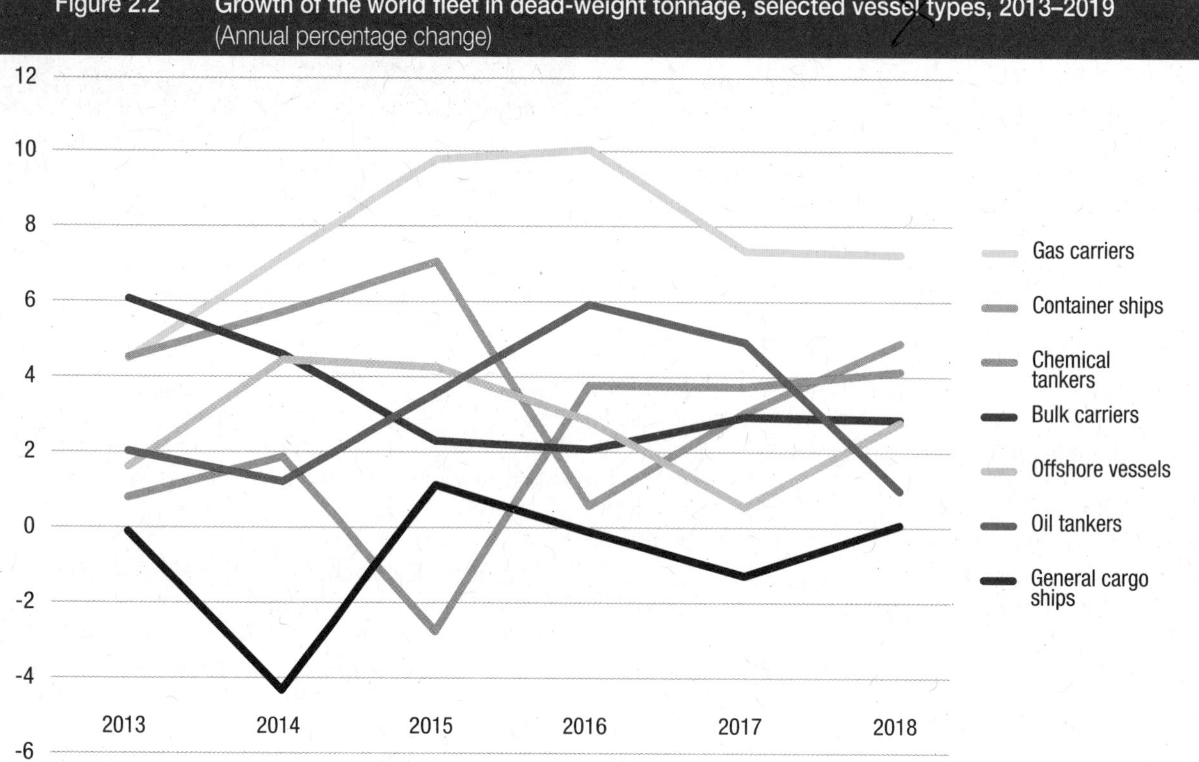

Sources: UNCTAD secretariat calculations, based on data from Clarksons Research and *Review of Maritime Transport*, various issues.
Notes: Propelled seagoing vessels of 100 gross tons and above as at 1 January; does not include inland waterway vessels.

2. Young fleets

The age of the world fleet has some implications for the sustainability of shipping, as younger vessels tend to be more efficient and less likely to break or cause environmental damage. A young fleet makes up most of the carrying capacity of the world fleet. The age of the fleet has implications for the sustainability of shipping and is an important factor to be considered in the transition to sustainable shipping operations – as these implications determine decisions to upgrade, renew and scrap the fleet, thereby affecting the supply of capacity, which also has an impact on freight rates and earnings.

In early 2019, the average age of the world merchant fleet was 21 years (dwt) (table 2.2), representing a slight increase over the previous year. However, this is not uniform across vessel types. As shown in figure 2.3, ships below 10 years of age represent a high proportion of the carrying capacity of bulk carriers (71 per cent), followed by container ships (56 per cent) and oil tankers (54 per cent). On the other hand, only 35 per cent of the carrying capacity of general cargo ships and 41 per cent of "other types" of vessels correspond to ships below 10 years of age, suggesting that these two segments are not undergoing fleet renewal.

The entry into force of the IMO 2020 regulation, which will limit the amount of sulphur for marine fuel oil to 0.50 per cent as of 1 January 2020, may disrupt the supply of vessels. In the short run, a reduction in the supply of vessels could occur due to the temporary withdrawal of vessels, particularly bigger ones, to be fitted for scrubbers. This is expected to cause vessels to be out of service for a few months and reduce carrying-capacity supply across the major segments by 0.5–1.4 per cent in 2019 and by 0.3–0.7 per cent in 2020 (Clarksons Research, 2019a).

Scrapping of less fuel-efficient vessels in the form of older ships may also increase, with an estimated projection of 26 million dwt equivalent in 2019 and 44 million dwt equivalent in 2020, reducing the growth in the world fleet by 0.8 per cent in 2020, notably 1.1 per cent across the bulker fleet, 0.8 per cent across the tanker fleet, and 0.7 per cent across the container ship fleet (Clarksons Research, 2019a). A more detailed discussion on the potential implications of the IMO 2020 regulation is set out in section D.2.

B. SHIPBUILDING, NEW ORDERS AND DEMOLITION

1. Bulk carriers, oil tankers and container ships take the lead in shipbuilding

In 2018, China, Japan and the Republic of Korea retained their leadership in global ship production (table 2.3), representing together 90 per cent of shipbuilding activity and individually, 40 per cent (China), 25 per cent (Japan) and 25 per cent (Republic of Korea). In 2018, China built 60 per cent of the global delivery of bulk

Table 2.2 Age distribution of world merchant fleet by vessel type, 2018–2019
(Percentage of total ships and dead-weight tonnage)

Country grouping and vessel type		Years					Average age	Average age
		0–4	5–9	10–14	15–19	20 +	2019	2018
World								
Bulk carriers	Percentage of total ships	22.84	44.09	14.64	8.70	9.74	9.72	9.07
	Percentage of dead-weight tonnage	25.12	46.28	14.15	7.53	6.92	8.88	8.27
	Average vessel size (dwt)	81 482	77 757	71 592	64 156	52 622		
Container ships	Percentage of total ships	16.68	21.77	31.32	13.95	16.28	12.34	11.89
	Percentage of dead-weight tonnage	27.58	28.52	27.06	10.52	6.32	9.44	9.02
	Average vessel size (dwt)	83 362	66 050	43 565	38 031	19 579		
General cargo	Percentage of total ships	4.71	14.60	14.38	7.11	59.20	26.39	25.64
	Percentage of dead-weight tonnage	9.34	25.85	17.23	9.57	38.01	18.95	18.37
	Average vessel size (dwt)	8 770	7 507	5 255	6 360	2 725		
Oil tankers	Percentage of total ships	14.67	21.73	18.22	9.40	35.98	18.87	18.53
	Percentage of dead-weight tonnage	22.54	31.41	24.97	15.74	5.35	10.11	9.97
	Average vessel size (dwt)	82 577	78 314	73 092	90 578	8 241		
Other	Percentage of total ships	12.62	19.01	13.45	8.27	46.65	22.85	22.39
	Percentage of dead-weight tonnage	22.00	19.32	19.57	10.92	28.19	15.44	15.44
	Average vessel size (dwt)	10 461	6 548	8 839	8 136	4 214		
All ships	Percentage of total ships	12.72	21.56	15.29	8.53	41.91	20.98	20.48
	Percentage of dead-weight tonnage	23.76	35.76	19.73	10.76	9.99	10.44	10.06
	Average vessel size (dwt)	44 370	39 985	30 696	30 946	6 342		
Developing economies – all ships								
	Percentage of total ships	12.92	22.92	14.83	7.75	41.58	20.06	19.61
	Percentage of dead-weight tonnage	22.85	35.94	15.90	10.35	14.97	11.18	10.85
	Average vessel size (dwt)	34 032	31 822	21 007	26 505	7 124		
Developed economies – all ships								
	Percentage of total ships	13.69	22.39	17.85	10.62	35.45	19.64	19.13
	Percentage of dead-weight tonnage	24.75	36.02	22.37	10.95	5.92	9.72	9.33
	Average vessel size (dwt)	58 320	50 545	40 750	35 471	7 175		
Countries with economies in transition – all ships								
	Percentage of total ships	5.95	9.25	7.69	3.80	73.31	29.94	29.38
	Percentage of dead-weight tonnage	9.00	25.75	22.60	15.09	27.55	16.45	16.06
	Average vessel size (dwt)	13 224	21 478	23 065	28 397	2 648		

Source: Clarksons Research.
Notes: Propelled seagoing vessels of 100 gross tons and above; beginning-of-year figures.

Figure 2.3 Age distribution of the merchant fleet, as at 1 January 2019
(Percentage of dead-weight tonnage)

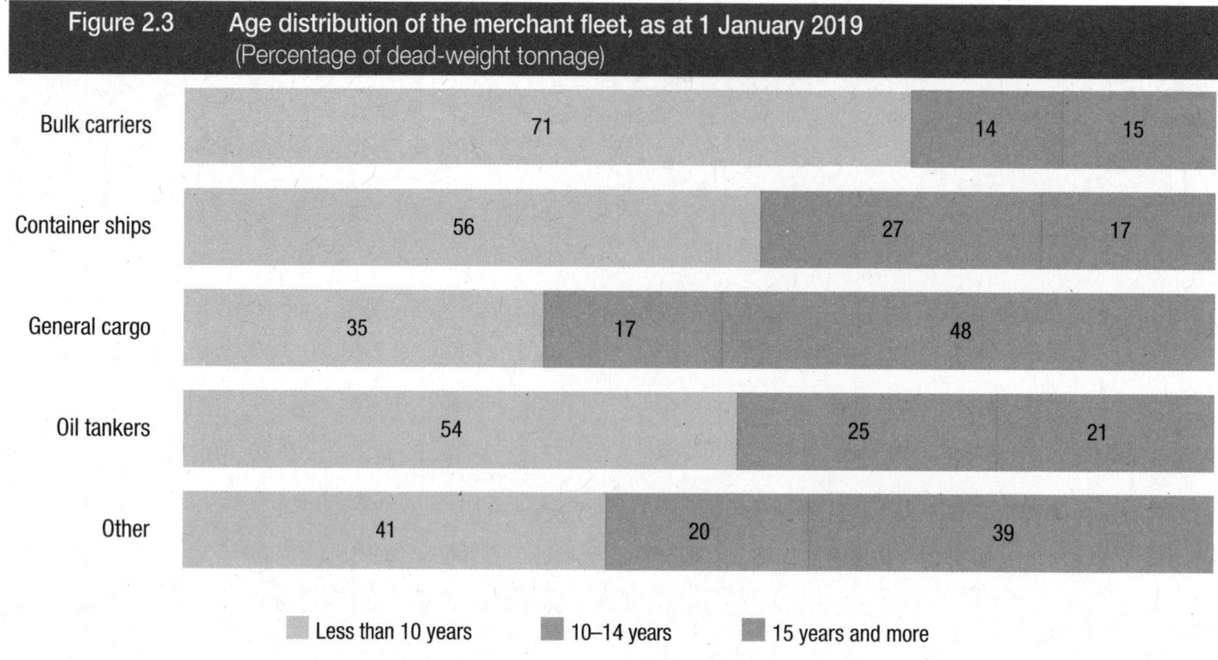

Source: UNCTAD secretariat calculations, based on data from Clarksons Research.

carriers, 49 per cent of container ships, 47 per cent of general cargo ships and 45 per cent of offshore vessels. The Republic of Korea led globally in newbuildings of gas carriers (with a share of 64 per cent), followed by oil tankers (42 per cent). The top segment in Japan was chemical tankers, which represented 45 per cent of global newbuilding deliveries, and bulk carriers, 33 per cent.

Ships delivered in 2018 were mostly bulk carriers (26.7 per cent of total gross tons), followed by oil tankers (25 per cent), container ships (23.5 per cent) and gas carriers (13 per cent) (table 2.3). Between 2014 and 2018, dry bulk carriers recorded the most newbuilding deliveries, although they experienced a downturn trend starting in 2016 (figure 2.4). Subsequently, oil tankers recorded the second-highest delivery level since 2016, overtaking container ships, which stood third, followed by gas carriers. The trendline during this period suggests an increasing number of container ships and gas carriers and a decreasing number of oil tankers and dry bulk carriers. This could be attributed to a demand for container ships of large capacity (above 15,000 TEUs), which grew by 33 per cent in 2018 (Clarksons Research, 2019b) and lower growth in demand for oil tankers and bulk carriers due to existing oversupply capacity (BIMCO, 2019; Gasparoti and Rusu, 2018).

Table 2.3 Deliveries of newbuildings by major vessel types and countries of construction, 2018
(Thousand gross tons)

	China	Japan	Philippines	Republic of Korea	Rest of world	World total	Percentage
Oil tankers	4 505	2 819	288	6 046	865	**14 524**	25.0
Bulk carriers	9 274	5 134	654	352	91	**15 505**	26.7
General cargo ships	416	159	-	74	234	**884**	1.5
Container ships	6 630	3 020	992	2 632	341	**13 614**	23.5
Gas carriers	762	1 754	52	4 709	26	**7 302**	12.6
Chemical tankers	466	647	-	274	64	**1 452**	2.5
Offshore vessels	774	18	-	472	453	**1 718**	3.0
Ferries and passenger ships	162	72	2	51	1 573	**1 860**	3.2
Other	270	816	-	24	76	**1 186**	2.0
Total	**23 260**	**14 440**	**1 988**	**14 633**	**3 724**	**58 045**	**100.0**
Percentage	40.1	24.8	3.4	25.2	6.4	**100.0**	

Source: Clarksons Research.

Notes: Propelled seagoing merchant vessels of 100 gross tons and above. For more data on other shipbuilding countries, see http://stats.unctad.org/shipbuilding.

Figure 2.4 Deliveries of newbuildings for selected vessel types, 2014–2018
(Thousand gross tons)

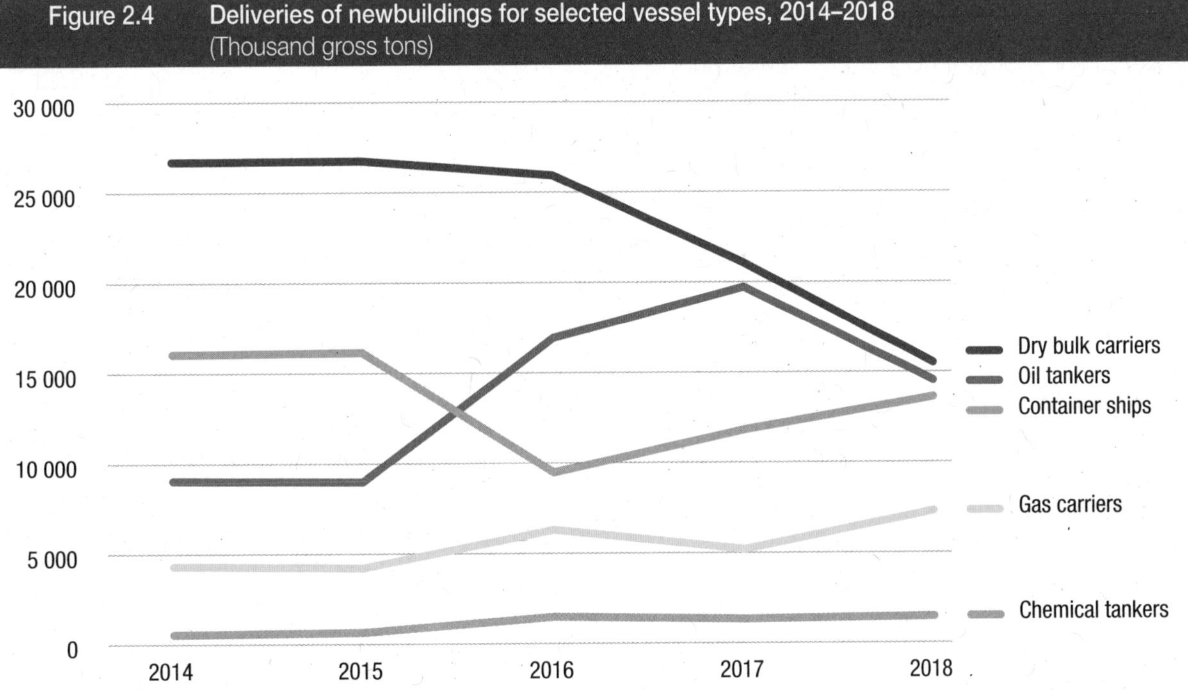

Source: UNCTAD, *Review of Maritime Transport*, various issues; based on data from Clarksons Research.

2. Vessel orders

Orders for the delivery of bulkers and oil tankers declined, in favour of orders for large and feeder vessels servicing container ships. World tonnage on order for all main vessel types further decreased in the 12 months to January 2019 (figure 2.5), reflecting a drop in orders since 2016 (Barry Rogliano Salles, 2019). The reduction is particularly marked for dry bulk carriers (37 per cent) and oil tankers (48 per cent).

In the container ship segment, it is expected that most orders will cover large vessels (above 10,000 TEUs of capacity) and feeder ships (below 3,000 TEUs of capacity) (IHS Markit, 2019; Clarksons Research, 2019c). The gas tanker segment could also witness an increase in the number of orders, as this fleet may not suffice to meet the growing demand for trade in liquefied natural gas.

The shipbuilding sector has been undergoing reforms to ensure competitiveness in a context of declining orders, mitigate the impact on a labour-intensive sector and develop a modern vessel-construction model fit for the future. In several Asian countries, Governments have taken various initiatives to support the shipbuilding industry. The use of public funds to finance shipbuilding prompted a complaint at WTO against the Republic of Korea in November 2018, on grounds that it may grant subsidies that may have a substantial impact on the price of ships, ship engines and maritime equipment, affecting trade flows in these products. At the same time, the shipbuilding industry in several European countries has called for increased Government support to help achieve the target of zero-emission shipping by 2050 (JOC.com, 2018a, 2018b).

Instances of consolidation have also been observed in the shipbuilding industry, namely in China and the Republic of Korea, where Korea Development Bank, which is the main shareholder of Daewoo Shipbuilding and Marine Engineering, has agreed to sell 55.7 per cent of its controlling stake in the yards to Hyundai Heavy Industries (Splash247.com, 2019a). This would result in control of 20 per cent of the global market for new ships, and an even bigger share of the market for liquefied natural gas carriers (*The Wall Street Journal*, 2019). Another potential merger between two main shipbuilders in China, namely China State Shipbuilding Corporation and China Shipbuilding Industry Corporation, is also being planned (Splash247.com, 2019b).

3. Sustainable ships: The path to developing zero-emission vessels

The entry into force of several global environmental instruments and the adoption of voluntary standards in the sector will have an impact on the maritime transport industry, particularly in the shipbuilding subsector, which will be responsible for incorporating these new standards into the design and construction of ships. Accordingly, considerable investments are going into research and development for better hydrodynamics, more energy-efficient engines, lower carbon fuels and carbon-free fuels for ships (United Kingdom Chamber of Shipping, 2018). For example, the Green Maritime Methanol consortium of leading international maritime companies, shipowners, shipyards, manufacturers, ports and research institutions, supported by the Ministry of Economic Affairs and Climate Policy of the Netherlands have joined forces to investigate the

Figure 2.5 World tonnage on order, 2000–2019
(Thousand dead-weight tons)

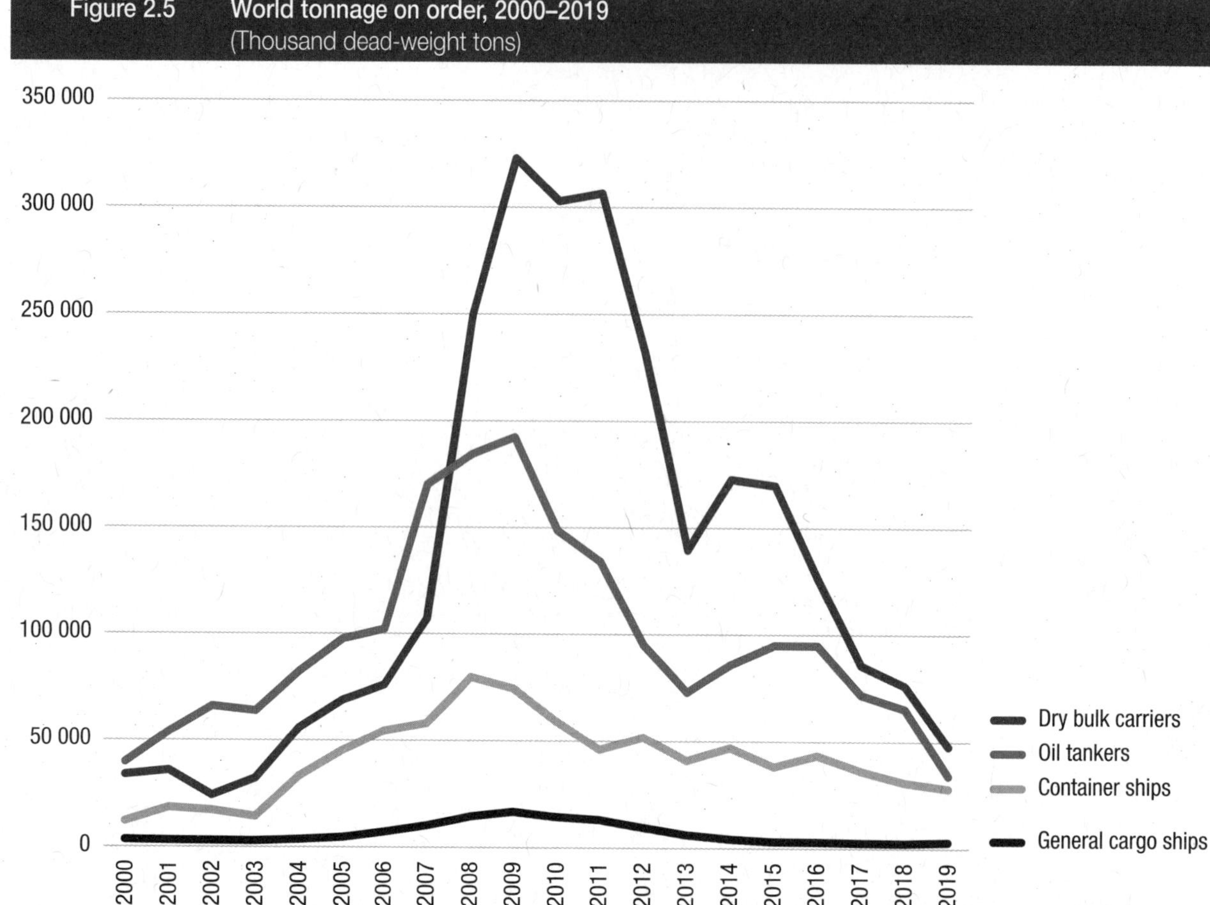

Source: UNCTAD secretariat calculations, based on data from Clarksons Research.
Notes: Propelled seagoing merchant vessels of 100 gross tons and above; beginning-of-year figures.

feasibility of methanol as a sustainable alternative transport fuel in the maritime sector in 2019 (Hellenic Shipping News Worldwide, 2019a). In another example, Maersk invested approximately $1 billion per year in innovation and technology between 2014 and 2019 to improve the technical and financial viability of carbon-free solutions and develop and deploy energy-efficient solutions (Novethic, 2019). Table 2.4 outlines the measures being considered to produce cleaner and more energy-efficient vessels.

In addition, as the sector is increasingly heading towards decarbonization, voluntary ship environmental evaluation schemes are also emerging. Examples include the Clean Shipping Index, Clean Cargo Working Group, Environmental Ship Index, Green Award and Ship Energy Efficiency Management Plan. Shipbuilding countries, for which the sector is of national importance in terms of direct financial returns, employment and supply-chain contributions, are also exploring options to remain competitive in this new context.

Table 2.4 Efficiency-improvement measures to achieve zero-emission shipping by 2050

Technological measures to improve ship-design efficiency	Use of alternative zero-carbon fuels or energy sources
Light construction materials	Batteries to power ships
Slender design	Hydrogen fuel cells
Propulsion-improvement devices	Hydrogen as fuel for internal combustion engines
Bulbous bows	Ammonia fuel cells
Air lubrication systems	Ammonia as fuel for internal combustion engines
Advanced hull coating	Synthetic diesel
Ballast water-system design	Synthetic methane
Energy-efficiency measures	Advanced biofuels
Engine and auxiliary systems improvement	Electricity to power ships
	Wind assistance

Sources: Organization for Economic Cooperation and Development and International Transport Forum, 2018, *Decarbonizing Maritime Transport: Pathways to Zero-carbon Shipping by 2035*; European Federation for Transport and Environment, 2018, *Road Map to Decarbonizing European Shipping*; University Maritime Advisory Services, 2019, How can shipping decarbonize?

Important elements that could mainstream sustainability considerations into shipbuilding and equipment manufacturing and help seize new opportunities include the following: building awareness about emerging standards among marine equipment manufacturers and suppliers; promoting research and development in environmentally friendly ship-related technologies, energy saving and carbon emissions reduction for ships; developing environmentally friendly maritime expertise; and promoting partnerships with technical and training institutes to spur innovation and the uptake of energy-saving and eco-friendly technologies (Global Environment Facility et al., 2018a; Lee and Nam, 2017).

The implementation of activities that can support the shipping industry's transition to a low-carbon future will require cooperation among stakeholders in the industry. This would have cost implications, require the development of human and technological capabilities, and involve technology adoption and transfer, especially in developing countries. Several initiatives have emerged in recent years to help Governments and maritime stakeholders achieve these objectives. There are several examples. First, the Global Maritime Energy Efficiency Partnerships Project, launched in 2015, aims to support increased uptake and implementation of energy-efficiency measures for shipping. It is actively involved in capacity-building for maritime administrations on data collection with regard to fuel oil consumption and emissions, which is an obligation derived from MARPOL, annex VI. Second, the Global Industry Alliance to Support Low-carbon Shipping, launched in 2017, is a public–private partnership initiative involving leading shipowners and operators, classification societies, engine and technology builders and suppliers, big data providers, and port and oil companies. They are working to eliminate common barriers to the uptake and implementation of energy-efficient technologies and operational measures. In March 2019, the Panama Canal Authority became the first developing country entity to join the Alliance. Third, an initiative called Green Voyage-2050 was launched in May 2019 to promote and test technical solutions to reduce emissions, as well as enhance knowledge and information sharing to support the IMO greenhouse gas reduction strategy. As part of this initiative, eight countries from five regions (Africa, Asia, the Caribbean, Latin America and the Pacific), will assume pilot roles and take action at the national level. The project will also build capacity in developing countries, including in small island developing States and the least developed countries, to fulfil their commitments to meet climate-change and energy-efficiency goals for international shipping. (For further information on regulatory activities related to greenhouse gas emissions reduction, see chapter 4.)

4. Ship demolition: Making ship recycling more environmentally friendly and safer

From a sustainability perspective, ship demolition has been associated with adverse environmental effects on ecosystems and occupational health hazards. Scrapping is a segment of the maritime supply chain dominated by developing countries due to several factors, including lower labour costs, a high proportion of utilization of steel from recycled ships for domestic manufacturing and, at times, weak enforcement of regulations.

Most of the tonnage sold for demolition relates to oil tankers, bulk carriers and container ships. However, in contrast with prior figures identifying bulk carriers as the most frequent vessel type sold for demolition, oil tankers took the lead in 2018 (table 2.5).

In 2019, Bangladesh, India, Pakistan and Turkey maintained their leadership in this segment of the maritime supply chain (table 2.5). However, for the

Table 2.5 Reported tonnage sold for demolition by major vessel type and country of demolition, 2018
(Thousand gross tons)

	Bangladesh	India	Pakistan	Turkey	China	World total	Percentage
Oil tankers	5 989	1 946	2 824	66	14	**10 884**	**59.5**
Bulk carriers	1 115	465	829	18	53	**2 495**	**13.6**
General cargo ships	127	149	57	65	5	**405**	**2.2**
Container ships	620	402	38	54	152	**1 284**	**7.0**
Gas carriers	347	455	48	3	97	**951**	**5.2**
Chemical tankers	43	167	28	28	2	**268**	**1.5**
Offshore vessels	181	581	72	143	30	**1 156**	**6.3**
Ferries and passenger ships	..	171	..	14	..	**185**	**1.0**
Other	210	353	47	29	5	**673**	**3.7**
Total	**8 632**	**4 690**	**3 943**	**418**	**359**	**18 300.9**	**100.0**
Percentage	**47.2**	**25.6**	**21.5**	**2.3**	**2.0**	**100**	

Source: Clarksons Research.

Notes: Propelled seagoing vessels of 100 gross tons and above. Estimates for all countries available at http://stats.unctad.org/shipscrapping.

Figure 2.6 Reported tonnage sold for demolition, selected countries, 2014–2018

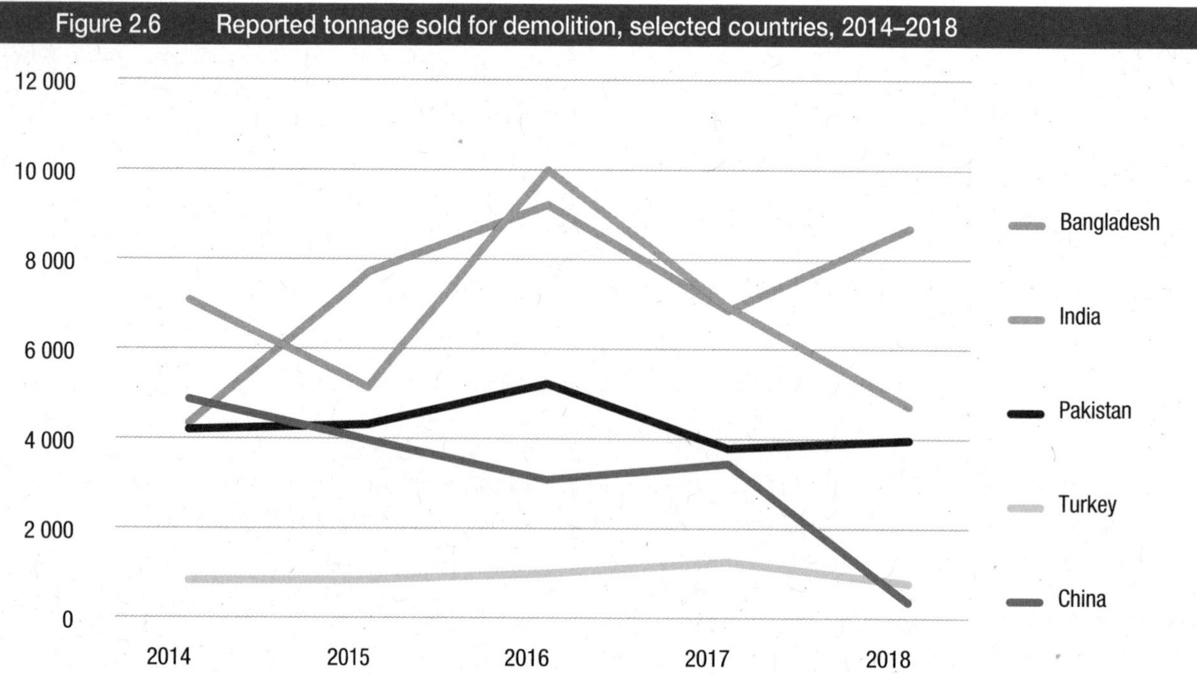

Source: UNCTAD, *Review of Maritime Transport*, various issues, based on data from Clarksons Research.

first time, Bangladesh became the main country of demolition. Figures for the period 2014–2018 show that China and India, and to a lesser extent, Turkey, show a decrease in scrapping activity (figure 2.6). Recent regulatory developments and voluntary initiatives by the industry to make ship recycling more environmentally friendly and safe to humans explain these trends.

In recent years, several countries have tightened regulations pertaining to ship demolition. This move is linked to the anticipation of the entry into force of the IMO Hong Kong [China] International Convention for the Safe and Environmentally Sound Recycling of Ships of 2009, as well as a European Union regulation in force since 31 December 2018. The latter requires certification to include shipyards in the list of yards where European Union-flagged ships can be dismantled and introduces requirements relating to shipping companies.

Voluntary initiatives by industry associations and other domestic policy priorities are also inducing changes in the sector. The latter is the case of China, whose ban on the entry of all foreign ships to China for recycling, represents one of a wide range of measures aimed at controlling environmental pollution in the country. India is pursuing the voluntary application of requirements of the Hong Kong [China] International Convention for the Safe and Environmentally Sound Recycling of Ships of 2009 and to achieve this, is investing heavily in introducing upgrades to its facilities (Splash247.com, 2019c; *The Economist*, 2019). Preparations for the entry into force of the IMO 2020 regulation could affect scrapping activity in 2019, as the scrapping of old vessels of smaller tonnage will probably increase to avoid the costly investment of upgrading them.

C. SHIP OWNERSHIP AND REGISTRATION

1. Five countries own more than half of the world fleet

As of 1 January 2019, the top five shipowning economies were Greece, Japan, China, Singapore and Hong Kong China, accounting for more than 50 per cent of the world's tonnage (table 2.6). Data for the last five years reveal that Germany, Japan and the Republic of Korea have been losing ground, while Greece, Singapore, China and Hong Kong, China have sustained an increasing trend (figure 2.7).

More than 70 per cent of the fleet (tonnage) is registered under a foreign flag. In a minority of countries (10 out of the leading 35 shipowning countries), however, the number of vessels flying under the national flag represent more than half of their fleet. These are as follows: the Islamic Republic of Iran (98 per cent), Indonesia (93 per cent), Viet Nam (81 per cent), Thailand (73 per cent), Hong Kong, China (72 per cent), Saudi Arabia (72 per cent), Malaysia (72 per cent), India (66 per cent), Italy (61 per cent) and Singapore (56 per cent) (table 2.6). Malaysia had the largest increase in the share of its nationally flagged fleet, from about 50 per cent in January 2018 to 72 per cent in January 2019.

In terms of the commercial value of the fleet, the top five shipowning countries in 2019, representing 45 per cent of the world total, are Greece, Japan, the United States, China and Norway. Greece is among the leading owners of oil tankers, bulk carriers and gas carriers; Japan and

Table 2.6 Ownership of world fleet ranked by dead-weight tonnage, 2019

	Country or territory of ownership	Number of vessels			Dead-weight tonnage				
		National flag	Foreign flag	Total	National flag	Foreign flag	Total	Foreign flag as a percentage of total	Total as a percentage of total
1	Greece	670	3 866	4 536	60 776 654	288 418 535	349 195 189	82.60	17.79
2	Japan	875	2 947	3 822	35 532 308	189 588 907	225 121 215	84.22	11.47
3	China	3 987	2 138	6 125	90 930 376	115 370 656	206 301 032	55.92	10.51
4	Singapore	513	1 214	2 727	71 287 105	50 198 543	121 485 648	41.32	6.19
5	Hong Kong, China	890	738	1 628	72 311 219	25 817 099	98 128 318	26.31	5.00
6	Germany	212	2 460	2 672	8 365 247	88 167 113	96 532 360	91.33	4.92
7	Republic of Korea	774	873	1 647	12 418 609	4 282 908	76 701 517	83.81	3.91
8	Norway	367	1 671	2 038	1 758 664	59 356 435	61 115 099	97.12	3.11
9	United States	822	1 153	1 975	9 518 623	48 859 083	58 377 706	83.69	2.97
10	Bermuda	14	518	532	337 958	57 894 249	58 232 207	99.42	2.97
11	Taiwan Province of China	134	871	1 005	5 651 439	45 439 668	51 091 107	88.94	2.60
12	United Kingdom	327	1 000	1 327	6 665 237	42 008 100	48 673 337	86.31	2.48
13	Denmark	26	954	980	29 405	42 974 866	43 004 271	99.93	2.19
14	Monaco	-	448	448	-	42 277 013	42 277 013	100.00	2.15
15	Belgium	107	191	298	10 155 219	20 011 240	30 166 459	66.34	1.54
16	Turkey	484	1 038	1 522	7 164 081	20 445 631	27 609 712	74.05	1.41
17	India	854	165	1 019	16 602 223	8 256 940	24 859 163	33.21	1.27
18	Switzerland	30	405	435	1 225 335	23 412 718	24 638 053	95.03	1.26
19	Russian Federation	1 356	351	1 707	7 772 112	14 975 374	22 747 486	65.83	1.16
20	Indonesia	2 063	82	2 145	20 768 274	1 526 652	22 294 926	6.85	1.14
21	Netherlands	708	487	1 195	5 802 564	12 348 682	18 151 246	68.03	0.92
22	United Arab Emirates	117	796	913	418 544	17 689 385	18 107 929	97.69	0.92
23	Saudi Arabia	133	151	284	12 877 984	5 214 501	18 092 485	28.82	0.92
24	Islamic Republic of Iran	172	64	236	3 981 632	13 927 633	17 909 265	77.77	0.91
25	Italy	514	178	692	12 058 223	5 803 985	17 862 208	32.49	0.91
26	Brazil	300	101	401	4 859 921	8 807 661	13 667 582	64.44	0.70
27	France	93	342	435	574 475	12 659 787	13 234 262	95.66	0.67
28	Cyprus	128	172	300	3 950 928	7 076 469	11 027 397	64.17	0.56
29	Viet Nam	880	140	1 020	7 736 562	1 896 794	9 633 356	19.69	0.49
30	Canada	217	156	373	2 636 754	6 460 998	9 097 752	71.02	0.46
31	Malaysia	458	141	599	6 283 692	2 448 601	8 732 293	28.04	0.44
32	Oman	5	44	49	5 704	7 871 432	7 877 136	99.93	0.40
33	Qatar	63	68	131	1 143 727	5 877 576	7 021 303	83.71	0.36
34	Thailand	337	69	406	5 036 967	1 826 924	6 863 891	26.62	0.35
35	Sweden	85	213	298	931 752	5 682 725	6 614 477	85.91	0.34
	Subtotal, top 35 shipowners	**19 715**	**26 205**	**45 920**	**507 569 517**	**1 364 874 883**	**1 872 444 400**	**72.89**	**95.41**
	Rest of world and unknown	*2 841*	*2 923*	*5 764*	*34 528 774*	*55 608 866*	*90 137 640*	*61.69*	*4.59*
	World total	**22 556**	**29 128**	**51 684**	**542 098 291**	**1 420 483 749**	**1 962 582 040**	**72.38**	**100.00**

Source: UNCTAD secretariat calculations, based on data from Clarksons Research.

Notes: Propelled seagoing vessels of 1,000 gross tons and above, as at 1 January 2019. For the purposes of this table, second and international registries are recorded as foreign or international registries, whereby, for example, ships belonging to owners in the United Kingdom registered in Gibraltar or the Isle of Man are recorded as being under a foreign or international flag. In addition, ships belonging to owners in Denmark and registered in the Danish International Ship Register account for 43.7 per cent of the Denmark-owned fleet in dead-weight tonnage, and ships belonging to owners in Norway registered in the Norwegian International Ship Register account for 26.6 per cent of the Norway-owned fleet in dead-weight tonnage. For a complete listing of nationally owned fleets, see http://stats.unctad.org/fleetownership.

Figure 2.7 Percentage of world fleet ownership, selected countries, 2015–2019

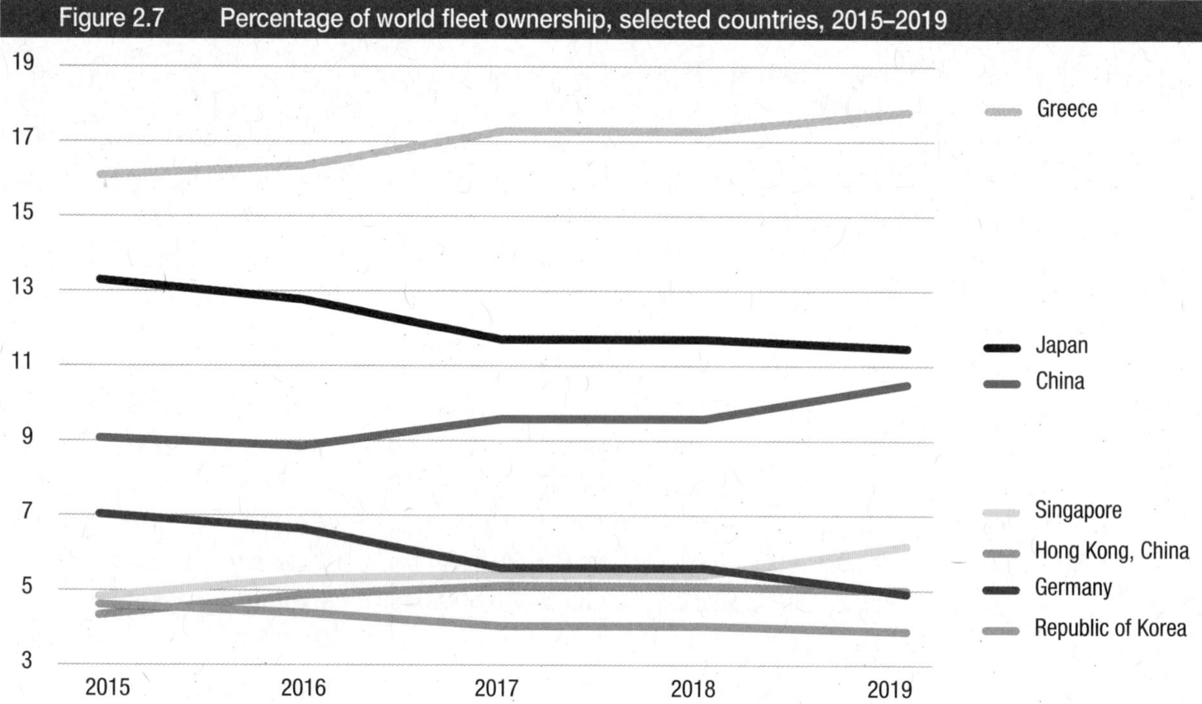

Source: UNCTAD, *Review of Maritime Transport*, various issues, based on data from Clarksons Research.

China, of bulk carriers; Germany, of container ships; and the United States, of ferries and passenger ships (table 2.7).[4]

2. Sustainability considerations result in expanded regulatory control by the flag State

Owners can choose to register their ships in national registers, which are often run by public administrations, or in open registries that are often privately operated as commercial operations with a strong service orientation as competitive advantage. Most owners prefer to register their ships in another country.

The registration segment of the maritime supply chain has been traditionally dominated by developing countries with their open registries. Historically, the decision to "flag out" was associated with reducing operational costs through lower registration costs, the recruitment of foreign labour, lower taxes, at times lower compliance with environmental and safety regulations (Non-governmental Organization Shipbreaking Platform, 2015) and avoidance of political restrictions. Nowadays, other factors are also considered when deciding to flag out. These include efficiency (for instance, reducing delays due to port inspections because of a ship register's good reputation), certification, links to a supportive cluster of financial and logistic services (enabling higher logistics performance) and the presence of a cybersecurity framework.

Maintaining their leadership, Panama, Liberia and the Marshall Islands are ranked first, second and third among the top 35 flags States, in terms of tonnage (table 2.8). In terms of fleet value, Panama, the Marshall Islands and the Bahamas are the leading flags of registration (table 2.9). In the case of Panama, the vessel types representing most of the value are bulk carriers; in the case of the Marshall Islands, bulk carriers and oil tankers; and in the case of the Bahamas, chemical tankers and ferries and passenger ships.

Flag States have an important role to play in enforcing sustainable shipping because they exercise regulatory control (i.e. apply the law and impose penalties in case of non-compliance) over the world fleet on issues such as ensuring safety of life at sea, protection of the marine environment, and the provision of decent working and living conditions for seafarers. Several methods are used to assess the performance of flag States based on different criteria. For instance, the grey, black and white lists under the Paris Memorandum of Understanding on Port State Control measure flag performance from the angle of the outcome inspections at the port (Paris Memorandum of Understanding on Port State Control, 2019). These inspections examine compliance with

[4] The aggregate fleet values published by Clarksons Research are calculated from estimates of the value of each vessel based on type, size and age. Values are estimated for all oil/product tankers, bulk carriers, combined carriers, container ships and gas carriers, with reference to matrices based on representative newbuildings and on second-hand and demolition values provided by Clarksons Platou brokers. For other vessel types, values are estimated with reference to individual valuations, recently reported sales and residual values calculated from reported newbuilding prices. As coverage concerning specialized and non-cargo vessels may not be complete, figures might not accurately represent the total value of the world merchant fleet above 100 gross tons. Desktop estimates are made on the basis of prompt charter-free delivery, as between a willing buyer and a willing seller for cash payment under normal commercial terms. For the purposes of this exercise, all vessels are assumed to be in good and seaworthy condition.

Table 2.7 Top shipowning countries, as at 1 January 2019
(Million dollars)

Country or territory	Oil tankers	Bulk carriers	General cargo ships	Container ships	Other vessel types	Gas carriers	Chemical tankers	Offshore vessels	Ferries and passenger ships	Other /not available	Total
Greece	30 569	37 218	197	7 463	17 842	13 593	1 049	175	2 522	503	93 288
Japan	8 634	35 492	3 577	9 489	34 910	12 268	4 866	4 828	3 080	9 868	92 102
United States	5 562	4 102	984	1 112	76 499	1 831	1 893	24 346	47 625	804	88 260
China	9 666	27 833	5 341	14 385	24 044	3 472	2 959	9 605	5 145	2 863	81 270
Norway	5 423	3 942	1 021	2 108	40 306	6 130	2 533	25 856	2 467	3 320	52 800
Singapore	10 481	12 674	980	5 715	14 565	3 342	4 692	5 804	118	609	44 415
Germany	2 416	6 694	3 957	17 685	12 037	1 842	925	758	8 116	395	42 789
United Kingdom	3 375	4 164	995	3 446	25 811	5 012	1 686	11 714	4 530	2 869	37 791
Hong Kong, China	6 244	12 461	774	9 073	5 869	1 322	291	125	2 982	1 149	34 422
Bermuda	5 507	5 200	0	1 328	14 293	8 190	432	5 602		69	26 329
Republic of Korea	4 475	7 830	949	2 623	9 733	3 922	1 749	538	505	3 019	25 610
Denmark	3 952	1 669	806	9 655	7 102	2 200	900	2 850	1 029	123	23 183
Netherlands	449	857	3 680	416	17 025	674	1 387	12 335	522	2 109	22 428
Switzerland	673	1 107	268	5 274	10 768	237	241	3 388	6 892	11	18 090
Italy	2 219	1 273	2 563	5	11 380	357	617	2 829	7 103	475	17 440
Brazil	907	196	20	214	15 588	140	90	15 284	72	2	16 925
Taiwan Province of China	1 635	7 438	626	4 144	871	434	208	40	87	102	14 713
France	144	424	221	4 154	8 139	453	127	5 635	1 682	241	13 082
Monaco	6 042	3 874		828	972	872	34		33	33	11 716
Turkey	1 345	3 456	2 060	1 273	2 525	163	1 187	763	387	24	10 658
Malaysia	303	231	109	60	9 125	1 958	129	6 848	15	175	9 828
Russian Federation	3 455	329	1 094	79	4 471	1 520	672	1 391	93	794	9 428
Belgium	3 885	1 430	725	343	1 895	1 230	97	25		542	8 278
Indonesia	1 754	811	1 076	772	3 586	462	366	994	1 723	41	7 999
Qatar	104	95	0	38	7 727	7 492	6	226		3	7 963
Other	19 064	15 836	8 746	3 808	52 621	7 508	4 688	25 606	11 744	3 076	100 076
World total 2019 (million dollars)	**138 283**	**196 638**	**40 769**	**105 490**	**429 704**	**86 623**	**33 825**	**167 566**	**108 472**	**33 219**	**910 885**
Growth 2019/2018 (percentage)	5.8	-0.9	-6.1	5.1	2.1	10.4	1.6	-4.5	6.6	4.6	1.9

Source: UNCTAD secretariat calculations, based on data from Clarksons Research.

Note: Value is estimated for all commercial ships of 1,000 gross tons and above.

requirements pertaining to the condition of the ship, its equipment, operations and social conditions (as per the International Labour Organization Maritime Labour Convention). In case of non-compliance, ships can be denied entry to a port, inspected at length, or detained when attempting to enter a port. The Shipping Industry Flag State Performance Table: 2018/2019 of the International Chamber of Shipping contains additional criteria such as the average age of the fleet and ratification of International Labour Organization conventions.

Given the increased awareness of environmental considerations and the probability of increased environmental standards, the scope of regulatory control by the flag State is likely to expand. Current developments suggest an increasing expectation for expanded compliance enforcement by flag States. Examples of such developments include the following new requirements: issuing a statement of compliance of ships with emissions, based on fuel consumption (IMO fuel oil consumption data collection system); reporting on emissions (European Union system for monitoring, reporting and verification) or proving compliance with environmental and other regulations to call at ports in the United States (United States Coast Guard Qualship 21 certification scheme/2019–2020 roster) (Hellenic Shipping News Worldwide, 2019b; Safety4sea, 2019a).

Table 2.8 Leading flags of registration by dead-weight tonnage, 2019

	Flag of registration	Number of vessels (percentage)	Vessel share of world total	Dead-weight tonnage (1,000 dwt)	Share of world total dead-weight tonnage (percentage)	Cumulated share of dead-weight tonnage	Average vessel size (dwt)	Growth in dead-weight tonnage 2019/2018 (percentage)
1	Panama	7 860	8.16	333 337	17	16.87	44 930	-0.57
2	Marshall Islands	3 537	3.67	245 763	12	12.43	69 878	3.23
3	Liberia	3 496	3.63	243 129	12	12.30	69 704	7.98
4	Hong Kong, China	2 701	2.80	198 747	10	10.06	75 083	8.17
5	Singapore	3 433	3.57	129 581	7	6.56	39 785	1.16
6	Malta	2 172	2.26	110 682	6	5.60	51 890	1.39
7	China	5 589	5.80	91 905	5	4.65	19 646	8.16
8	Bahamas	1 401	1.45	77 844	4	3.94	56 449	1.26
9	Greece	1 308	1.36	69 101	3	3.50	64 339	-4.28
10	Japan	5 017	5.21	39 034	2	1.97	10 263	4.23
11	Cyprus	1 039	1.08	34 588	2	1.75	34 110	-1.36
12	Isle of Man	392	0.41	27 923	1	1.41	71 232	2.28
13	Indonesia	9 879	10.26	23 880	1	1.21	4 674	5.54
14	Danish International Ship Register	566	0.59	22 444	1	1.14	41 717	15.86
15	Norwegian International Ship Register	611	0.63	19 758	1	1.00	32 550	1.08
16	Madeira	465	0.48	19 107	1	0.97	41 179	-1.14
17	India	1 731	1.80	17 354	1	0.88	10 633	-6.41
18	United Kingdom	1 031	1.07	17 041	1	0.86	19 930	1.64
19	Italy	1 353	1.41	13 409	1	0.68	12 015	-11.82
20	Saudi Arabia	374	0.39	13 128	1	0.66	45 583	-2.97
21	Republic of Korea	1 880	1.95	13 029	1	0.66	7 915	-6.65
22	United States	3 671	3.81	11 810	1	0.60	6 373	-1.03
23	Belgium	201	0.21	10 471	1	0.53	60 180	18.88
24	Malaysia	1 748	1.82	10 162	1	0.51	7 202	1.45
25	Russian Federation	2 739	2.84	9 132	0	0.46	3 416	5.05
26	Bermuda	148	0.15	9 088	0	0.46	62 245	-15.62
27	Germany	609	0.63	8 470	0	0.43	16 607	-16.74
28	Viet Nam	1 868	1.94	8 469	0	0.43	4 844	3.27
29	Antigua and Barbuda	780	0.81	7 501	0	0.38	9 715	-13.88
30	Turkey	1 234	1.28	7 489	0	0.38	7 866	-5.76
31	Netherlands	1 217	1.26	7 192	0	0.36	7 016	-1.78
32	Cayman Islands	170	0.18	6 743	0	0.34	42 678	8.76
33	Registre international français	94	0.10	6 231	0	0.32	66 287	3.91
34	Taiwan Province of China	389	0.40	5 751	0	0.29	19 105	19.35
35	Thailand	825	0.86	732	0	0.29	8 367	-8.66
	Top 35 total	**71 528**	**74.28**	**1 875 024**	**94.87**	**94.87**		
	Rest of world	***24 767***	***25.72***	***101 467***	***5.13***	***5.13***		
	World total	**96 295**	**100.00**	**1 976 491**	**100.00**	**100.00**	**25 024**	**2.61**

Source: UNCTAD secretariat calculations, based on data from Clarksons Research.

Notes: Propelled seagoing merchant vessels of 100 gross tons and above, as at 1 January. For a complete listing of countries, see http://stats.unctad.org/fleet.

Table 2.9 Leading flags of registration, ranked by value of principal vessel type, 2019 (United States dollars)

Flag of registration	Oil tankers	Bulk carriers	General cargo ships	Container ships	Gas carriers	Chemical tankers	Offshore vessels	Ferries and passenger ships	Other/not applicable	Total
Panama	12 783	44 379	3 871	14 555	5 505	10 611	8 943	21 185	7 815	129 648
Marshall Islands	23 637	28 792	487	6 314	4 631	1 341	15 145	20 085	2 607	103 040
Bahamas	7 595	4 982	86	425	123	28 627	11 517	23 885	2 757	79 996
Liberia	17 412	22 108	1 091	15 973	2 263	150	5 287	11 812	1 741	77 837
Hong Kong, China	10 467	26 125	1 849	18 073	1 906	46	5 201	306	123	64 095
Malta	9 736	11 221	1 664	8 401	1 899	11 609	4 569	4 875	950	54 924
Singapore	11 138	13 039	1 191	11 109	3 141		5 756	6 558	1 724	53 657
China	4 928	13 892	2 827	2 615	1 511	4 526	705	6 784	2 663	40 451
Greece	9 210	3 547	38	257	68	1 576	4 506	1	96	19 299
Italy	1 185	831	2 521	103	467	12 474	286	521	473	18 862
Subtotal top 10	**108 090**	**168 918**	**15 625**	**77 826**	**21 514**	**70 959**	**61 915**	**96 013**	**20 949**	**641 809**
Other	***30 193***	***27 720***	***25 143***	***27 664***	***12 311***	***37 513***	***24 708***	***71 553***	***12 270***	***269 075***
World total	**138 283**	**196 638**	**40 768**	**105 490**	**33 825**	**108 472**	**86 623**	**167 566**	**33 219**	**910 884**

Source: UNCTAD secretariat calculations, based on Clarksons Research data, as at 1 January 2019 (estimated current value).

D. CONTAINER SHIPPING

The container shipping industry has been undergoing a challenging phase in recent years, driven by a persistent market imbalance between trade and fleet supply capacity that has been intensifying with the influx of mega vessels, rising trade tensions and increased protectionism, as well as changing environmental regulations. These factors have increased the volatility of freight rates and transport costs in 2018/2019, a feature that will continue through 2020.

1. Freight rates: Mixed results

In 2018, container freight rates showed mixed results. Weak trade growth and the sustained delivery of mega container ships in an overly supplied market exerted further pressure on fundamental market balance, resulting in lower freight rates in general. However, towards the second half of the year, a temporary surge in seaborne trade was triggered by an increase in shipments from China to the United States before the potential application of higher tariffs on Chinese imports and more effective capacity management from carriers.

As illustrated in figure 2.8, container fleet supply capacity increased in 2018 by 6 per cent, compared with 4 per cent in 2017. Such capacity surpassed expansion in global seaborne container trade, which increased by 2.6 per cent as of 1 January 2019, reaching an estimated total volume of 152 million TEUs (see chapter 1).

Imbalances between supply and demand drove down freight rates on mainlane container trade routes during the first half of 2018, reaching as low as $1,200 per FEU on the Shanghai–United States West Coast routes and $2,200 per FEU on the Shanghai–United States East Coast routes (JOC.com, 2019a). These routes were faced with low volumes and excess capacity due to the continual deployment of mega large vessels. At the beginning of 2019, 25 per cent of capacity deployed on the Trans-Pacific route was accounted for by container ships of more than 12,000 TEUs of capacity, up from 19 per cent at the start of 2018 and 7 per cent at start of 2016 (Clarksons Research, 2019d). In the face of declining rates and a difficult and unpredictable environment, carriers reorganized to reduce capacity, increasing cascading practices and introducing a series of blank, or cancelled, sailings hence disrupting regular schedules on these routes. (For further information, see Universal Cargo, 2016).

In the latter half of the year, mixed trends in freight rates were observed across the trade lanes. Demand on Trans-Pacific routes grew to avoid anticipated United States tariffs on imports from China scheduled for January 2019, which were subsequently delayed. Spot rates on the Shanghai–United States West Coast route reached a six-year high in late 2018, rising 11 per cent in the last quarter in comparison with the same period in 2017, to an average $2,286 per forty-foot equivalent unit (FEU) (Clarksons Research, 2019d). This brought the full-year 2018 average to $1,736 per FEU, up 17 per cent from the yearly average in 2017. Average spot rates for the Shanghai–United States East Coast route reached $2,806 per FEU, an increase of 14 per cent from 2017 average (table 2.10).

The Far East–Europe routes witnessed decreasing average freight rates. The Shanghai–Northern Europe route averaged $822 per TEU in 2018, down 6.2 per cent compared with the 2017 average, and the

Figure 2.8 Growth of demand and supply in container shipping, 2007–2018
(Percentage)

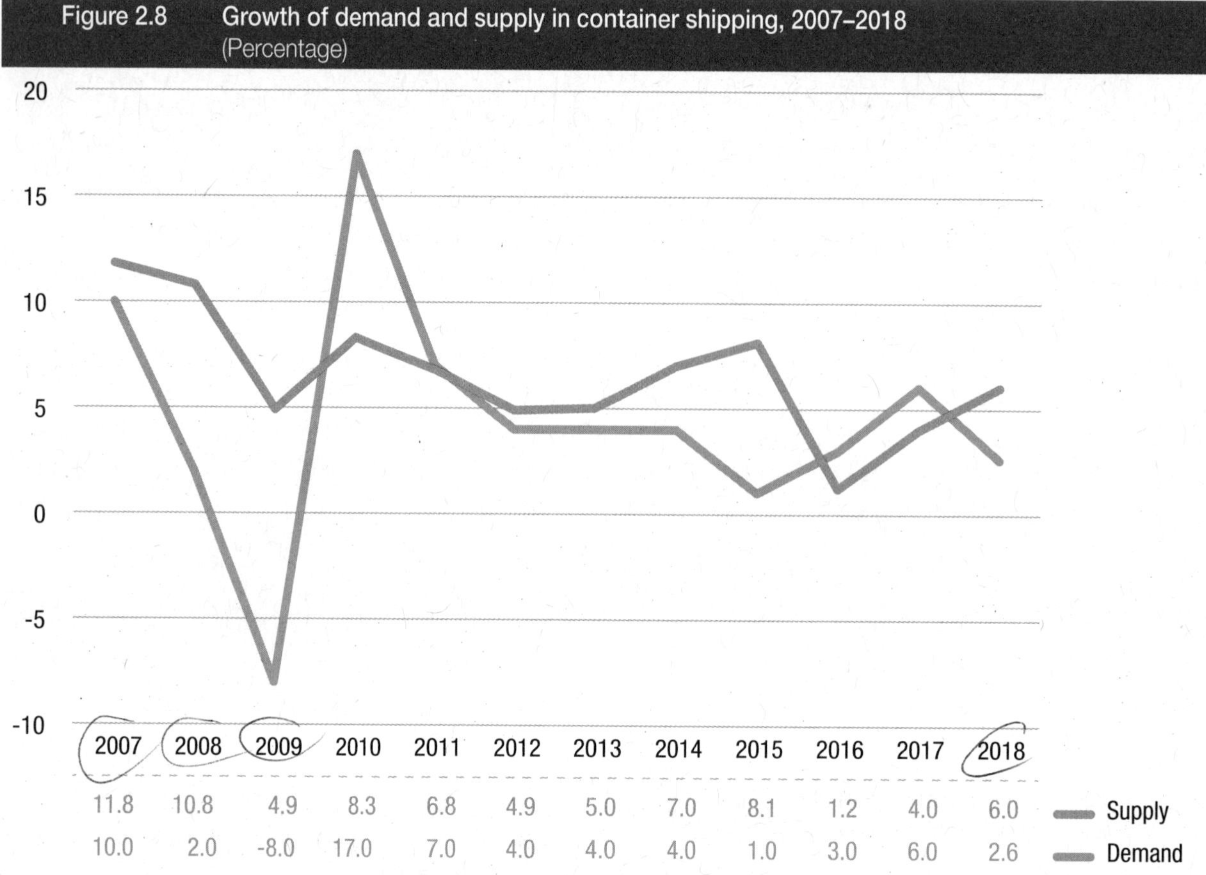

	2007	2008	2009	2010	2011	2012	2013	2014	2015	2016	2017	2018
Supply	11.8	10.8	4.9	8.3	6.8	4.9	5.0	7.0	8.1	1.2	4.0	6.0
Demand	10.0	2.0	-8.0	17.0	7.0	4.0	4.0	4.0	1.0	3.0	6.0	2.6

Source: UNCTAD secretariat calculations. Demand is based on data from figure 1.5, and supply is based on data from Clarksons Research, *Container Intelligence Monthly*, various issues.

Notes: Supply data refer to total capacity of the container-carrying fleet, including multipurpose and other vessels with some container-carrying capacity. Demand growth is based on million TEU lifts.

Figure 2.9 New ConTex index, 2010–2019
(Index base: October 2007 – 1,000 points)

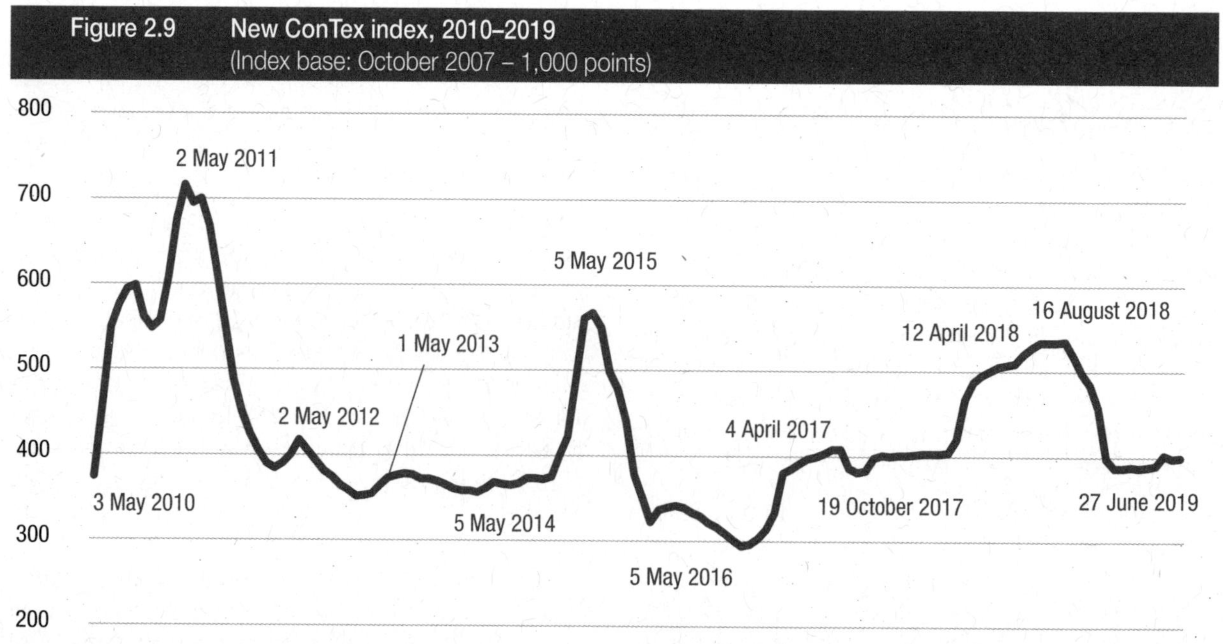

Source: UNCTAD secretariat calculations, based on data from the New ConTex index produced by the Hamburg Shipbrokers Association. See www.vhss.de.

Notes: The New ConTex is based on assessments of current-day charter rates of six selected container ship types, which are representative of their size categories: Type 1,100 TEUs (charter period of one year), Type 1,700 TEUs (charter period of one year), Type 2,500 TEUs (charter period of two years), Type 2,700 TEUs (charter period of two years), Type 3,500 TEUs (charter period of two years) and Type 4,250 TEUs (charter period of two years).

Table 2.10 Container freight market rates, 2010–2018

Freight market	2010	2011	2012	2013	2014	2015	2016	2017	2018
Trans-Pacific	(Dollars per 40-foot equivalent unit)								
Shanghai–United States West Coast	2 308	1 667	2 287	2 033	1 970	1 506	1 272	1 485	1 736
Percentage change	68.2	-27.8	37.2	-11.1	-3.1	-23.6	-15.5	16.7	16.9
Shanghai– United States East Coast	3 499	3 008	3 416	3 290	3 720	3 182	2 094	2 457	2 806
Percentage change	47.8	-14.0	13.56	-3.7	13.07	-14.5	-34.2	17.3	14.2
Far East–Europe	(Dollars per 20-foot equivalent unit)								
Shanghai–Northern Europe	1 789	881	1 353	1084	1161	629	690	876	822
Percentage change	28.2	-50.8	53.6	-19.9	7.10	-45.8	9.7	27.0	-6.2
Shanghai–Mediterranean	1 739	973	1 336	1 151	1 253	739	684	817	797
Percentage change	24.5	-44.1	37.3	-13.9	8.9	-41.0	-7.4	19.4	-2.4
North–South	(Dollars per 20-foot equivalent unit)								
Shanghai–South America (Santos)	2 236	1 483	1 771	1 380	1 103	455	1 647	2 679	1 703
Percentage change	-8.0	-33.7	19.4	-22.1	-20.1	-58.7	262.0	62.7	-36.4
Shanghai–Australia/New Zealand (Melbourne)	1 189	772	925	818	678	492	526	677	827
Percentage change	-20.7	-35.1	19.8	-11.6	-17.1	-27.4	6.9	28.7	22.2
Shanghai–West Africa (Lagos)	2 305	1 908	2 092	1 927	1 838	1 449	1 181	1 770	1 920
Percentage change	2.6	-17.2	9.64	-7.9	-4.6	-21.2	-18.5	49.9	8.5
Shanghai–South Africa (Durban)	1 481	991	1 047	805	760	693	584	1 155	888
Percentage change	-0.96	-33.1	5.7	-23.1	-5.6	-8.8	-15.7	97.8	-23.1
Intra-Asian	(Dollars per 20-foot equivalent unit)								
Shanghai–South-East Asia (Singapore)	318	210	256	231	233	187	70	148	146
Percentage change		-34.0	21.8	-9.7	0.9	-19.7	-62.6	111.4	-1.4
Shanghai–East Japan	316	337	345	346	273	146	185	215	223
Percentage change		6.7	2.4	0.3	-21.1	-46.5	26.7	16.2	3.7
Shanghai–West Japan	Not available	Not available	Not available	Not available	Not available	Not available	Not available	215	223
Percentage change	Not available	Not available	Not available	Not available	Not available	Not available	Not available	Not available	3.7
Shanghai–Korea, Republic of	193	198	183	197	187	160	104	141	163
Percentage change		2.6	-7.6	7.7	-5.1	-14.4	-35.0	35.6	15.6
Shanghai–Persian Gulf/Red Sea	922	838	981	771	820	525	399	618	463
Percentage change		-9.1	17.1	-21.4	6.4	-36.0	-24.0	54.9	-25.1

Source: Clarksons Research, *Container Intelligence Monthly*, various issues.

Note: Data are based on yearly averages.

average rates on the Shanghai–Mediterranean route declined by 2.4 per cent reaching $797 per TEU. This decline is partly attributable to weaker performance in European economies such as Germany and the United Kingdom, as well as the economic crisis in Turkey (see chapter 1) and the continued oversupplied routes. These were driven mainly by the upsizing of vessels. Container ships of capacities greater than 15,000 TEUs accounted for 53 per cent of total capacity deployed on these trade routes at the end of 2017, up from 44 per cent at the end of 2017 and 33 per cent at the end of 2016 (Clarksons Research, 2019d).

In 2018, freight rate movements on the non-mainlane container trade routes were also mixed, with variation between routes. Rates on the Shanghai–Australia route went up 22 per cent, averaging $827 per TEU in 2018. On the other hand, rates on the North–South routes weakened, generally due in part to a drop in Latin American and sub-Saharan Africa imports attributed to weakened economic activities in those regions, namely in Nigeria and South Africa and in Argentina, Brazil and the Bolivarian Republic of Venezuela (see also chapter 1), while the total deployment of vessels continued to increase. As such, the rates on the Shanghai–South America (Santos) route averaged $1,703 per TEU in 2018, down 36.4 per cent from 2017, and the rates on the Shanghai–South Africa (Durban) route averaged $888 per TEU, down 23.1 per cent from 2017.

In addition, higher average bunker prices (31.5 per cent higher in 2018, compared with 2017) added pressure to operating expenses of carriers and contributed to weakening their operating margins (Barry Rogliano Salles, 2019). An increase in bunker prices, which were not fully offset by an increase in freight rates, had a negative impact on profits.

However, a rise in freight rates and demand in late 2018, combined with better supply management, enabled some container carriers to improve their results. In 2018, CMA CGM recorded revenues of $23.5 billion, up 11.2 per cent. Maersk Line, including Hamburg Süd, posted revenues of $28.4 billion, an increase of 29 per cent, and Hapag-Lloyd, $13.6 billion, compared with $11.2 billion in 2017.[5]

Compliance with the IMO 2020 regulation will bring new challenges in the shipping industry, particularly in container shipping.

Charter rates and earnings improved on a full-year average basis in 2018 but deteriorated during the second half of the year. Despite strong regional trade volumes and limited capacity expansion in the small sizes of vessels, rates and earnings made progress in the first half of the year, dropping to just above operating expenses in the second half, as carriers consolidated into larger alliances and were able to use their bargaining power to keep rates under pressure (Barry Rogliano Salles, 2019). The 12-month charter rate increased to an average of 502 points in 2018, compared with 378 in 2017 (figure 2.9).

It remains to be seen how freight rates will hold in 2019–2020. Intensified trade tensions, which had helped boost container ship freight rates at the end of 2018 and improved carriers' profitability (Universal Cargo, 2019), could have a negative impact on the development of freight markets in 2019 and 2020. Demand for cargo may be affected at a time when the industry is confronted with new challenges and additional costs of complying with the new IMO 2020 regulation on sulphur fuel limits that will be applied on 1 January 2020 (Universal Cargo, 2019). Capacity management will therefore be key to reconciling slow growth in demand, high supply capacity and high operating costs. Non-mainlane routes are expected to remain the principal driver of growth in 2019 and 2020 (Clarksons Research, 2019c).

2. IMO 2020 regulation: A game changer for the shipping industry

As noted previously, 1 January 2020 will mark the full implementation of the IMO 2020 regulation reducing the content of sulphur in fuel oil from 3.5 per cent applied since 2012, to 0.5 per cent in 2020 (see chapter 4). This will significantly reduce the amount of sulphur oxides emanating from ships, improve air quality in port cities and coastal areas and meet global climate change objectives.

Maritime shipping relies heavily on fossil fuels. About 3.5 million barrels of high sulphur residual fuel oil (bunker fuel) per day were consumed by the sector in 2017, which represent about 50 per cent of the global fuel oil demand (McKinsey and Company, 2018). Most of this fuel oil has high sulphur content, which results in the emission of sulphur oxides into the atmosphere. The sector consumes just over 1 million barrels per day of marine gas oil, which is a lower-sulphur, higher-value distillate oil (Hellenic Shipping News Worldwide, 2018). This represents only 5 per cent of the global demand for diesel and gas oil, the majority of which is consumed in the heavy-duty trucking sector (Hellenic Shipping News Worldwide, 2018).

Bringing emission levels to under 0.5 per cent mass/mass will mark the beginning of a new era that will bring about fresh challenges and require a radical change by the shipping industry. This section will emphasize the impact of this change on the container segment, which in turn will have repercussions on transport costs and the price that shippers will pay and may therefore have an impact on the price of goods to consumers.

For carriers to comply with the new IMO 2020 regulation, three main options are currently available. As outlined below, each has its advantages, disadvantages and cost implications (CAI International, 2019).

Option 1. The most direct option is for carriers to switch to low-sulphur fuels such as low-sulphur residual fuel oil, very-low-sulphur fuel oil, or low-sulphur distillates such as marine gas oil. This would inevitably entail additional costs and higher freight rates, given that the price of high-sulphur fuel is lower than that of low-sulphur fuels, as the latter are more costly to produce. As a reference, the price of low-sulphur fuel stood at about $600–$700 per metric ton in March and April 2019, while that of the traditional bunker fuel oil was about $400–$450 per metric ton (Seeking Alpha, 2019), and the price differential between high-sulphur bunkers and marine gas oil was about $170 and $320, respectively, per metric ton (JOC.com, 2019a). Ensuring the availability of low-sulphur fuels and bridging the gap between demand and supply of these fuels will be among the main concerns of carriers in the near future. Refineries have a key role to play in increasing the production of low-sulphur marine fuels. Big refiners such as Exxon Mobil, British Petroleum and

[5] Data were derived from the annual reports of various companies.

Compañía Española de Petróleos, commonly known as Cepsa, are preparing to produce a large quantity of such fuel as the IMO 2020 deadline draws near (Forbes, 2019a; gCaptain.com, 2019).[6]

Option 2. Carriers could continue to use cheaper high-sulphur fuel oil and install scrubbing equipment to remove sulphur from the ship engines' exhaust system (CAI International, 2019). However, installing these scrubbers will come at a cost. Various sources have estimated that installing scrubbers can cost between $2 million and $10 million (IncoDocs, 2019; Seeking Alpha, 2019). They are also made by a limited number of manufacturers around the world that may not be able to meet all demand. Hence, as mentioned previously, this would influence the carriers to turn to scrapping, in particular for older vessels of smaller tonnage, with more ships likely to be scrapped towards the end of 2019 (IncoDocs, 2019). Another concern for ships fitted with scrubbers would be the availability of high-sulphur fuel oil to meet the demand and the impact on price if refiners move to significantly restrict the sale of such fuel oil.

Option 3. Carriers can also use cleaner alternative fuels such as liquefied natural gas or methanol. However, it is estimated that liquefied natural gas production could cover only 10 per cent of the required shipping fuel by 2040 (CAI International, 2019). In addition, ships fitted with liquefied natural gas tanks will require more physical space on board, taking up almost 3 per cent of a vessel's TEU slots. As a result, this will reduce the number of containers that can be carried. Also, due to the expected large increase in demand for liquefied natural gas fuels, it has been reported that the price of liquefied natural gas may increase as much as 50 per cent (IncoDocs, 2019). As for other alternative sources of fuel, such as biofuels and hydrogen, they are mostly sin the research and development stages.

Therefore, compliance with the IMO 2020 regulation will bring new challenges in the shipping industry, particularly in container shipping. Key issues for consideration may include higher costs and price volatility, as well as reduced capacity and increased transit time,

Higher costs and price volatility

Container shipping industry costs associated with meeting the IMO 2020 mandate are estimated to range from $5 billion to tens of billions of dollars (JOC.com, 2018c). Cost increases would mainly reflect increases in fuel prices and investments made to ensure compliance. For context, a round trip from Asia to Northern Europe could cost an additional $1 million to $2.5 million after implementation of the sulphur emission rules (Bunker Trust, 2019; The Loadstar, 2018). Calculations by MDS Transmodal using its online bunker adjustment factor calculator suggest that a switch from intermediate fuel oil with a maximum viscosity of 380 centistokes (IFO 380) to marine gas oil on a benchmark Far East–Europe service using ships with a capacity of 18,500 TEUs would increase the bunker cost per TEU by $62 for the headhaul direction and $39 for the backhaul direction (MDS Transmodal, 2019).

These additional costs may have an impact on the price to be paid by the end user (Forbes, 2019b), as carriers will attempt to pass on increased costs to shippers through various forms, including new bunker surcharge formulas (IHS Markit et al., 2019). It is argued that if these costs are not passed on to shippers, profit margins in the container shipping industry would be reduced and may lead to bankruptcies of the most financially vulnerable carriers (Safety4sea, 2019b). This may also prompt further consolidation in the container shipping industry.

> Additional costs may have an impact on the price to be paid by the end user, as carriers will attempt to pass on increased costs to shippers through various forms, including new bunker surcharge formulas.

In recent years, carriers have been struggling to find ways to cover their losses and have applied various bunker charge programmes to mitigate these costs. For example, in 2018, carriers turned to a cost-recovery programme applying emergency bunker surcharges and passed the costs on to shippers (Forbes, 2019b). Shippers may be at risk of receiving a new set of emergency bunker surcharges that is projected to be 15–20 per cent higher once the regulations enter into force (Forbes, 2019b). Six global container lines – Maersk Line, Mediterranean Shipping Company, CMA CGM/American President Lines, Hapag-Lloyd, Orient Overseas Container Line and Ocean Network Express (ONE) – had already outlined a new price mechanism for the bunker adjustment factor (also known as marine fuel recovery at Hapag-Lloyd or the bunker recovery charge) that would replace the old formulas on 1 January 2020 to cover fuel costs, as prices are expected to surge because of tighter environmental standards from 2020. For example, Maersk Line and the Mediterranean Shipping Company have estimated at least a $2 billion increase in cost due to the various changes made to their fleet and its fuel supply, while Hapag-Lloyd estimates that using low-sulphur fuel will add about $100 per TEU (JOC.com, 2019b).

However, shippers have complained that the carriers' methods of calculating the bunker adjustment factor to help them cope with unexpected fuel price fluctuations are usually not transparent, they lack uniformity and

6 Other sources include company websites.

could comprise an element of revenue generation, rather than serving solely to recover real bunkers costs (The Loadstar, 2018).

Reduced capacity and increased transit time

Another effect that may emerge with the application of the IMO 2020 regulation are the temporary and long-term disruptions in supply capacity. As noted earlier, supply capacity may be temporarily reduced due to the time that vessels will be out of service to install the scrubbers. Estimates show that container capacity may be reduced by 1.2 per cent in 2019 for scrubber retrofitting (Clarksons Research, 2019a).

In the long term, however, supply capacity will be permanently eliminated because of the space that scrubbers and liquefied natural gas tanks would occupy on the vessel, and old vessels that will be phased out or scrapped.

Lastly, practices by carriers such as blank sailing and slow steaming could become more common as a means of lowering fuel costs. These practices will also reduce supply capacity while increasing transit times (Forbes, 2019b). This in turn will have an impact on the number of direct port calls, which may decrease and trigger a greater need for trans-shipment (World Maritime News, 2019).

In conclusion, in an already uncertain climate of demand growth, additional uncertainty arising from factors relating to supply, fuel costs and investment in new technologies such as scrubbers, could drive up the costs of complying with the IMO 2020 regulation and make freight rates more difficult to predict. At the same time, compliance with the IMO 2020 regulation would be a practical test as to how the shipping market, as well as shippers and consumers, would respond and adapt to changes, namely in the context of the IMO strategy aimed at reducing greenhouse gas emissions from ships by at least 50 per cent by 2050, compared with the 2008 level.

3. Increasing consolidation and market concentration in container shipping

Consolidation in the global container shipping industry has gathered pace in recent years, leading to mergers and acquisitions between container lines and a reshuffling of shipping alliances. Three alliances dominate the container shipping market and capacity deployed on the three major East–West trade routes (figure 2.10). Since 2014, the top 10 container shipping lines (figure 2.11), most of which are part of these alliances, increased their combined market share from 68 per cent to 90 per cent, and their deployed capacity from some 55 million TEUs to 96.4 million TEUs.

Container shipping is an increasingly concentrated sector in terms of operations and alliances, ship deployment and major ports of call. Data related to annual deployed capacity by operators for Pacific routes provide an indication of how maritime transport services have evolved between 2006 and 2019. Under most criteria, the level of concentration has increased over the years (table 2.11).

For instance, using several measurements as per table 2.11, the level of concentration increased in 2019 in the case of the Pacific Islands, in comparison with 2006. However, the level of concentration decreased for one measurement (number of companies).

However, consolidation could increase pressure faced by smaller operators and have an impact on freight rates, as well as on the frequency, efficiency, reliability and quality of services in small and remote islands and in the least developed countries, given their increased vulnerability to reduced connectivity and access to transport services, hence, the need to monitor its evolution and impact (UNCTAD, 2017, 2018b).

A case in point are markets for the island regions in the Caribbean, the Indian Ocean, and the Pacific (figure 2.12). A comparison of 2006 and 2019 shows that there are fewer operators today, each carrying higher average volumes per company. The decline in percentage terms is similar in all regions, considering that the initial scenario in the Caribbean (2006) is already more concentrated than that of the Pacific and Indian Ocean islands.

From the perspective of shippers that are clients of an alliance, the participation of shipping lines in an alliance has led to more deep-sea maritime services, ships per service, higher vessel size and lower average round-trip duration, compared with services offered

Table 2.11 Concentration indicators in liner shipping for Pacific routes, 2006 and 2019

Concentration indicators	2006	2019	Trend
Share of top shipping company (percentage)	29	33	Concentration increased
Share of top four shipping companies (percentage)	57	60	Concentration increased
Herfindahl–Hirschman Index	1 253	1 497	Concentration increased
Number of companies	22	24	Concentration decreased
Gini coefficient	0.53	0.59	Concentration increased

Source: UNCTAD secretariat calculations, based on data from MDS Transmodal, February 2019.

Figure 2.10 Market share of the three container shipping alliances in major East–West trade routes, deployed capacity in TEUs, as of February 2019

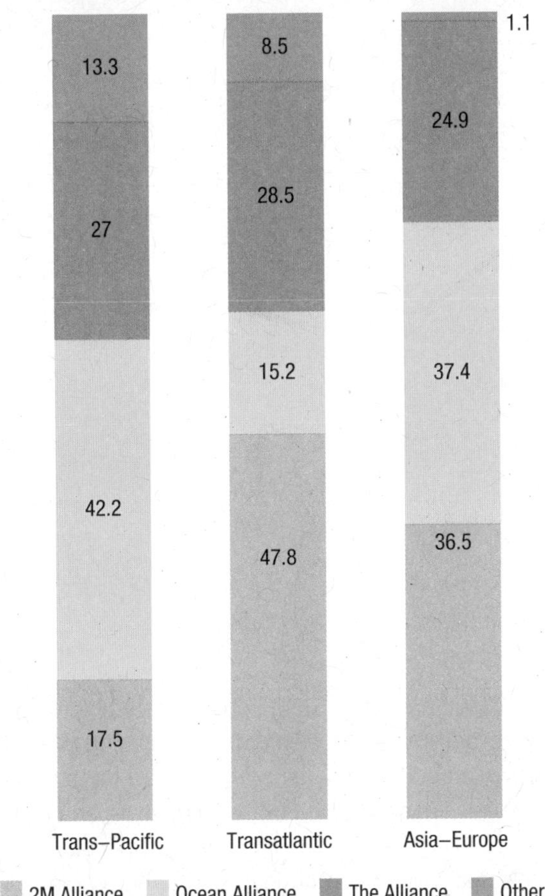

Source: UNCTAD secretariat calculations, based on data from MDS Transmodal Container Ship Databank, February 2019.

Note: 2M alliance includes Maesrk and Mediterranean Shipping Company; Ocean Alliance includes COSCO, CMA CGM and Evergreen; The Alliance includes ONE, Yang Ming and Hapag-Lloyd.

Figure 2.11 Top 10 deep-sea container shipping lines and market share in deployed capacity February, 2019 (Percentage)

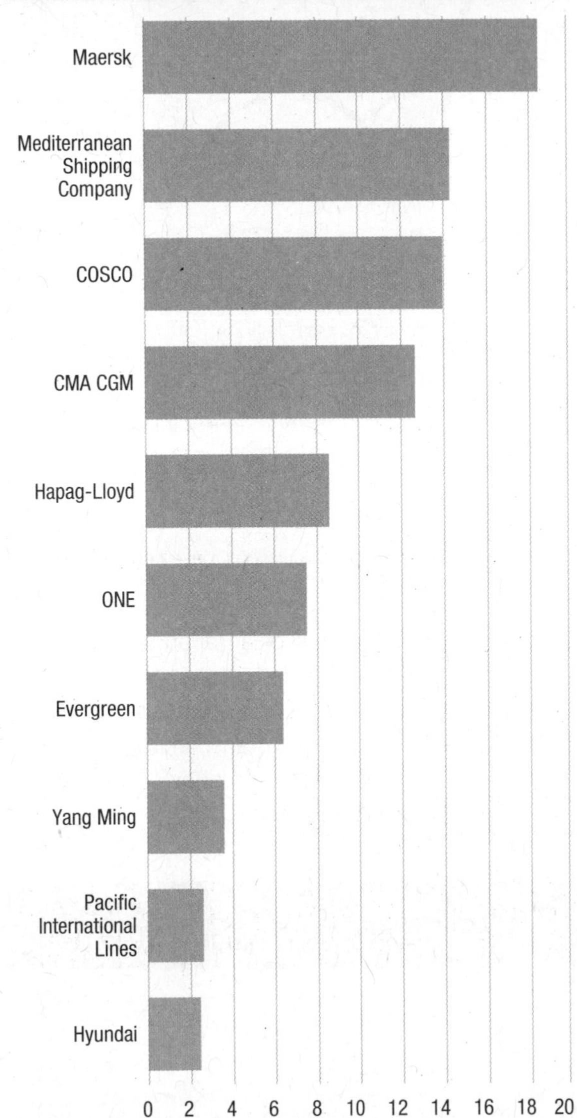

Source: UNCTAD secretariat calculations, based on data from MDS Transmodal Container Ship Databank, February 2019.

Note: Data refer to fully cellular container ship tonnage and do not include intraregional services.

Table 2.12 Major changes in deep-sea maritime services offered by all operators, 2014–2019

	Services offered by all operators			Services offered by all operators that are members of an alliance			Services offered by all operators that are not members of an alliance		
	2014 Q1	2019 Q1	Percentage change	2014 Q1	2019 Q1	Percentage change	2014 Q1	2019 Q1	Percentage change
Number of services	504	455	-9.7	150	285	90.0	431	223	-48.3
Number of ships per service	7	8	12.3	8	9	8.5	7	5	-23.0
Average ship size (TEUs)	4 869	6 636	36.3	5 933	7 823	31.8	4 453	3 040	-31.7
Average round trip (days)	64	65	1.9	66	64	-2.5	63	68	7.5

Source: UNCTAD secretariat calculations, based on data from MDS Transmodal Container Ship Databank, February 2019.

Abbreviations: Q, quarter.

Figure 2.12 Container shipping operators by annual deployed capacity, 2006–2019
(Operators per million 20-foot equivalent units)

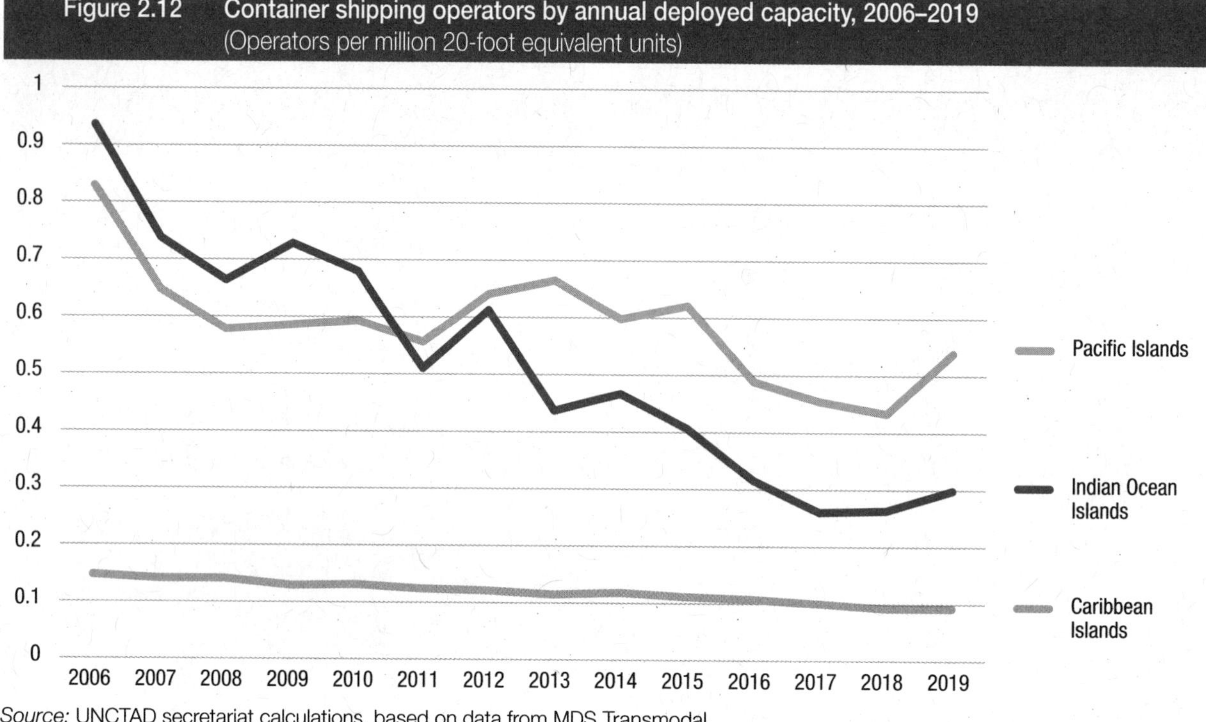

Source: UNCTAD secretariat calculations, based on data from MDS Transmodal.

by operators not members of an alliance since 2014 (table 2.12). This suggests greater flexibility and adaptability to changing market conditions. However, perceived container shipping transparency, especially with regard to surcharges, is a matter of concern for shippers (World Maritime News, 2019).

E. PORT SERVICES AND INFRASTRUCTURE SUPPLY

1. Increased sustainability expectations

Ports are infrastructure assets that play a key role in international trade. As shown in chapter 1, global port traffic has been expanding over the years, reflecting growth in the economy and in trade. As a sea–land interface and point of convergence between various modes of transport, ports act as gateways to trade, providing access to global markets, including for landlocked countries.

Ports are increasingly expected to align their performance with sustainability expectations, namely, to deliver optimum economic and social gains while causing minimum environmental damage. This is forcing them to rethink their strategies and operations.

From the perspective of optimum economic gains, ports face pressures to improve efficiency and reduce costs. In a context characterized by heightened intra-port and inter-port competition (see section below) and larger vessels, shipping operators expect ports to increase their capacity to handle higher cargo volumes in an optimum way.

Developing and improving port infrastructure and facilities are important elements of port strategies to improve attractiveness as ports of call for shipping companies. This concerns both the physical and digital infrastructures. Table 2.13 summarizes the objectives of selected investment projects that were carried out between 2017 and 2019, with a view to developing or upgrading port infrastructure and service.

Along with improved economic efficiency, ports are expected to deliver on other sustainability parameters, such as security and safety, social inclusiveness, resource conservation and environmental protection. This is because ports can produce negative environmental impacts on the one hand, and are directly or indirectly affected by climate change on the other.

Ports are highly exposed to climate-related events such as sea-level rise, strong exposure to winds, changes in storm patterns and coastal currents, and flooding. These can increase the risk of delays, cause significant logistic and service disruptions, and damage to coastal transportation infrastructure, resulting in significant economic costs and affecting the trading and development prospects of most vulnerable regions (box 2.1). A recent study estimated that global damage due to sea-level rise and related extreme events could amount to $10.8 trillion per year, about 1.8 per cent of global GDP, for a scenario of 1.5 degrees Celsius warming by 2100. If warming is not mitigated, the costs could reach even higher levels (Jevrejeva et al., 2018).

Table 2.13 Type of infrastructure investment in ports and examples of ports and projects, 2017–2019

Investment related to developing or upgrading	Project objectives	Examples, projects or results
Maritime access	Dredging and/or increasing cargo-handling capacity through automation (investment in cranes)	Investments in port and terminal infrastructure to accommodate larger vessels in Zhuhai, China; resulted in 70 per cent increase in container traffic
Equipment and superstructure		3.5 billion Euros invested in Tanger Med Port complex expansion; expected to triple handling capacity from 3 million to 9 million TEUs
Expansion of port capacity to accommodate larger vessels		Dredging investments in Port of Hamburg, Germany; Tanjung Pelepas, Malaysia; Jan de Nul, Bangladesh; and Rotterdam, Netherlands
		Investment in Port of Piraeus, Greece (2018): 6 electric rubber-tyred gantry cranes, 30 terminal tractors and 30 terminal chassis; upgrade of terminal operating system to cope with increased traffic and in anticipation of new services in medium-term derived from takeover by COSCO
		Investment in new cranes in Port of Savannah, United States and Sines, Portugal
Smooth transport flows within port area	Reducing congestion and cargo dwell times	Improving facilities to ensure fluidity in storing and handling return of empty containers
		Improving ability to share information among different facilities to increase port efficiency (artificial intelligence and blockchain investments in Port of Rotterdam)
Connections to/from port using different modes of transport (hinterland strategies)	Improving intermodal capabilities	Improvements in hinterland connectivity in Tangshan, China; results: attract more service calls and services (30.7 per cent increase in container traffic)
Sites for port-related logistic and manufacturing activities in port area	Developing functional and spatial clusters of industrial or services activities that are directly or indirectly linked to maritime transport to increase traffic or business opportunities for port and to diversify revenue sources	Special economic zones in several ports in China and in Port Klang, Malaysia
		Development of e-logistics facilities such as e-commerce parcel-sorting hubs in Portugal and United Kingdom
Energy-related infrastructure	Developing facilities for bunkering; adapting to make liquefied natural gas available as marine fuel	Facilities currently under construction in ports of Cologne, Germany; Marseille Fos and Dunkirk, France; Antwerp, Belgium; and Barcelona, Spain
Reducing environmental footprint of port and shipping operations	Reducing emissions in port vicinity	Electrification (Turkey)
		Predictive capacity to calculate when vessels approaching port will arrive at berth (Port of Rotterdam)

Sources: European Seaports Organization, 2018; Lloyd's List, 2018a, 2018b, 2019; International Association of Ports and Harbours, 2019; and International Port Collaborative Decision-making Council (www.ipcdmc.org/organisation).

Box 2.1 Adapting coastal transport infrastructure to the impacts of climate change: The special case of small island developing States

Adaptation and resilience measures are essential to reducing the negative impacts of climate change. However, a recent UNCTAD port industry survey on the impacts of climate change on adaptation for ports revealed large gaps in terms of relevant information available to seaports of all sizes and across regions, with implications for effective climate risk assessment and adaptation planning. Relevant information and adequate climate adaptation efforts are urgently needed, especially for ports in developing regions, including small island developing States.

Adaptation is an urgent imperative for small island developing States, as they are often particularly exposed and vulnerable to the impacts of climate change while, at the same time, critically dependent on coastal transport infrastructure for external trade, food, energy and tourism. Climate-related events, which are expected to increase in severity and frequency, may cause major disruptions to the connectivity of small island developing States to international markets, as well as to related economic sectors such as tourism.

From 2015 to 2017, UNCTAD implemented a technical assistance project with a focus on climate change impacts and adaptation for coastal transport infrastructure in the Caribbean (see https://sidsport-climateadapt.unctad.org/ and chapter 4 of this report), drawing on earlier work and in collaboration with a range of partners. Key project outcomes include an assessment of operational disruptions and marine flood risk for eight ports and airports in Jamaica and Saint Lucia, as well as a transferable methodology to assist policymakers in small island developing States in taking effective adaptation action.

Sources: Asariotis et al., 2017; Intergovernmental Panel on Climate Change, 2018; UNCTAD, 2018c, 2018d, 2018e.

Ports also face increased scrutiny to reduce externalities – pollution, noise and environmental impact – from their operations. As major hubs of economic activity that are usually located near highly populated areas, seaports are an important source of air pollution for coastal areas and urban communities. With growing port activities and more attention focused on reducing emissions from the maritime transport sector, ports are seeking to understand the magnitude of their air emissions and pollution and the impact of alternative actions to reduce them.

Possible sources of emissions in ports include the following: seagoing vessels, domestic vessels (fireboats, pilot boats, police boats, push-boats, tugboats, tenders), cargo-handling equipment, heavy- and light-duty vehicles, locomotives, electrical grids, power plants, industrial and manufacturing facilities, administrative offices, and logistics infrastructure or warehouses (Global Environment Facility et al., 2018a, 2018b; Safety4Sea, 2019c).

A variety of measures can be taken to reduce port emissions:

- Exploring the potential of using alternative fuels, introducing differentiated port dues, providing onshore power supply, switching to low-sulphur fuels at berth and establishing speed limits in ports.
- Improving the exchange of information between ports and ships so than ships can sail at optimal speed (virtual arrival).
- Giving preferential treatment to harbour crafts with engines that meet stringent emissions standards.
- Strengthening port State control inspection regimes for visiting ships, relating to compliance with MARPOL, annex VI.
- Designating additional emission-control areas, leading to stricter environmental emission standards enforced at certain ports (ships going through them should use fuel with a sulphur content lower than 0.10 per cent (below the 0.5 per cent limit applicable on 1 January 2020).

2. Increased competition and competitiveness drive port infrastructure and services supply

Intra- and inter-port competition are key features of the supply of port infrastructure and services. Intra-port competition stems from the diversity of actors involved in the administration of different terminals and services within a port. This is a consequence of the increased use of concessions for the management of terminals and port services. Table 2.14 identifies the 21 main global players in this field, which control 80 per cent of global terminal operations, and indicates their current throughput and scope for capacity expansion.

Technology underpinning productivity (i.e. reduced times for loading and unloading) and fees associated with services are important differentiating factors at the intra-port level. The use of specialized terminals by type of cargo is increasingly being used to raise operational efficiency in the handling of cargo. For example, in the port of San Antonio, Chile, each terminal handles a different type of cargo.

Compared with intra-port competition, inter-port competition is affected by other variables besides technology, namely conditions of access to transport networks, and economic and regulatory issues (see table 2.15).

Terminal operators are also engaging in consolidation, motivated by the interest of ports to attract shipping companies as ports of call; increase port throughput, efficiency and economies of scale; and diversify

Table 2.14 Top 21 global terminal operators, throughput and capacity, 2018
(Million 20-foot equivalent units)

Ranking 2018 (throughput)	Company	Headquarters	Million TEUs	Percentage share	Growth/ decline (million TEUs)	Growth/ decline 2017–2018	Million TEUs	Growth/ decline 2017–2018 (percentage)
1	COSCO	China	105.8	13.5	14.5	15.9	130.0	17.8
2	Hutchison Ports	Hong Kong, China	82.6	10.5	0.2	0.3	112.0	1.6
3	PSA International	Singapore	80.1	10.2	6.2	8.4	112.6	7.9
4	APM Terminals	Netherlands	78.6	10.0	2.3	3.1	99.7	-2.0
5	DP World	United Arab Emirates	70.0	8.9	1.3	1.9	89.7	3.2
6	Terminal Investment Limited	Switzerland	47.7	6.1	3.7	8.4	62.4	8.7
7	China Merchants Ports	China	34.5	4.4	3.5	11.4	42.9	5.2
8	CMA CGM	France	25.6	3.3	0.9	3.5	38.4	1.6
9	Eurogate	Germany	13.7	1.7	-0.1	-1.1	22.6	-7.0
10	SSA Marine	United States	12.6	1.6	1.3	11.4	20.2	2.5
11	NYK Lines (Nippon Yusen Kabushiki Kaisha)	Japan	10.6	1.4	-0.4	-3.4	23.8	34.6
12	Evergreen	Taiwan Province of China	10.4	1.3	0.1	0.9	17.2	3.6
13	International Container Terminal Services	Philippines	9.7	1.2	0.6	6.4	17.9	13.7
14	Hyundai	Republic of Korea	7.6	1.0	1.4	23.1	12.3	10.8
15	HHLA (Hamburger Hafen und Logistik)	Germany	7.4	1.0			10.3	8.4
16	MOL (Mitsui Osaka Shosen Kaisha Lines)	Japan	7.3	0.9	0.2	3.4	10.0	4.8
17	Yildirim/Yilport	Turkey	6.4	0.8	0.3	4.4	10.1	-0.2
18	Bollore	France	5.3	0.7	0.5	11.5	9.4	6.2
19	Yang Ming	Taiwan Province of China	4.4	0.6	-0.3	-5.5	8.4	-5.9
20	"K" Line (Kawasaki Kisen Kaisha)	Japan	3.3	0.4	-0.2	-5.3	5.7	44.1
21	SAAM Puertos (Sudamericana Agencia Aéreas y Marítimas)	Chile	3.2	0.4	0.1	4.9	5.2	8.4
	Global operators total		**626.6**	**80.0**	**43.70**	**7.50**		

Source: Drewry, 2019, *Global Container Terminal Operators Annual Review and Forecast 2019*.

Table 2.15 Inter-port competition: Factors that influence port competition and competitiveness

Factors	Impact on port competition and competitiveness
Logistics related to maritime transport access	Operational capacity of port to receive larger vessels perceived as an imperative to maintain port competitiveness, for example in Asia and Europe Operational incapacity of port to receive larger vessels results in losing maritime connections, for example, as in Port of Santos, Brazil, or the need for trans-shipment, inducing higher freight costs Vertical integration between shipping companies and terminal operators can affect competition if all terminals in a port are controlled by the same company, and that company merges with a shipping company. In this case, the merged entity will have an incentive to discriminate against other shipping companies by providing lower quality services or charging higher prices.
Logistics related to land transport access	Land transport access to and from port is as important for competitiveness of port as access to maritime transport networks Negative impact on activities of terminal operator likely, even if operator is highly efficient, owing to lack of or ineffective connection between terminal and centres of production, distribution and consumption Need for public policies aimed at developing competitive freight markets that comprise whole logistics chain, for instance aligning incentives related to railways concessions and port concessions, for example in Brazil
Economic factors	Domestic regulation to ensure adequate fees for services rendered in relation to operational costs and to avoid anticompetitive behaviour necessary to oversee role of ports as public utilities, particularly in context of greater participation of private sector and increased consolidation among key actors
Regulatory frameworks	Legal certainty (predictability in treatment of goods by customs authorities) is factor of competitiveness; unpredictability associated with higher costs

Source: UNCTAD, forthcoming, *Challenges in Competition and Regulation of Port Infrastructure and Services and Maritime Transport: Focus on the Latin American Region*.

business opportunities. Between 2018 and 2019, several alliances and joint ventures were established between terminal operators to allow the joint operation of berths and between liner companies and terminal operators.

In Hong Kong, China, four terminal operators joined forces to operate 23 berths. Given that almost all the berths and terminals at the Port of Hong Kong, China are grouped under the Hong Kong [China] Seaport Alliance, the competition agency of Hong Kong, China has launched an investigation. Further, the authorities of Taiwan Province of China have announced the formation of joint ventures between port and terminal operators in that province to run several terminals in Kaohsiung.

In December 2018, pan-Japanese liner group ONE and the Port of Singapore Authority launched a joint venture to operate four berths at Pasir Panjang Terminal, Singapore. Instances of mergers and joint ventures between ports in China (regional hubs merging with smaller ports and between ports and terminals) have also been reported, resulting in the emergence of larger port groups (International Association of Ports and Harbours, 2019).

Terminal operators are also pursuing vertical integration – integrating logistic networks to expand activities beyond the port gate to diversify sources of revenue – and are competing with liner shipping companies with the same aim. This is illustrated by the acquisition in 2018 by DP World of Unifeeder, a Danish logistics company that operates a container feeder and shortsea network in Europe. Some of the concerns associated with these developments and their impact on terminal operations in Australia are described in box 2.2.

Box 2.2 Significant increases in container terminal operations in Australia generate concern of competition agency

The Australian Competition and Consumer Commission has expressed concern over unilateral infrastructure surcharges imposed by the two main terminal operators, Patrick and DP World Australia, since late June 2010, to recover landside investments. DP World Australia at Melbourne, for example, introduced a charge of $A3.45 (about US$2.87) per box in 2017 and increased it to $A85.30 (about US$58) in 2019 – an increase of more than 2,000 per cent. In Brisbane, DP World set charges at $A18 (about US$12) per box in 2010 and increased them to $A65.15 (about US$44) in 2019. Sydney also witnessed a steep rise in charges: DP World increased charges of $A21.16 (about US$14.4) per box to $A63.80 (US$44.5) per box. In practice, users – shippers and trucking companies – have no choice in the selection of terminal operators; therefore, they cannot avoid imposed surcharges.

The Commission believes these charges are disproportionately affecting the competitiveness of small trucking companies, as they are forced to pass on the extra costs to shippers, unlike bigger operators. Exporters have also expressed concerns, indicating that the extra charges are eroding their trade competitiveness.

In July 2019, fees to use the vehicle booking system that enables trucking companies to organize the receival and delivery of ocean shipping containers were also increased. The costs to transport operators of using such systems for the allocation of container slots with the two major container stevedores in Australia, DP World and Patrick Terminals, have risen 87.95 per cent and 73.33 per cent respectively.

Sources: Freightwaves 2019a, 2019b, 2019c.

F. OUTLOOK AND POLICY CONSIDERATIONS

Maritime businesses, including shipping companies and ports, face mounting sustainability expectations and more stringent environmental standards. In this context, the maritime transport sector is expected to deliver economic and social gains, with minimum environmental damage. This is producing a sea change in the sector, transforming operations across different segments of the maritime supply chain. One example of this trend is the pressure on the sector to switch to cleaner fuels, owing to growing environmental concerns.

From this perspective, the entry into force of the IMO sulphur cap of 0.5 per cent for marine fuel oil in January 2020 is a major game changer, with potential far-reaching implications on the cost, price volatility and supply of maritime transport. There are several sources of concern. One relates to higher and more volatile freight and charter rates stemming from the additional costs of more expensive fuel options; another relates to investments that are being made to ensure compliance, while yet another relates to the possibility that active supply capacity may be reduced owing to short-term disruptions in vessel supply. Such disruptions can occur in the following circumstances: the installation of scrubbers on younger ships accounting for greater carrying capacity, scrapping of less fuel-efficient vessels, blank sailings and slow steaming.

The entry into force of this regulation brings uncertainty to future shipping operations. From the perspective of carriers, this uncertainty relates to the installation of scrubbers and the availability of alternative fuels. From the perspective of shippers, emerging concerns relate to clarity of application of bunker fuel surcharges and how the entry into effect of this regulation will affect international shipping costs. It is argued that if the additional costs are not passed on to shippers, profit margins, particularly in the container shipping segment, could be reduced and lead to further consolidation and bankruptcy of the most financially vulnerable carriers.

To cope with low and volatile freight rates, reduced earnings and profitability caused by structural oversupply and weak growth in demand, container shipping companies have continued to engage in consolidation. In February 2019, the 10 deep-sea container-shipping lines represented 90 per cent of deployed capacity and dominated the major East West trade routes through three alliances.

Consolidation can increase the pressure faced by smaller operators and may have an impact on freight rates, frequency and efficiency, reliability and quality of services in small and remote islands and the least developed countries. Between 2006 and 2019, the level of concentration in terms of operations and alliances, ship deployment and major ports of call increased in the Pacific Islands. Data suggest that between 2006 and 2019, the number of companies providing transport services on Pacific routes decreased. At the same time, each company providing services on those routes was carrying bigger cargo volumes.

However, from the perspective of customers of the alliances, the participation of shipping lines in an alliance appears to provide more services, ships per service, higher vessel sizes and smaller average round-trip durations, compared with services offered by operators that are not members of an alliance, suggesting greater flexibility and adaptability to market conditions.

Patterns of the participation of developing countries in the maritime transport supply chain have changed over the last 50 years. The trends mentioned in this report suggest that the segments in which they have traditionally led are being affected and transformed because of sustainability considerations. For instance, the entry into force of several global environmental instruments and the adoption of voluntary standards in the sector are likely to have an impact on shipbuilding. This is because shipbuilding will be responsible for incorporating these elements into the design and construction of ships. Shipbuilding countries, for which the sector is of national importance in terms of direct financial returns, employment and supply-chain contributions, are exploring options to remain competitive in this new environment. These would include the following:

- Making an in-depth assessment of operations and services being provided by shipyards.
- Raising awareness about emerging standards among marine equipment manufacturers and suppliers.
- Developing environmentally friendly maritime expertise.
- Forging partnerships with maritime experts, technical and training institutes to promote innovation and the uptake of energy-saving and eco-friendly technologies.

The registration segment of the maritime supply chain has been traditionally dominated by developing countries and their open registries. Given the increased awareness of environmental considerations and the probability of stricter environmental standards, the scope of regulatory control by the flag State is likely to expand. Other decisive factors influencing the decision to flag out to open registries and to build awareness of emerging standards should be considered part of the strategy to retain competitiveness in this segment of the maritime supply chain.

Developing countries have also traditionally dominated ship demolition. Recent regulatory developments and industry voluntary initiatives aimed at making ship recycling more environmentally friendly and safer for humans could change this. Some of the countries that have traditionally participated in this supply chain segment – China, India and Turkey, for example – have shown declining demolition figures in recent years.

For port infrastructure and service providers, greater sustainability means improved economic efficiency, resilience, and environmental and social sustainability. In an increasingly competitive environment, both at the intra-port and intra-port levels, the port sector is witnessing increased consolidation, alliances and vertical integration in connection with logistic activities.

To achieve greater sustainability in the port sector, it is essential to make further investments to upgrade port infrastructure and operations. To carry out activities that will reduce externalities such as air pollution, it is necessary to develop capabilities and encourage the uptake of energy-efficient technologies and operational measures aimed at reducing emissions. Public and private cooperation is key in this regard. A challenge faced by shipping and port businesses is that of ensuring technology uptake and transfer to avoid falling behind in maritime sector capabilities and of increasing financing and investment with a view to developing and upgrading infrastructure and services. It is important to make transport infrastructure climate-proof, strengthen resilience, finance research and development for innovation, develop human capital development and reinforce regulatory and institutional frameworks for compliance.

Advancing towards sustainable shipping offers opportunities for developing countries. By moving towards cleaner transport alternatives and applying new technologies, several problems can be addressed simultaneously, for example, improving efficiency in transport operations, lowering energy consumption, mitigating climate change, and reducing local air pollution and traffic congestion. This is particularly important for developing countries, as they can consider integrating relevant sustainability principles and criteria at early stages of infrastructure investment and planning, given their stage of development and current focus on infrastructure development.

Further, many developing countries have expressed heightened interest in harnessing the potential of the blue economy. The sustainable use of ocean resources to ensure economic growth and improved livelihoods, jobs and ocean ecosystem health involves a wide range of activities. These include coastal tourism, the exploitation and conservation of living marine resources (fisheries management), the use of non-living marine resources (seabed mining), and activities relating to the maritime supply chain (port activities, shipbuilding and repair and shipping services).

To leverage opportunities and address challenges from a sustainable development policy perspective, there is a need to adopt a systemic approach to assess how best to support the development of national port and shipping sectors so as to promote competitiveness and connectivity, and seafaring and shipping-related work as viable employment options, and, at the same time, tackle environmental challenges. Understanding how sustainability parameters affect sectoral performance at the national level and linkages across segments is a key element of this assessment. So are leveraging on digitization as an enabling force and promoting cooperation within the ports and towards external actors.

REFERENCES

Asariotis R, Benamara H and Mohos-Naray V (2017). Port industry survey on climate change impacts and adaptation. UNCTAD Research Paper No. 18.

BIMCO (2019). Tanker shipping: While we wait for 2020 to kick in, it's all about politics. 12 June.

Barry Rogliano Salles (2019). Annual Review 2019: Shipping and Shipbuilding Markets.

Bunker Trust (2019). IMO 2020 costs could force liner market into further consolidation, says Drewry. 3 April.

CAI International (2019). How will IMO 2020 affect ship capacity and freight rates? CAI Transportation Blog. Available at http://blog.capps.com/how-will-imo-2020-affect-ship-capacity-and-freight-rates.

Clarksons Research (2019a). Scrubber Count Update and IMO 2020 Market Impact Assessment. July. Update No. 3.

Clarksons Research (2019b). *Container Intelligence Quarterly*. Second Quarter.

Clarksons Research (2019c). *Container Intelligence Monthly*. Volume 21, May.

Clarksons Research (2019d). *Container Intelligence Quarterly*. First quarter.

Drewry (2019). *Global Container Terminal Operators Annual Review and Forecast 2019*. London.

European Federation for Transport and Environment (2018). *Road Map to Decarbonizing European Shipping*. Brussels.

European Seaports Organization (2018). *The Infrastructure Investment Needs and Financing Challenge of European Ports*. Brussels.

Forbes (2019a). IMO 2020: What shippers need to know now. 8 April.

Forbes (2019b). Exxon Mobil eyes marine fuels business expansion as IMO 2020 deadline looms. 13 March.

Freightwaves (2019a). Australian shippers in uproar on DP World fees. 18 April. Available at www.freightwaves.com/news/maritime/20190419-major-cash-grab-underway (accessed 10 September 2019).

Freightwaves (2019b). Marine terminal operators sting Australian shippers and truckers with huge surcharges. 19 April.

Freightwaves (2019c). Marine box terminal operators hit truckers with huge Vehicle Booking System fee hikes. 4 July.

Gasparoti C and Rusu E (2018). An overview on the shipbuilding market in the current period and forecast. *EuroEconomica*. 1(37):254–271.

gCaptain.com (2019). BP [British Petroleum] introduces new IMO 2020-compliant bunker fuel. 11 March.

Global Environment Facility, United Nations Development Programme, IMO Global Maritime Energy Efficiency Partnerships Project and Institute of Marine Engineering, Science and Technology (2018a). *Ship Emissions Toolkit: Guide No.3 – Development of a National Ship Emissions Reduction Strategy*. Elephant Print. Lewes, East Sussex.

Global Environment Facility, United Nations Development Programme, IMO Global Maritime Energy Efficiency Partnerships Project and International Association of Ports and Harbours (2018b). *Port Emissions Toolkit: Guide No.1 – Assessment of Port Emissions*. Elephant Print. Lewes, East Sussex.

Hellenic Shipping News Worldwide (2018). IMO 2020: Mayhem or opportunity for the refining and marine sectors? 6 September.

Hellenic Shipping News Worldwide (2019a). Major Dutch maritime companies join Green Maritime Methanol Project. 22 February.

Hellenic Shipping News Worldwide (2019b) Liberian flag added to QUALSHIP 21. 12 April.

International Association of Ports and Harbours (2019). *Ports and Harbours*. Volume 64. No. 2. March/April.

IHS Markit (2019). Shipping and Shipbuilding Outlook. March.

IHS Markit, JOC.com, Gemini Shippers Group and Seabury Maritime (2019). IMO 2020: What every shipper needs to know. White Paper. March. Micropress Printers. Suffolk, United Kingdom.

IncoDocs (2019). IMO 2020: How regulations will impact the shipping industry. 9 April.

Intergovernmental Panel on Climate Change (2018). Global Warming of 1.5°C. An Intergovernmental Panel on Climate Change Special Report on the impacts of global warming of 1.5°C above pre-industrial levels and related global greenhouse gas emission pathways, in the context of strengthening the global response to the threat of climate change, sustainable development and efforts to eradicate poverty. World Meteorological Organization. Geneva. Available at www.ipcc.ch/sr15/ (accessed 10 September 2019).

International Chamber of Shipping (2019). *Shipping Industry Flag State Performance Table: 2018/2019*. London.

Jevrejeva S, Jackson LP, Grinsted A, Lincke D and Marzeion B (2018). Flood damage costs under the sea level rise with warming of 1.5 °C and 2 °C. *Environmental Research Letters*. 13(7):074014. 4 July.

JOC.com (2018a). Are they container lines or quasi-utility companies? 14 November.

JOC.com (2018b). EU [European Union] scrutiny of Asia container shipping subsidies builds. 7 December.

JOC.com (2018c). Low-sulphur BAFs [bunker adjustment factors] rattle already volatile container shipping. 25 September.

JOC.com (2019a). Scrubber retrofits put pressure on ocean reliability. 21 April.

JOC.com (2019b). Low-sulphur BAFs [bunker adjustment factors] offer shippers path to hedge exposure. 1 May.

Lee T and Nam H (2017). A study on green shipping in major countries: In the view of shipyards, shipping companies, ports and policies. *The Asian Journal of Shipping and Logistics.* 33(4):253–262.

Lloyd's List (2018a). One Hundred Ports 2018.

Lloyd's List (2018b). 37 Piraeus (Greece): Throughput 2017: 4,145,079 TEUs, up 10.9% (2016: 3,736,644 TEUs), 31 August.

Lloyd's List (2019). Tanger Med volumes to grow by 1m TEUs per year. 12 July.

McKinsey and Company (2018). IMO 2020 and the outlook for marine fuels. September.

MDS Transmodal (2019). IMO 2020 to result in 50% hike in bunker costs on Far East–Europe trade lane: Launch of online BAF Calculator to increase bunker cost transparency for shippers and lines. 16 July.

Non-governmental Organization Shipbreaking Platform (2015). *What a Difference a Flag Makes: Why Shipowners' Responsibility to Ensure Sustainable Ship Recycling Needs to Go beyond Flag State Jurisdiction*. Brussels.

Novethic (2019). Maersk, the world's leading container shipping company, aims for carbon neutrality in 2050. 11 January.

Organization for Economic Cooperation and Development and International Transport Forum (2018). *Decarbonizing Maritime Transport: Pathways to Zero-carbon Shipping by 2035*. Paris.

Paris Memorandum of Understanding on Port State Control (2019). White, Grey and Black List for the period 1 July 2019–1 July 2020. Available at www.parismou.org/detentions-banning/white-grey-a (accessed 11 September 2019).

Safety4sea (2019a). 58% of flag States could be removed from STCW [Standards of Training, Certi Watchkeeping for Seafarers] White List. 10 May.

Safety4sea (2019b). BIMCO: Container shipping will face a challenging 2019. 19 February.

Safety4Sea (2019c). European Commission study supports Mediterranean ECA [emissions control area]. 30 March.

Seeking Alpha (2019). IMO 2020: An overview of the its [sic] effects in shipping, oil and other industries. 29 March.

Splash247.com (2019a). Hyundai Heavy given go-ahead to take over DSME. 31 January.

Splash247.com (2019b). Merger talk heats up between China's top shipbuilders in wake of Korean yard consolidation. 1 February.

Splash247.com (2019c). Calls grow for Beijing to scrap ship recycling ban. 10 January.

The Economist (2019). The world's biggest ship-breaking town is under pressure to clean up. 7 March.

The Loadstar (2018). Shippers are being "left in the dark" as carriers look to recover IMO 2020 costs. 3 October.

The Wall Street Journal (2019). Korea's [Republic of Korea's] Mega-merger of shipyards set to dominate global shipbuilding. 6 February.

United Kingdom Chamber of Shipping (2018). IMO agrees at least 50 per cent reduction in carbon emissions from shipping by 2050. 13 April.

UNCTAD (2017). *Review of Maritime Transport 2017* (United Nations publication. Sales No. E.17.II.D.10, New York and Geneva).

UNCTAD (2018a). Market consolidation in container shipping: What next? UNCTAD Policy Brief No. 69.

UNCTAD (2018b). *Review of Maritime Transport 2018* (United Nations publication. Sales No. E.18.II.D.5. New York and Geneva).

UNCTAD (2018c). *Climate Change Impacts on Coastal Transportation Infrastructure in the Caribbean: Enhancing the Adaptive Capacity of Small Island Developing States (SIDS) – Saint Lucia – A case study*. UNCTAD/DTL/TLB/2018/3. Geneva.

UNCTAD (2018d). *Climate Change Impacts on Coastal Transportation Infrastructure in the Caribbean: Enhancing the Adaptive Capacity of Small Island Developing States (SIDS) – Jamaica: A case study*. UNCTAD/DTL/TLB/2018/2. Geneva.

UNCTAD (2018e). *Climate Change Impacts on Coastal Transportation Infrastructure in the Caribbean: Enhancing the Adaptive Capacity of Small Island Developing States (SIDS): Climate Risk and Vulnerability Assessment Framework for Caribbean Coastal Transport Infrastructure*. UNCTAD/DTL/TLB/2018/1. Geneva.

UNCTAD (forthcoming). *Challenges in Competition and Regulation of Port Infrastructure and Services and Maritime Transport: Focus on the Latin American Region*.

Universal Cargo (2016). What is blank sailing? 26 November.

Universal Cargo (2019). Two big problems ocean freight shipping faces in 2019. 31 January.

University Maritime Advisory Services (2019). How can shipping decarbonize? Available at https://u-mas.co.uk/Latest/Post/411/How-can-shipping-decarbonise-A-new-infographic-highlights-what-it-d-take-to-decarbonise-shipping-by-2050 (accessed 13 September 2019).

World Maritime News (2019). Drewry: Sulphur cap to trigger slow steaming, trans-shipment. 18 March.

This chapter looks at different performance indicators relating to the maritime transport sector. The aim is to help policymakers and port and maritime authorities assess and track the performance of their countries' ports and shipping businesses and provide analytical tools to guide their policymaking in the field of maritime transport through a set of key performance indicators that are relevant to the sustainable development of the maritime sector.

The various indicators featured in the chapter are indicative of how the *Review of Maritime Transport* can support ongoing performance-tracking analysis. This year, a particular focus is given to port performance and connectivity, building on a new port liner shipping connectivity index for more than 900 ports, new statistics on port calls and time spent in port, as well as insights gained from the UNCTAD Train for Trade Port Management Programme.

Shipping connectivity and port-waiting time are proxy measures of efficiency, access to markets, infrastructure endowment, supply-side capacity, trade facilitation and other sustainability parameters. The data suggest that geography, trade volumes and port efficiency matter for a country's shipping connectivity. Several small island developing States are among the countries with the lowest shipping connectivity, as they are often confronted with a vicious cycle wherein low trade volumes discourage investments in better maritime transport connectivity, and faced with low connectivity, merchandize trade becomes costly and uncompetitive.

With regard to turnaround times, in 2018, ships spent a median time of 23.5 hours (0.97 days) in port. Typically, dry bulk carriers spent 2.05 days in port, container ships, 0.7 days. A shorter time in port is a positive indicator that could signal the level of port efficiency and trade competitiveness. The 10 lowest-ranking economies are all developing countries or least developed countries, while the economies with the fastest turnaround times are mostly advanced economies with large volumes or small economies that handle low cargo volumes at each port call.

PERFORMANCE INDICATORS

Horizon 2030

LINER SHIPPING CONNECTIVITY

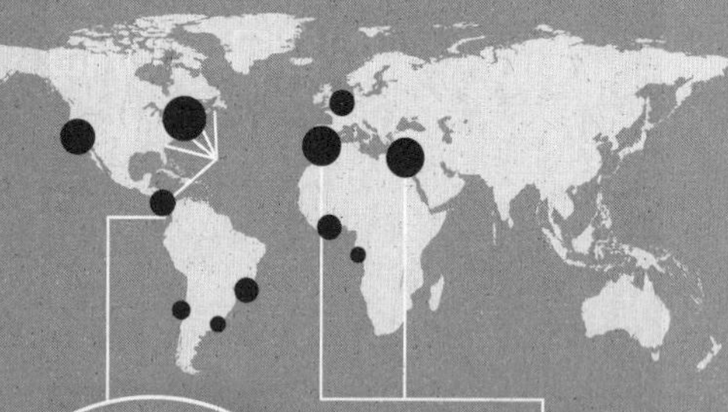

After the Panama Canal expansion in 2017, the liner shipping connectivity index for the East Coast in North American ports increased.

Port Said, Egypt and Tanger Med, Morocco are the leading African ports in the Mediterranean region.

PORT TURNAROUND TIMES

A shorter time in port is a positive indicator of a port's efficiency and trade competitiveness.

in 2018

- **2.05** days for dry bulk
- **0.70** day for container ships
- **0.94** day for liquid bulk

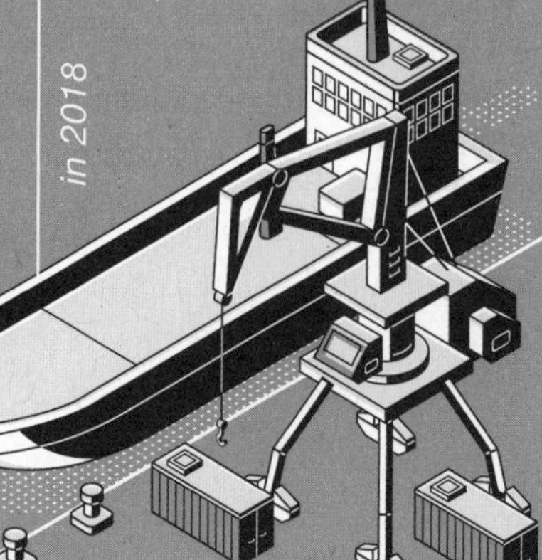

ENVIRONMENTAL INDICATORS

Three vessel indicators can be used to assess the world shipping fleet's impact on the environment.

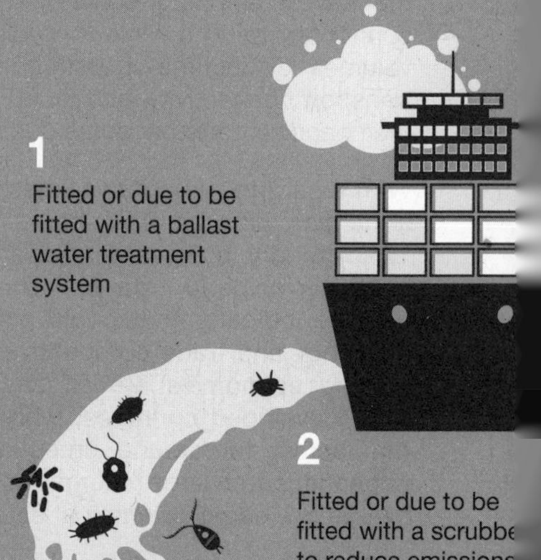

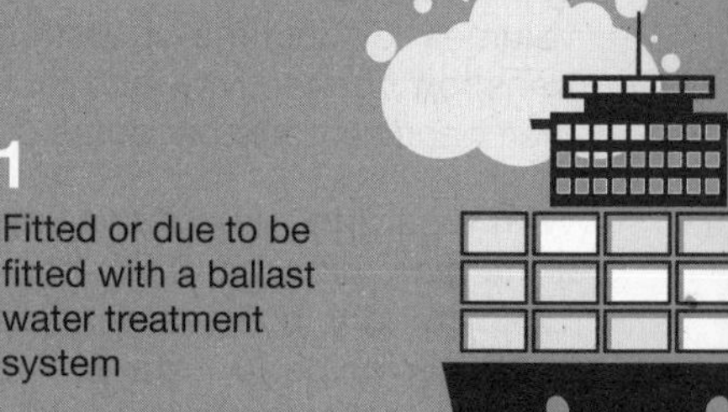

1

Fitted or due to be fitted with a ballast water treatment system

2

Fitted or due to be fitted with a scrubbe to reduce emissions of sulphur

3

Compliant with tier III regulations to reduce nitrogen-oxide emissions

A. MARITIME TRANSPORT PERFORMANCE MEASUREMENT

Maritime transport is a complex area of activity, owing to the inherently international nature of shipping and its multi-stakeholder dimension. These characteristics create an analytical challenge that is compounded by the role of the sector as an input production factor supporting other economic sectors and areas of activity, such as trade, fishing, tourism and energy. Such intricacies also underscore the critical importance of hard facts and data to support sound policymaking across different portfolios to ensure that balanced policy trade-offs are achieved.

Performance indicators are important analytical tools that can facilitate an understanding of the nature and scale of issues facing the shipping industry and ports, and help assess the potential impact of alternative policy options. Indicators are also necessary for self-evaluation and benchmarking, two factors that are integral to policymaking, as they help assess progress towards set goals and targets. Bearing in mind the strategic and practical usefulness of performance indicators, indicators with multidimensional metrics spanning a range of factors, such as efficiency, cost-effectiveness, productivity, profitability, connectivity, access, social inclusiveness and environmental sustainability, are increasingly considered necessary for maritime business and its users, as well as for Governments and policymakers. Data at the country level are becoming ever more important to help establish the nature and scale of maritime transport activity and underlying trends, as well as to interpret the results and implications for policymakers, especially in developing countries. Maritime transport indicators that support performance monitoring, measurement, reporting and evaluation are attracting more and more attention and interest.

Other factors such as the implementation of the 2030 Agenda for Sustainable Development and the Sustainable Development Goals have also reinforced the momentum of performance indicators that would help track and assess the performance of shipping and ports, as well as determine progress towards achieving objectives and targets. UNCTAD contributes to Sustainable Development Goal reporting on various indicators, including on transport (UNCTAD, 2019a). Further, the *Review of Maritime Transport* has a role to play with regard to maritime transport performance indicators, monitoring, reporting and benchmarking.

This chapter capitalizes on existing data from various issues of the *Review of Maritime Transport* to support performance-based approaches to maritime transport. Drawing upon over five decades of maritime transport work – monitoring trends and compiling and analysing data – the chapter offers a one-stop shop to country-level maritime transport indicators, while emphasizing the perspective of developing countries and the sustainability dimension. Some indicators are augmented by new data and information received from partners that are exploiting digital innovations and technologies.

This year, chapter 3 provides an assessment of selected performance indicators for maritime transport, notably shipping connectivity, port turnaround times, port performance and environmental indicators for the shipping fleet. In the coming years, the Review will cover additional indicators, including the environmental and social dimensions of shipping and ports, and expand the corresponding statistical coverage on its maritime statistics portal.

In this respect, UNCTAD has developed various tools and programmes to assist member States in their effort to improve their transport performance towards achieving their goals and objectives in sustainable transport, including maritime transport. Among these programmes is the UNCTAD Framework for Sustainable Freight Transport, which aims to provide useful guidance and practical tools to support stakeholders in mainstreaming sustainability considerations into their freight transport-related policies, plans, operations and investment decisions (UNCTAD, 2019b). Articulated around 6 steps, 1 set of cross-cutting enabling factors and 27 detailed substeps, the Framework for Sustainable Freight Transport provides a modular step-by-step process that details how to plan, design, develop and implement tailored sustainable freight transport strategies (see www.sft-framework.org/; accessed 16 September 2019).

In addition, the Framework offers guidance and practical tools to help relevant stakeholders and decision-makers, from both the public and the private sectors, take adequate response measures that promote sustainable freight transport systems. The main tools include the *Self-assessment Questionnaire*, a filterable and extensive list of some 250 key performance indicators and a catalogue containing over 300 sustainable freight transport measures. The key performance indicators identified in the Framework enable users to analyse the current situation and monitor developments. These can be filtered by mode of transport, scope and dimensions of sustainability. Of the total set of 250 indicators provided by the tool, 152 can be applied to maritime transport.

Combining the bottom-up approach of the Framework for Sustainable Freight Transport with a top-down approach of global and comparable performance indicators, such as those discussed in this chapter, will help policymakers make informed decisions in support of their port and shipping businesses. UNCTAD will continue to engage with relevant data providers, research institutions and academia to make use of the latest available information and statistics, providing unbiased analysis and advice to the extent possible. Future issues of the Review will cover a variety of different indicators, including environmental and social dimensions of shipping and ports, given their critical importance in meeting the Sustainable Development Goals.

B. LINER SHIPPING CONNECTIVITY

The position of a country or port in the global container shipping network – that is to say, its connectivity – is an important determinant of accessibility to global trade, trade costs and competitiveness. To provide an indicator for this connectivity, UNCTAD in 2004 developed the liner shipping connectivity index (UNCTAD, 2017a), which aims to capture a country's level of integration into the existing global liner shipping network by measuring liner shipping connectivity. In 2019, UNCTAD expanded the coverage of the index and introduced a new port liner shipping connectivity index for more than 900 ports. (See box 3.1.)

The liner shipping connectivity index can be considered a proxy for the accessibility to global trade. The higher the level, the easier it is for a country to access the global maritime freight transport system, including in terms of

Box 3.1 Liner shipping connectivity index: A proxy for maritime transport connectivity

The liner shipping connectivity index indicates a country's integration level into global liner shipping networks. The index is set at 100 for the maximum value of country connectivity in 2006, which was represented by China. The index was updated and improved in 2019, with further country coverage, incorporating an additional component (the number of country pairs with a direct connection), and newly generated for 2006 onwards, setting the new index at 100 for the country with the highest average in 2006. The new time series replaces the previous liner shipping connectivity index of UNCTAD, which had been generated from 2004 onwards. Readers interested in the earlier time series, covering 2004 until 2018, may contact rmt@unctad.org. The current version of the index is generated from the following six components: number of scheduled ship calls per week in the country concerned, deployed annual capacity in TEUs (total deployed capacity offered in the country), number of regular liner shipping services to and from the country, number of liner shipping companies that provide services to and from the country, average size in TEUs of the ships deployed by the scheduled service with the largest average vessel size and number of other countries that are connected to the country through direct liner shipping services (a direct service is defined as a regular service between two countries; it may include other stops in between, but the transport of a container does not require trans-shipment).

The index is generated for all countries that are serviced by regular containerized liner shipping services. For each component, the country's value is divided by the maximum value of the component in 2006, and the average of the six components for the country is calculated. The country average is then again divided by the maximum value of the average in 2006 and multiplied by 100. The result is a maximum index of 100 in the year 2006. This means that the index for China in 2006 is 100, and all other indices are in relation to this value.

In collaboration with MDS Transmodal, UNCTAD in 2019 updated and improved the liner shipping connectivity index. For example country coverage was expanded to include several small island developing States, and a component covering the number of countries that can be reached without the need for trans-shipment was added. The other five components – number of companies that provide services, number of services, number of ships that call per month, total annualized deployed container-carrying capacity and ship sizes – remain unchanged.

Applying the same methodology as for the country-level liner shipping connectivity index, UNCTAD generated a new port liner shipping connectivity index for more than 900 container ports annually, from 2006 to 2019. This new index at the port level responds to frequent requests received by UNCTAD from port authorities and shippers. Each one of the six components of the port index covers a key aspect of a connectivity:

- A large number of scheduled ship calls allows for high service frequency for imports and exports. In Shanghai, for example, 298 container ship port calls are scheduled per month, that is to say, about 10 per day. The average port in the world receives 12 ships per month, and the median port, 5. This means that a typical port can expect one container ship call about every six days.
- A high deployed total capacity allows shippers to trade large volumes of imports and exports. For example, the value for Shanghai is 68 million TEUs; the global average per port is 1.6 million TEUs.
- A high number of regular services to and from the port is associated with shipping options to reach different overseas markets. For example, 265 services are offered to and from Shanghai; the global average for all ports is 10 services.
- A high number of liner shipping companies that provide services is an indicator of the level of competition in the market. For example, 68 carriers provide services to and from Shanghai; the global average for all ports is six. The global median is three companies; in other words, half of the world's container ports are serviced by three or fewer companies.
- Large ship sizes are associated with economies of scale on the sea leg and with potentially lower transport costs. For example, in 2019, 10 ports accommodated ships services with an average size of 20,182 TEUs: Antwerp, Belgium; Dalian, China; Hamburg, Germany; Ningbo, China; Piraeus, Greece; Qingdao, China; Rotterdam, the Netherlands; Shanghai, China; Singapore, Singapore; and Xingang, China. In the UNCTAD database of 960 ports for 2019, the average size of the ships on the services with the largest vessels is 3,836 TEUs.
- A high number of destination ports that can be reached without the need for trans-shipment is an indicator of fast and reliable direct connections to foreign markets. Counting on a direct regular shipping connection has empirically been shown to help reduce trade costs and increase trade volumes (Hoffmann et al., 2019; Wilmsmeier and Hoffmann, 2008). For example, Shanghai has direct connections with 295 partner ports, which means that an exporter from Shanghai can sell to clients in 295 overseas port destinations without the need for trans-shipment. The average port has 28 direct connections, while the median port has 14.

Source: UNCTAD, Division on Technology and Logistics, based on information from MDS Transmodal.

Figure 3.1 Liner shipping connectivity index, top 10 economies, 2006–2019

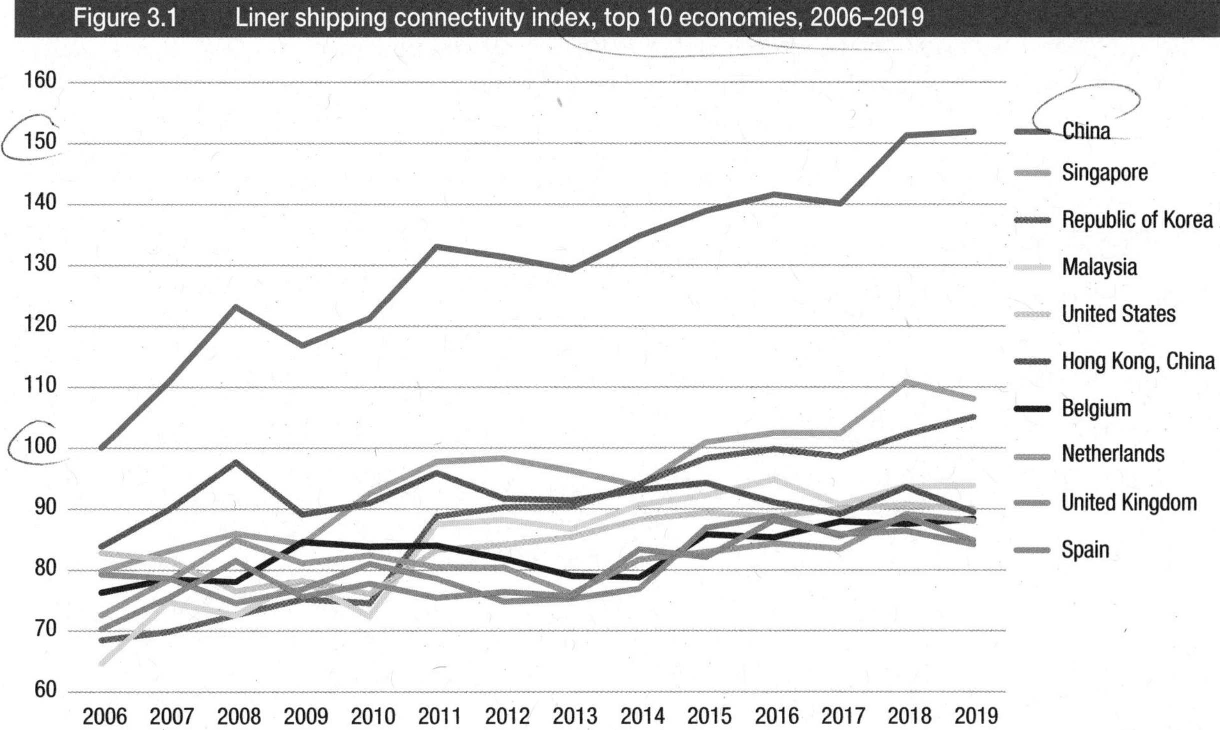

Source: UNCTAD, based on data from MDS Transmodal. For the complete data set for all countries, see https://unctadstat.unctad.org/wds/TableViewer/tableView.aspx?ReportId=92.

capacity, transport options and frequency, and thus effectively participate to international trade. Therefore, the index can be considered both as a measure of connectivity to maritime shipping and as a measure of competitiveness and trade facilitation.

1. A growing connectivity divide

In 2019, 5 of the 10 most connected economies are in Asia, 4 are in Europe and 1 is in North America (figure 3.1). Since 2006, the most connected country – China – improved its liner shipping connectivity index by 51 per cent; the average index went up by 24 per cent, while the lowest index in 2019 was below the lowest index in 2006. The least connected countries saw little improvement during the period; they include small island developing States, meaning that trade in shipped goods remains problematic in those countries, with economic knock-on effects. Put differently, there is a growing connectivity divide – an increasing difference between the most and least connected countries. The divide can be explained by the enhanced competitiveness of the most connected countries, namely through improved hard and soft port and trade-facilitation infrastructure, while the least connected countries have not found the resources for such investments and thus have not been able to attract additional regular container shipping services. For a more detailed analysis of trends in the country liner shipping connectivity index and its components, see UNCTAD, 2017a.

> There is a growing connectivity divide – an increasing difference between the most and least connected countries.

2. Ports connect to compete

The port-level liner shipping connectivity index is generated for all container ports of the world that receive regular container shipping services. (For the complete data set of more than 900 ports, from 2006 to 2019, see http://stats.unctad.org/maritime). Trends in selected maritime regions relating to the port-level index are discussed below.

On the West Coast of North America, the three most connected ports in 2019 are in the United States, followed by Manzanillo, Mexico and Vancouver, Canada. Mexican ports have seen particularly high growth rates during the last decade, as they serve as entry points for Mexican imports and exports and as trans-shipment hubs for Central American trade with Asia. Over the last three years, West Coast ports in North America have lost steam compared with ports on the East Coast, which gained competitiveness owing to the expanded Panama Canal. All sea routes from China to the East Coast of North America have become cheaper, compared with railway services that connect Chicago or New York with Los Angeles or Long Beach.

On the East Coast of North America, the 10 most connected ports are located in the United States. Halifax, Canada is ranked eleventh in the region, and Veracruz, Mexico, fourteenth. The liner shipping connectivity index in most North American East Coast ports was stagnant until 2016, and only after the Panama Canal expansion in 2017 did the index for the East Coast in North American ports increase, especially in New York/New Jersey, Savannah and Charleston, United States, which are now the top three ports on the East Coast of North America.

In Central America and the Caribbean, the most connected ports in 2019 are Cartagena, Colombia; Manzanillo, Mexico; and Balboa, Panama. Cartagena's connectivity has strengthened since 2017, following the expansion of the Panama Canal. Five of the top 10 ports of the region are in Panama, including Rodman port (ranked ninth), which only began operations as a container port in 2018. Colón, on the Caribbean side of Panama (ranked seventh), also witnessed improvement, as its index more than doubled in 2017.

Tanger Med recorded the world's highest absolute increase in its index during the first decade of its operations since 2007.

On the West Coast of South America, Callao, Peru; Guayaquil, Ecuador; and San Antonio, Chile are the most connected ports in the region in 2019. Chilean ports represent 7 of the top 10 most connected ports in the region, including ports that have started receiving regular container shipping services in the last decade only (Coronel and Lirquén). As Chilean ports share the fleet assignment to Chile, their individual indices are lower than those of Callao or Guayaquil, where there is less inter-port competition at the national level. Port Callao has almost doubled its liner shipping connectivity index since 2006, following port reforms and private sector investments, as well as a growing domestic market and some trans-shipment traffic.

On the East Coast of South America, 8 of the 10 most connected ports are in Brazil, led by Santos. Buenos Aires, Argentina and Montevideo, Uruguay are ranked second and third, respectively. Montevideo has a much smaller national market than ports in Argentina and Brazil, but it manages to attract large portions of trans-shipment traffic, as well as transit cargo destined for the Plurinational State of Bolivia and Paraguay. The cabotage restrictions in the region also increase the prospects of Montevideo becoming a trans-shipment hub, in competition with ports in Argentina and Brazil. Shipping a container between two Argentinean ports, for example, is normally done on vessels flying under the flag of Argentina, while from Montevideo, it is possible to provide such services to secondary ports in Argentina with internationally flagged ships (UNCTAD, 2017b).

In Northern Europe, the ports of Antwerp, Belgium and Rotterdam, the Netherlands closely compete for first position, with Antwerp leading in recent years, followed by Hamburg, Germany in third position. Two ports in the Baltic Sea (Aarhus, Denmark and Gdansk, Poland) have joined the league of the top 10. In the United Kingdom, the new London Gateway port has within a few years

Figure 3.2 Liner shipping connectivity index for the top 10 ports in Western Africa, 2006–2019

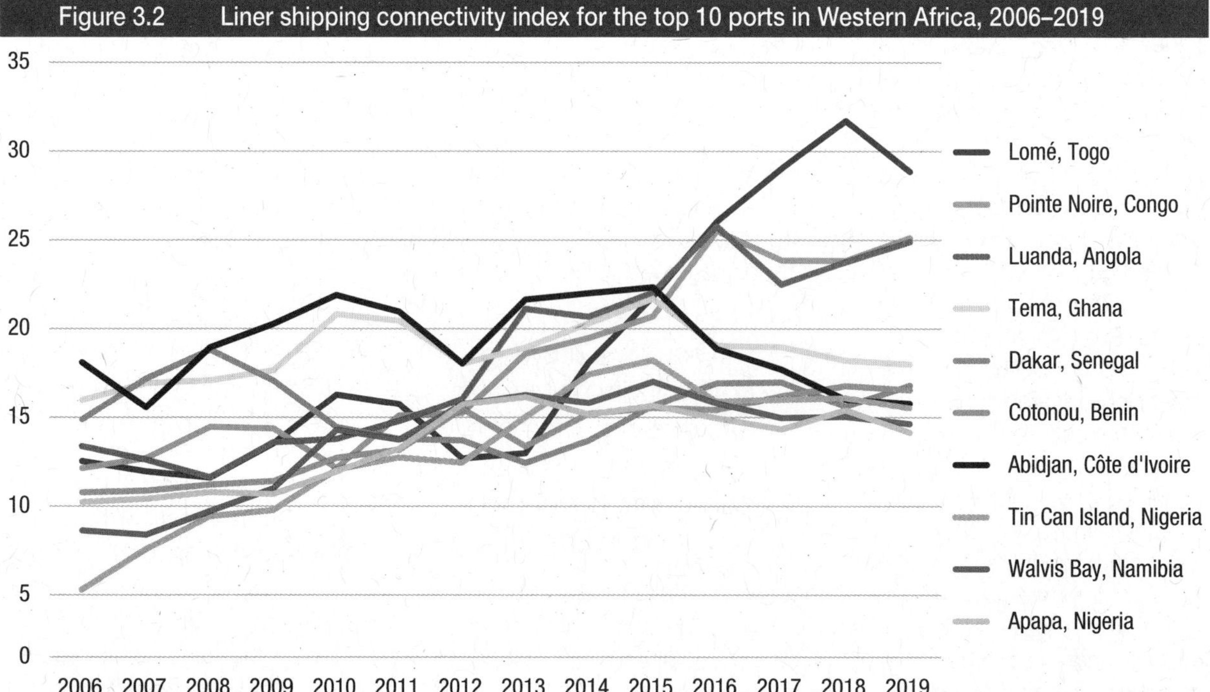

Source: UNCTAD secretariat calculations, based on data from MDS Transmodal. Underlying data for these and all other ports are available at http://stats.unctad.org/maritime.

climbed to second position in the country, overtaking Southampton, Tilbury and others.

In the Mediterranean, Piraeus, Greece emerged as the most connected port in 2019, followed by Valencia, Algeciras and Barcelona, Spain. In Piraeus, COSCO holds a 51 per cent controlling share and increasingly uses the port for its own trans-shipment services. Port Said, Egypt and Tanger Med, Morocco are the leading African ports in the Mediterranean region; Tanger Med recorded the world's highest absolute increase in its index during the first decade of its operations since 2007. Both Port Said and Tanger Med provide extensive trans-shipment services, benefiting from their geographical position and private sector investments from major global port operators.

In Western Africa, Lomé, Togo has emerged as the leading hub port. It is followed by Pointe Noire, Congo and Luanda, Angola (figure 3.2). Spurred by modernization reforms and benefitting from the congestion at the port of Lagos, Nigeria, Lomé port has been rapidly expanding in recent years. Another factor influencing the good performance of leading ports in the region is that they managed to attract direct services from China, boosting their indices, given the additional services and the larger vessels deployed on these routes (Wolde Woldearegay et al., 2016). Abidjan, Côte d'Ivoire, which was still ranked number one in the region in 2016, slipped to seventh position in 2019. Lagos dropped from the ranking of the 10 most connected ports of the region in 2006 to sixteenth position in 2019, while two other Nigerian ports (Tin Can Island and Apapa) joined the ranking. Within the African continent, Western Africa has relatively low connectivity, as its geographical position does not link it to any major North–South or East–West shipping routes.

In Southern Africa, 4 of the top 10 ports of the region are in South Africa, namely Durban, Cape Town, Coega and Port Elizabeth. The other ports among the top 10 are in Mozambique (Maputo, Beira and Nacala) and Madagascar (Toamasina and Mahajanga), all of which have significantly lower indices than the top four South African ports. In Southern Africa, port connectivity is closely associated with a country's own trading volumes as well as trade from neighbouring landlocked countries, while trans-shipment services are not a major factor (Hoffmann et al., 2019; Humphreys et al., 2019).

In Eastern Africa, the most connected ports are Port Louis, Mauritius and Pointe de Galets, Reunion. Both ports provide trans-shipment services to other Eastern and Southern African ports. The liner shipping connectivity index of Mombasa, Kenya and Dar es Salaam, United Republic of Tanzania have been relatively stagnant, except for a temporary peak in Mombasa in 2018. Both ports are important gateways to Eastern African countries' overseas trade, including the landlocked countries of Burundi, Rwanda and Uganda, yet they are highly congested, limiting their potential for improved connectivity. Policy measures that could help improve port connectivity in Eastern Africa include expanding and further modernizing existing ports, investing in new ports, encouraging inter-port competition among neighbouring countries, improving intermodal connections and trade, and facilitating transit (Humphreys et al., 2019; UNCTAD, 2017a).

In the Red Sea, the leading ports are Jeddah and King Abdullah, Saudi Arabia and Djibouti, Djibouti. All three ports mostly provide trans-shipment services, competing with ports in Asia and Eastern Africa for this business. The other ports of the region in Eritrea, the Sudan and Yemen cater mostly for national trade; they have recorded lessening connectivity in the past few years caused by lower trade volumes stemming from economic and political developments in the region.

In Southern Africa, the top four ports of the region are in South Africa – Durban, Cape Town, Coega and Port Elizabeth.

In the Persian Gulf, the port of Jebel Ali, United Arab Emirates, has the highest index. Dammam, Saudi Arabia; Khalifa, United Arab Emirates; and Salalah, Oman are competitors in the trans-shipment cargo sector, albeit with lower levels of connectivity. The other ports in the region, in Bahrain, the Islamic Republic of Iran, Iraq and Qatar have experienced volatile connectivity. Bandar Abbas, Islamic Republic of Iran experienced a slump in connectivity in 2014 and 2015, following embargoes that discouraged container lines from providing direct calls to ports in that country. Bandar Abbas recovered from 2016 to 2018, but in 2019 again experienced a strong decline, recording its lowest index since 2006.

In South Asia, Colombo, Sri Lanka is the most connected port. The port provides services for goods imported to and exported from Sri Lanka, as well as trans-shipment services for other South Asian countries. The remaining top 10 ports of South Asia are in India (seven ports) and Pakistan (two ports). Chittagong, Bangladesh is ranked fourteenth in South Asia, and Male, Maldives is ranked eighteenth. The port of Mundra, India has seen the largest increase in its index but is still lagging behind Colombo. Colombo benefits from cabotage restrictions in India, as these discourage carriers from trans-shipping in Indian ports, for which they are required to use Indian-flagged ships (UNCTAD, 2017b).

In South-East Asia, Singapore reports the highest index, followed by Port Klang and Tanjung Pelepas, Malaysia. These three ports are important hub ports, largely serving the same trans-shipment markets. The index of Hai Phong, Viet Nam almost doubled between 2018 and 2019, as its new terminal became the first deep-water port in northern Viet Nam. The remaining ports in the region in Indonesia, the Philippines, Thailand and Viet Nam largely cater for their countries' own imports and exports and their indices have for the most part declined.

In mainland China, Shanghai and Ningbo have strengthened their lead since 2006, and today Shanghai is the most connected port in the world. Shanghai has overtaken Hong Kong, China, which was number one in 2006. Ningbo has doubled its liner shipping connectivity index since 2006. Together, mainland China ports accounted for 28.5 per cent of world container port traffic in 2018 (see chapter 1). Most of their traffic is composed of Chinese exports, combined with containerized imports and some domestic trans-shipment traffic.

In East Asia, the top four ports, not including mainland China, are Busan, Republic of Korea, which is ranked third in the world; followed by Hong Kong, China; Kaohsiung, Taiwan Province of China; and Yokohama, Japan. Overall, the East Asian ports outside mainland China recorded less growth in their indices than ports in mainland China. Kobe and Nagoya, Japan have seen a decline in their connectivity, reflecting slower growth in the Japanese economy and the fact that ports in Japan are not as competitive as trans-shipment centres.

Ports in Australia and New Zealand cater mostly for their own countries' imports and exports, and some trans-shipment services for the Pacific Island economies. In 2017 and 2019, the port of Tauranga, New Zealand accommodated mainline services with ships of capacities of over 9,000 TEUs. In Australia, Melbourne, Brisbane and Sydney have similar indices, as they are served largely by the same lines deploying the same ships along the country's east coast.

The Pacific Island economies are among those with the lowest container shipping connectivity (figure 3.3). Port Vila, Vanuatu receives about one container ship every three days, and there are only four companies that provide regular shipping services to the island. On Kiribati, only one operator offers regular liner shipping services, with one ship arriving about every 10 days, connecting Kiribati to only four other ports. Some of the Pacific Island economies also have among the fewest port calls (see next section about port calls and time in port). While most other regions have enjoyed improved connectivity, there has not been any systematic improvement in the Pacific small island developing States. They must deal with recurring low trade volumes that discourage shipping companies and ports from investing in better maritime transport connectivity, and they suffer from low shipping connectivity. As a result, trade in goods becomes costly and uncompetitive (UNCTAD, 2014, 2017a).

Governments and port authorities can foster port liner shipping connectivity through the following policy areas: digitalization; linkage of domestic, regional and global networks; ensuring competition; port modernization; trade and transport facilitation; sustainability; and monitoring performance (Benamara et al., 2019). The *Review of Maritime Transport* and complementary online statistical information and country profiles are aimed at supporting member States in this endeavour by providing regularly updated statistics and performance indicators.

Figure 3.3 Liner shipping connectivity index for top 10 ports in the Pacific Islands, 2006–2019

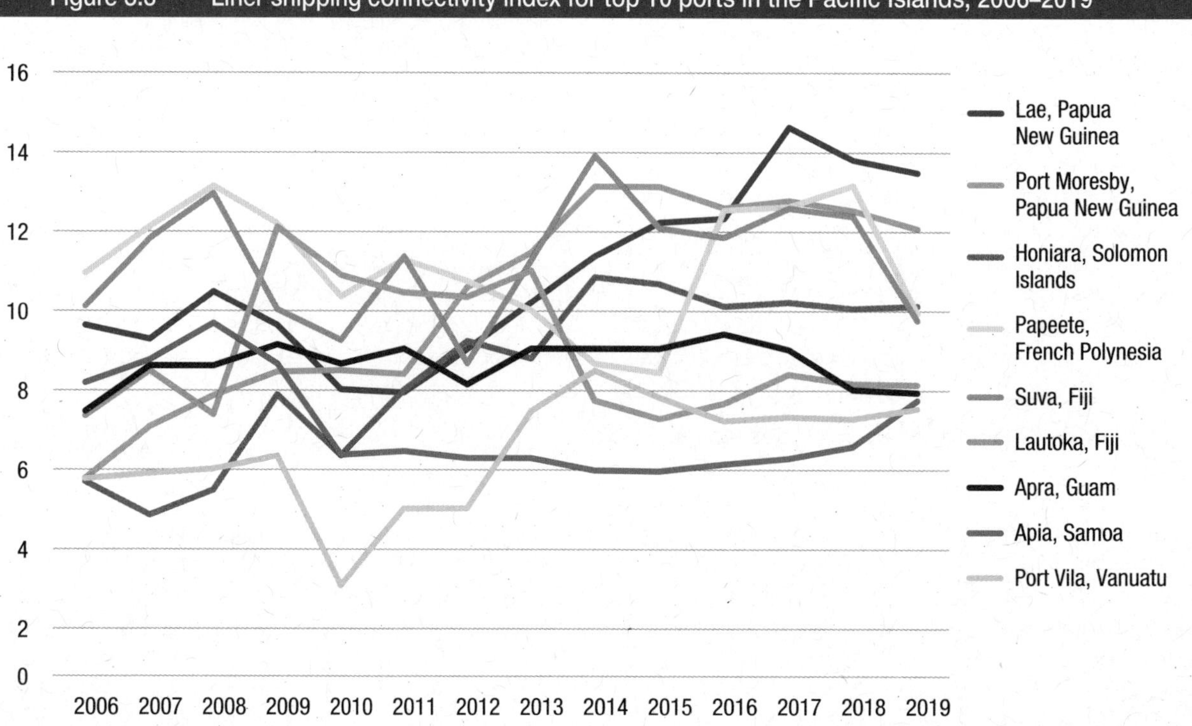

Source: UNCTAD secretariat calculations, based on data from MDS Transmodal. Underlying data for these and all other ports are available at http://stats.unctad.org/maritime.

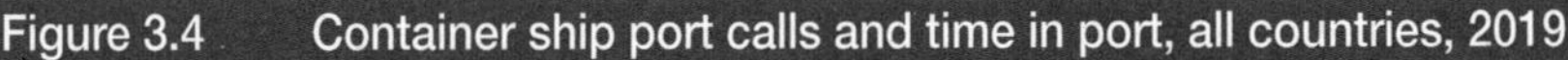

Figure 3.4 Container ship port calls and time in port, all countries, 2019

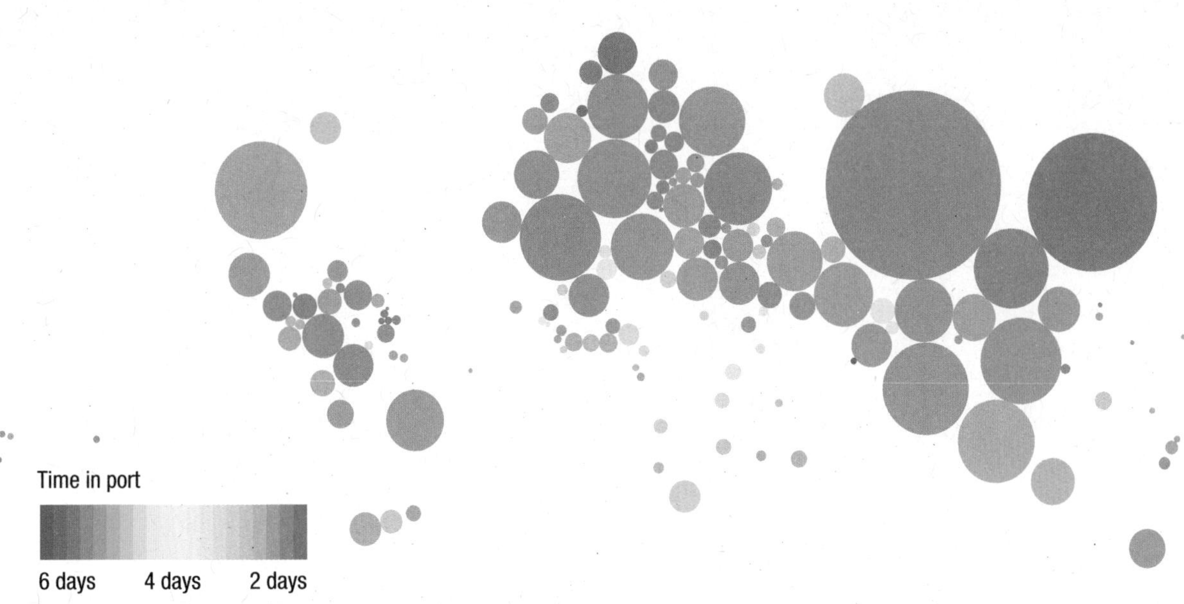

Source: UNCTAD secretariat calculations, based on data from Marine Traffic (www.marinetraffic.com).
Note: Ships of 1,000 gross tons and above.

C. PORT TURNAROUND TIMES

Port performance is a key indicator of trade efficiency that determines connectivity and trade costs (Micco et al., 2003; UNCTAD, 2017a). Every hour of ship time saved in a port helps ports, carriers and shippers save money on port infrastructure investments, capital expenditures on ships and inventory holding costs of merchandise goods.

Benefiting from a new data set provided by Marine Traffic, which draws on automatic identification system data produced by the world's commercial fleet, UNCTAD has undertaken a novel analysis on the time ships spend in port during port calls.[7] A number of significant variations can be observed between countries and vessel types.

1. Reducing the time in port to accommodate more ship calls

A shorter time in port is a positive indicator of a port's efficiency and trade competitiveness. In 2018, the median time of ship spent in port during one port call was 23.5 hours (0.97 days).[8] In general, dry bulk carriers spent 2.05 days during a port call, almost three times the median time of a container ship.

Table 3.1 lists the top 25 economies in terms of port calls and the median time of different ship types spent in their ports in 2018. Tables 3.2 to 3.5 present in more detail the data for different vessel types. Figure 3.4 illustrates the global distribution of port calls by container ships and the median time spent in ports. The predominance of Asia in port calls reflects the dominant role of Asian countries in containerized trade.

In 2018, tankers and other liquid bulk vessels spent a median of 0.94 days in port, ranging between 0.11 days (about 2.5 hours) in Peru and more than four days in Kenya (table 3.2). The best performing

[7] UNCTAD secretariat calculations are based on data provided by Marine Traffic (www.marinetraffic.com). Aggregated figures are derived from the fusion of automatic identification system data with port-mapping intelligence by Marine Traffic, covering ships of 1,000 gross tons and above. Passenger ships are not included in this analysis. Only arrivals have been taken into account to measure the number of port calls. Cases involving less than 10 arrivals or 5 vessels on a country level per commercial market as segmented are not included. The data will be updated every six months on the UNCTAD maritime statistics portal (http://stats.unctad.org/maritime).

[8] The present analysis reflects the median time. The average time vessels spend in port is longer for practically all countries and markets, due to statistical outliers – ships that spend weeks or months in a port, for example for repairs. The statistical distribution of time spent in ports has a "long tail". The global average time ships spent in port in 2018 was 42 hours, compared with a median time of 23.5 hours. To avoid any distortion by outliers of the results of the analysis, UNCTAD statistics report on the median time – not the average time – as the latter may be influenced by a few exceptional cases of ships being detained or staying longer than planned for other reasons. A longer time spent in port does not necessarily mean that the port is less efficient. Shipowners may choose to have their ships stay longer to purchase goods or bunkers or to undertake repairs. At the same time, a short stay may not only be due to fast and efficient operations, but simply result from being a small port with few port calls (i.e. no congestion). At such ports only a small number of containers are loaded or unloaded.

Table 3.1 Median time spent in port in top 25 economies by number of port calls and market segment, 2018

Economy	Number of port calls	Number of days					
		Liquid bulk carriers	Dry bulk carriers	Container ships	Break bulk carriers	Liquefied natural gas carriers	Liquefied petroleum gas carriers
China	205 448	1.10	2.00	0.62	1.17	1.21	1.00
Japan	180 400	0.31	0.90	0.35	1.12	0.99	0.32
Netherlands	100 343	0.49	0.84	0.78	0.40	1.30	0.94
United States	72 485	1.64	1.84	1.00	1.79	1.28	2.03
Russian Federation	68 211	1.04	2.50	1.40	1.56	1.10	1.34
Republic of Korea	65 762	0.79	2.34	0.60	1.29	1.03	0.72
Indonesia	62 059	1.28	3.55	1.09	1.26	1.38	1.13
Singapore	60 712	0.60	0.12	0.77	0.65	2.22	1.12
Spain	59 326	0.84	2.27	0.66	1.14	1.05	0.96
United Kingdom	58 203	1.06	2.73	0.73	1.46	1.43	1.08
Germany	50 264	0.36	2.48	0.79	0.50	..	0.75
Norway	49 339	0.61	0.87	0.33	0.34	0.32	0.75
Turkey	47 488	1.11	4.00	0.63	1.52	1.31	1.36
Italy	39 265	1.29	3.55	0.82	1.93	..	1.44
India	38 999	1.42	2.49	0.93	0.82	1.15	1.27
Malaysia	32 982	1.16	3.42	0.76	1.15	1.09	0.91
Belgium	31 811	1.30	3.88	1.02	1.43	1.18	1.40
Taiwan Province of China	30 729	1.05	2.14	0.46	1.26	0.99	0.98
Australia	29 783	1.34	1.65	1.20	1.79	1.22	0.90
Greece	28 535	0.54	0.35	0.95	1.07	0.99	0.88
Brazil	27 546	1.74	2.67	0.81	2.45	2.94	1.66
Canada	27 225	1.12	0.32	1.49	0.28	..	..
Thailand	26 206	0.68	3.07	0.79	1.59	1.23	0.57
Sweden	25 461	0.68	0.51	0.63	1.04	0.61	0.82
France	24 677	1.06	3.14	0.75	1.50	1.20	1.07
World total	**1 884 818**	**0.94**	**2.05**	**0.70**	**1.11**	**1.11**	**1.02**

Source: UNCTAD secretariat calculations, based on data from Marine Traffic (www.marinetraffic.com).

Notes: Ships of 1,000 gross tons and above, not including passenger ships. The total number of port calls is computed for roll-on roll-off vessels; the time spent in ports by such vessels is not. Ports with fewer than five port calls of this vessel type in 2018 are not included. For the complete table of all countries, see http://stats.unctad.org/maritime.

economies include two groups. One group represents countries with a high number of port calls. These include Japan, which, with 44,382 port calls, has the highest number of all countries in this segment, followed by the Netherlands (41,843 port calls) and Germany (14,394 port calls). The other group represents economies that have very few port calls, and small and relatively old ships, for example Switzerland. In both cases, highly efficient and mechanized liquid bulk operations in the ports ensure that tanker owners can expect their ships to spend less than half a day in port. Developing countries and the least developed countries, where a tanker is likely to spend two to four days loading or unloading its cargo, make up the lower half of the table. The possible reasons and potential policy solutions are discussed below, as they mostly apply to all vessel types equally.

Dry bulk carriers are the vessels with the highest median time (2.05 days) spent in port (table 3.3). While loading iron ore or coal can be done relatively quickly with conveyer-belt systems, unloading is usually a more time-consuming operation. Also, the value per ton of dry bulk cargo tends to be lower than for most other commodities, hence the inventory holding cost of staying longer in port is less for iron ore carriers than for container ships. The time spent in port ranges between 0.12 days per port call in Singapore and more than 11 days in the Sudan. In this market segment, too, the economies with the longest port turnaround times are developing countries or the least developed countries.

Table 3.2 Ten highest- and lowest-ranking economies: Median time spent in port by liquid bulk carriers, 2018

Economy	Ranking, from fastest to slowest	Median time in port (days)	Average size of vessels (gross tons)	Size of largest vessel (gross tons)	Average age of vessels (years)	Total number of port calls in 2018
Peru	1	0.11	24 356	83 850	14	2 521
Switzerland	2	0.23	1 869	5 000	25	394
Japan	3	0.31	7 913	166 093	12	44 382
Gibraltar	4	0.35	5 060	59 315	14	1 252
Germany	5	0.36	4 428	160 278	18	14 394
Cyprus	6	0.39	9 010	62 385	18	909
Faroe Islands	7	0.45	4 587	13 239	12	125
Iceland	8	0.48	8 896	30 641	14	242
Netherlands	9	0.49	9 440	170 004	15	41 843
Panama	10	0.49	13 730	165 125	21	2 713
Madagascar	142	2.49	13 467	42 826	6	131
Reunion	143	2.54	26 535	30 965	8	33
Senegal	144	2.79	25 289	85 362	11	265
Yemen	145	2.87	12 437	63 076	19	284
Congo	146	2.93	20 770	29 658	11	36
Somali	147	2.94	5 259	26 218	23	56
Iraq	148	3.13	71 414	172 146	13	1 380
Nigeria	149	3.15	20 250	157 831	16	1 507
United Republic of Tanzania	150	3.84	20 385	64 705	18	236
Kenya	151	4.03	36 933	64 705	11	198
World		**0.94**	**15 543**	**234 006**	**13**	**494 120**

Source: UNCTAD secretariat calculations, based on data from Marine Traffic (www.marinetraffic.com).

Note: Ships of 1,000 gross tons and above. Ports with fewer than five port calls of this vessel type in 2018 are not included. For the complete table of all countries, see http://stats.unctad.org/maritime.

Table 3.3 Ten highest- and lowest-ranking economies: Median time spent in port by dry bulk carriers, 2018

Economy	Ranking, from fastest to slowest	Median time in port (days)	Average size of vessels (gross tons)	Size of largest vessel (gross tons)	Average age of vessels (years)	Total number of port calls in 2018
Singapore	1	0.12	24 275	155 051	8	2 731
Canada	2	0.32	27 302	108 237	23	13 562
Greece	3	0.35	5 792	63 864	25	2 928
Sweden	4	0.51	6 838	51 147	28	1 443
Cabo Verde	5	0.53	27 721	107 666	12	158
Netherlands	6	0.84	36 464	134 692	10	4 355
Denmark	7	0.87	9 528	65 950	29	783
Norway	8	0.87	16 467	108 237	18	2 282
Japan	9	0.90	17 830	203 403	14	28 835
Barbados	10	0.94	9 790	25 769	18	17
Tunisia	123	6.45	19 814	36 426	12	303
Cameroon	124	6.74	25 953	36 467	11	250
Algeria	125	6.85	24 224	70 933	10	645
Iraq	126	8.22	29 970	44 625	9	132
Angola	127	8.56	24 753	41 091	10	53
Benin	128	9.02	27 263	36 353	11	110
Myanmar	129	9.07	25 037	36 339	11	65
Cuba	130	9.68	18 004	31 617	15	272
Libya	131	9.90	19 634	94 542	21	165
Sudan	132	11.25	27 085	45 026	12	112
World		**2.05**	**31 940**	**203 483**	**13**	**259 551**

Source: UNCTAD secretariat calculations, based on data from Marine Traffic (www.marinetraffic.com).

Note: Ships of 1,000 gross tons and above. Ports with fewer than five port calls in 2018 of this vessel type are not included. For the complete table of all countries, see http://stats.unctad.org/maritime.

Table 3.4 Ten highest- and lowest-ranking economies: Median time spent in port by container ships, 2018

Economy	Ranking, from fastest to slowest	Median time in port (days)	Average size of vessels (gross tons)	Size of largest vessel (gross tons)	Average age of vessels (years)	Total number of port calls in 2018
Faroe Islands	1	0.23	11 635	17 368	14	276
Saint Vincent and the Grenadines	2	0.28	13 325	18 358	11	114
Grenada	3	0.30	13 899	16 162	10	86
Gibraltar	4	0.31	11 187	35 878	14	40
Norway	5	0.33	8 377	21 586	15	3 536
Japan	6	0.35	17 334	217 617	12	38 238
Saint Lucia	7	0.40	12 620	16 162	11	137
Taiwan Province of China	8	0.46	29 444	217 617	14	15 616
Honduras	9	0.46	17 887	32 901	14	1 297
Denmark	10	0.49	21 242	214 286	13	1 171
Myanmar	147	2.77	14 676	25 165	19	355
Guinea-Bissau	148	2.86	13 278	25 294	17	59
Algeria	149	2.96	12 145	28 397	16	926
Bangladesh	150	2.97	18 306	94 511	12	1 338
Gambia	151	3.39	18 174	32 903	17	144
Guyana	152	3.53	22 575	27 279	8	65
Yemen	153	3.62	20 603	34 610	16	187
Tunisia	154	3.80	9 356	18 327	18	344
Sudan	155	4.31	26 581	73 899	16	182
Maldives	156	6.48	17 075	39 753	15	87
World		**0.70**	**38 520**	**217 673**	**13**	**454 016**

Source: UNCTAD secretariat calculations, based on data from Marine Traffic (www.marinetraffic.com).

Note: Ships of 1,000 gross tons and above. Ports with fewer than five port calls in 2018 of this vessel type are not included. For the complete table of all countries, see http://stats.unctad.org/maritime.

Table 3.5 Ten highest- and lowest-ranking economies: Median time spent in port by break bulk vessels, 2018

Economy	Ranking, from fastest to slowest	Median time in port (days)	Average size of vessels (gross tons)	Size of largest vessel (gross tons)	Average age of vessels (years)	Total number of port calls in 2018
Guernsey	1	0.12	1 800	2 597	21	208
French Polynesia	2	0.16	3 066	18 100	38	637
Gibraltar	3	0.20	3 828	21 483	13	498
Saint Kitts and Nevis	4	0.24	3 717	14 413	30	195
Canada	5	0.28	10 014	37 499	9	3 281
Saint Vincent and the Grenadines	6	0.31	8 742	16 137	21	189
Bahamas	7	0.32	4 070	39 771	24	548
Norway	8	0.34	2 802	51 065	22	32 692
Antigua and Barbuda	9	0.38	6 164	20 973	18	171
Paraguay	10	0.38	2 877	5 162	32	619
Gambia	165	3.43	7 211	19 883	20	46
Moldova	166	3.44	3 424	5 985	31	95
Maldives	167	4.51	6 065	22 998	25	70
Myanmar	168	4.63	10 107	23 132	16	72
Somalia	169	4.88	7 085	21 992	25	179
Syrian Arab Republic	170	4.98	5 797	32 333	31	135
Korea, Democratic People's Republic of	171	5.44	3 380	6 558	25	18
Yemen	172	5.62	5 966	23 856	26	186
Seychelles	173	5.72	5 242	20 886	26	168
Tuvalu	174	13.99	4 067	6 082	29	72
World		**1.11**	**5 438**	**91 784**	**19**	**430 344**

Source: UNCTAD secretariat calculations, based on data from Marine Traffic (www.marinetraffic.com).

Note: Ships of 1,000 gross tons and above. Ports with fewer than five port calls in 2018 of this vessel type are not included. For the complete table of all countries, see http://stats.unctad.org/maritime.

Of all vessel types, container ships spend the least median time in port (0.7 days). The data range between less 0.23 days on the Faroe Islands to 6.5 days on Maldives (table 3.4). Among the reasons for such results on Maldives is that container ships usually have to anchor in the port area and unload the container using their own gear onto barges, which then take the containers to the pier. With 87 container ship port calls in 2018, this means that in practice one or two ships are being serviced at a time. The 10 lowest-ranking economies in this segment, too, are developing countries or least developed countries, while the countries with the fastest turnaround times are mostly advanced economies with large volumes (Japan and Norway, for example) or small economies, where the short time spent by ships in port is the result of low frequencies – no waiting times or congestion – and low volumes loaded or unloaded at each port call.

Although break bulk general cargo ships do not account for a large share of seaborne trade (chapter 2, table 2.1), they represent a large share of the world fleet in terms of number of vessels and port calls. They carry all types of combined and general cargo and are important for smaller ports that lack sufficient volumes to attract more specialized vessels. The widest range of times spent in port has been observed for break bulk general cargo ships, between 0.12 days on Guernsey and two weeks on Tuvalu (table 3.5). The traffic in Guernsey includes frequent regular traffic with France and the United Kingdom, which does not require any customs or immigration formalities and thus allows the ships to start operations immediately after arriving in their dedicated terminals. Similarly, in Norway, with 32,692 port calls for this vessel type, ships provide frequent domestic services, with fast and efficient operations and no customs or immigration formalities. On Tuvalu, the median time a general cargo ship spent in port in 2018 was two weeks. Just 72 port calls were recorded during the year. Again, all economies in the lower half of the table are developing countries and least developed countries, including several small island developing States.

Carriers of liquefied natural gas and liquefied petroleum gas call in a few countries only, as this type of cargo requires highly specialized port facilities. In 2018, only 43 countries received liquefied natural gas carriers, and only 84 countries received liquefied petroleum gas carriers. For both vessel types, the median time spent in port is slightly more than one day, ranging from less than five hours in Peru to more than three days in Côte d'Ivoire, Ghana and Jordan. Countries with short turnaround port times include some with high numbers of port calls (Japan, the Republic of Korea, Norway and Thailand). Those economies in the lower half of table 3.4 concerning carriers of liquefied natural gas and liquefied petroleum gas are mostly developing countries and least developed countries with a low number of port calls for these vessel types (data on additional vessel types and countries are available at http://stats.unctad.org/maritime.

2. Ships spend less time in more efficient ports

Countries with more port calls usually have shorter turnaround times as well. Ports with shorter turnaround times are more attractive to shippers and the carriers; therefore, the number of port calls will tend to be higher compared with competing ports that have longer turnaround times. The causality goes both ways: If the turnaround time is shorter, a port with the same number of berths can accommodate more port calls. At the same time, countries that trade more and have more port calls will also generate more income to invest in efficient port operations. For container ships, for example, figure 3.5 depicts the correlation between the number of port calls, the size of the largest container ships that call in a country's ports and the median time container ships spend in the port.

If ships are larger, other things being equal, turnaround time should be longer, as there will be more cargo to be loaded and unloaded. At the same time, ports that can accommodate larger ships will usually also be more modern and efficient. UNCTAD analysis shows that there is a negative correlation between the size of the largest ship that calls at a country's port and the median time ships spend in port, while there is a slight positive correlation for most market segments between the average size of vessels and the time spent in port. In other words, being able to accommodate very large container ships is an indicator that a port is fast and efficient, while ports that receive large ships will on

Figure 3.5 Time in port and number of port calls by container ships, 2018

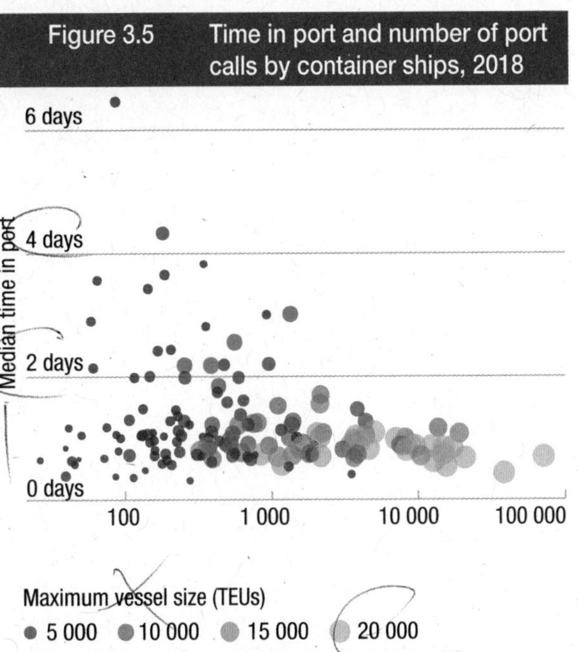

Source: UNCTAD secretariat calculations, based on dat Marine Traffic (www.marinetraffic.com).

Note: Ships of 1,000 gross tons and above.

Figure 3.6 Africa: Container ship port calls and time in port, 2018

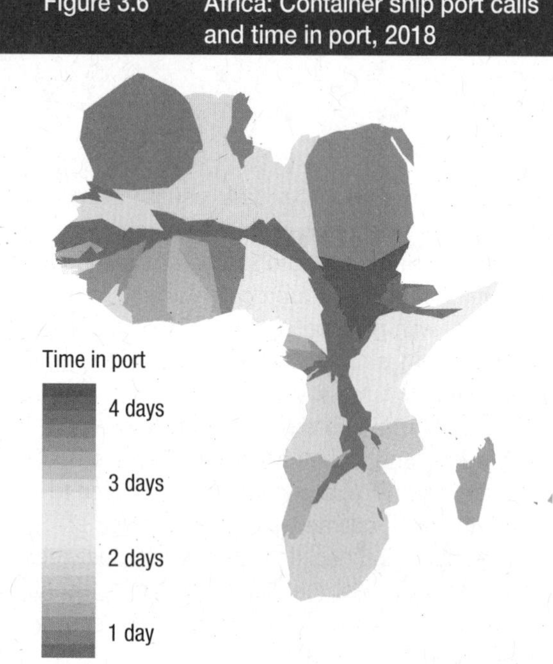

Source: UNCTAD secretariat calculations, based on data from Marine Traffic (www.marinetraffic.com).

Note: Ships of 1,000 gross tons and above.

average also take slightly longer to load and unload the higher cargo volumes.

In Africa, the countries with the most port calls are located at the geographical corners of the continent (figure 3.6). Egypt, Djibouti and Morocco benefit from their geographical position and attract container ships for trans-shipment services (see also previous section on liner shipping connectivity). South Africa provides hub port services, and its ports serve as gateways to containerized trade in South Africa and its neighbours. All four countries are also among those receiving the largest container ships in Africa.

In order to minimize the time a ship spends in port – for a given volume of cargo to be loaded or unloaded – port and maritime authorities and policymakers may consider the following three recommendations (Benamara et al., 2019). First, ships should only arrive when they need to arrive, as arriving too early implies additional costs in port as well as additional expenditures and more pollution, including air emissions. To arrive on time rather than in time is the aim of port-call-optimization initiatives (Lind et al., 2018, 2019; UNCTAD, 2019c). Second, once a ship arrives at the pier, operations should start immediately, without having to wait for authorities to clear paperwork or carry out other procedures. Implementing the IMO Convention on Facilitation of International Maritime Traffic and the Agreement on Trade Facilitation of the World Trade Organization can help in this regard (UNCTAD, 2016). Finally, port operations should be borne into account. Fast and reliable loading and unloading operations require investment in infrastructure and superstructures, as well as technological and human capacities. It is important to consider the total logistics costs when pondering such investments, including the daily costs of waiting times of ships and trucks, and the potential loss of trade competitiveness resulting from long port turnaround times (UNCTAD, 1998; World Bank, 2007).

D. SHIPPING FLEET: ENVIRONMENTAL INDICATORS

The environmental impact of shipping includes pollution caused by the invasion of non-native species following the discharge of untreated ballast water from ships. This is considered one of the greatest threats to the world's oceans and one of the major threats to biodiversity (see chapter 4). The International Convention for the Control and Management of Ships' Ballast Water and Sediments (2004) entered into force in September 2017. The Convention aims to prevent the risk of the introduction and proliferation of non-native species following the discharge of untreated ballast water from ships. One way to reduce this risk is to install ballast water treatment systems.

Air pollution from ships is another concern that has a major impact on health and the environment. Vessels emit large quantities of pollutants into the air, principally in the form of sulphur oxide, nitrogen oxide and particulate matter, which have been steadily growing and affect human health. Ships also generate 3 per cent of the world's total greenhouse gas emissions such as carbon dioxide, contributing to global warming and extreme weather effects. As noted in chapter 2, from 1 January 2020, IMO will enforce a new 0.5 per cent global sulphur cap on fuel content, a reduction in the present 3.5 per cent limit. The global fuel sulphur cap is part of IMO's response to heightening environmental concerns, contributed in part by harmful emissions from ships.

This section will look at three indicators applicable to vessels and which are of relevance in assessing the environmental impact of some of the world's shipping fleet:

- The vessel is fitted or is due to be fitted with a ballast water treatment system.
- The vessel is fitted or is due to be fitted with a scrubber to reduce sulphur emissions.
- The vessel is compliant with tier III regulations to reduce emissions of nitrogen oxide. (See table 3.6 and chapter 4 for further information).

In total, of the 95,402 ships in the UNCTAD maritime database, 7.66 per cent have installed or ordered a ballast water treatment system, 1.58 per cent have installed or ordered a system to reduce sulphur-oxide emissions, and 0.53 per cent have installed or ordered a system to reduce nitrogen-oxide emissions as of 1 January 2019.

There are significant differences between the fleets by flag of registration and country of ownership. The underlying causes of these differences are mainly the different vessel types and the trading routes. Tables 3.6, 3.7 and 3.8 are designed to encourage discussion rather than to draw conclusions. Some vessel types have less need for having certain systems installed than others, and some trading routes and ports do not require ballast water treatment.

The shipping industry is in a transformational phase, including in terms of environmental development. Providing some indicative data for policymakers, including flag States and ownership origin, to see where their countries' fleets stand, can be a useful initial indicator that could help stakeholders address some of the issues and apply purposeful transport policy or incentive schemes. Whether or not ships trade internationally and are bound by international conventions, policymakers in maritime authorities and port States have a role to play: setting strategies and encouraging, for example, the installation of modern systems to reduce the environmental impact of shipping or introducing regulations or tax or incentive schemes. Knowing how a country's national fleet compares with others as regards the installation of such systems is a first objective performance indicator.

1. Larger and newer ships tend to be equipped with more modern installations

Larger and newer ships that trade internationally are more likely to have ballast water treatment systems installed than smaller and older ships that may be deployed mostly in national waters. Accordingly, the ship types that have the largest share of ballast water treatment systems installed are liquefied gas carries (28.76 per cent), dry bulk carriers (23.32 per cent) and container ships (18.88 per cent) (table 3.6). Oil and chemical tankers have a higher average age (see also chapter 2, table 2.2.), which may partly explain why this vessel type has a smaller share of installed ballast water treatment systems. Ferries, general cargo ships and offshore supply vessels are more likely to be deployed in coastal or inter-island transport and may not need to treat their ballast water.

2. Differences by flag and country of ownership

Among the top 50 flag States by number of ships, the registries with the best performance for ballast water treatment systems are the Isle of Man (33.33 per cent), Hong Kong, China (30.47 per cent) and the Marshall Islands (28.66 per cent) (table 3.7). For ships that do not trade internationally, there tends to be less need for investing in such systems, as water ballast is not an issue. It is therefore not surprising that the national fleets of China, Indonesia, Japan and the United States have far lower environmental indices, as many of these ships are deployed in domestic shipping services. As regards scrubbers, the largest shares are those of Greece (9.25 per cent of its registered ships), followed by the Marshall Islands (8.64 per cent) and Malta (7.64 per cent). The fact that a vessel does not have a scrubber installed does not necessarily imply that the vessel does not comply with the sulphur cup, as it may also switch to alternative fuels. For systems to reduce nitrogen-oxide emissions, the two Norwegian international ship registers, the Danish International Ship Register and the Isle of Man have the most ships equipped with such systems. These leading flags of registration cater largely for ships that trade internationally.

Table 3.6 Selected environmental indicators by vessel type, 2019

Vessel type	Percentage of vessels fitted with ballast water treatment systems	Percentage of vessels fitted with scrubbers	Percentage of vessels compliant with tier III regulations to reduce nitrogen-oxide emissions
Bulk carriers	23.32	4.03	0.05
Chemical tankers	10.72	1.15	0.86
Container ships	18.88	5.05	0.19
Ferries and passenger ships	1.36	2.13	0.57
General cargo ships	2.16	0.65	0.21
Liquefied natural gas carriers	28.76	1.45	1.45
Offshore supply vessels	2.37	0.03	0.96
Oil tankers	11.99	3.71	0.46
Other/not available	2.82	0.30	0.19
Total	**7.66**	**1.58**	**0.53**

Source: UNCTAD secretariat calculations, based on data from Clarksons Research.

Notes: Propelled seagoing merchant vessels of 100 gross tons and above, beginning-of-year figures. Estimates include ships fitted with scrubbers, those pending scrubber installation and ships on order.

Table 3.7 Environmental indicators by flag State and top 50 economies by number of ships, 2019

Ranking by number of ships	Flag State	Percentage of vessels fitted with ballast water treatment systems	Percentage of vessels fitted with scrubbers	Percentage of vessels compliant with tier III regulations to reduce nitrogen-oxide emissions
1	Indonesia	0.23	0.01	0.00
2	Panama	13.96	1.83	0.37
3	Japan	2.30	0.04	0.02
4	China	2.79	0.27	0.17
5	United States	2.60	0.30	0.65
6	Marshall Islands	28.66	8.64	0.56
7	Liberia	19.51	4.44	0.34
8	Singapore	21.11	1.28	0.17
9	Russian Federation	2.20	0.00	0.15
10	Hong Kong, China	30.47	2.30	0.26
11	Malta	21.55	7.64	1.01
12	Korea, Republic of	5.48	0.16	0.05
13	Viet Nam	0.16	0.00	0.00
14	Malaysia	1.43	0.00	0.29
15	India	0.81	0.69	0.06
16	Philippines	2.53	0.00	0.00
17	Bahamas	22.07	4.26	2.34
18	Italy	2.95	2.28	0.07
19	Greece	12.23	9.25	0.46
20	Turkey	1.13	0.97	0.24
21	Netherlands	11.48	4.26	1.23
22	Cyprus	15.98	2.79	0.87
23	United Kingdom	11.05	3.78	0.87
24	Norway	6.35	0.52	8.95
25	Brazil	2.10	0.00	0.35
26	Thailand	2.05	0.24	0.00
27	Saint Vincent and the Grenadines	0.74	0.00	0.25
28	Antigua and Barbuda	1.91	0.76	0.13
29	Belize	0.38	0.00	0.00
30	Islamic Republic of Iran	0.13	0.00	0.00
31	Canada	2.84	2.09	0.60
32	Nigeria	0.30	0.00	0.00
33	Mexico	1.57	0.00	0.00
34	United Arab Emirates	0.00	0.00	0.00
35	Germany	3.44	3.28	1.64
36	Norwegian International Ship Register	25.62	4.11	11.66
37	Australia	0.52	0.17	0.86
38	Danish International Ship Register	12.77	5.14	3.90
39	Honduras	0.00	0.00	0.00
40	Sierra Leone	0.00	0.00	0.00
41	Spain	0.62	0.00	0.21
42	Madeira	15.09	2.59	0.65
43	France	2.50	2.05	0.00
44	Ukraine	0.00	0.00	0.00
45	Togo	0.00	0.00	0.00
46	Egypt	0.26	0.00	0.00
47	Isle of Man	33.33	2.82	3.85
48	Taiwan Province of China	7.14	3.70	0.00
49	Saudi Arabia	2.95	1.07	0.00
50	Bangladesh	0.54	0.00	0.00
	Subtotal top 50 registries	**8.50**	**1.71**	**0.53**
	Rest of world and unknown flag	*2.17*	*0.76*	*0.49*
	World total	**7.66**	**1.58**	**0.53**

Source: UNCTAD secretariat calculations, based on data from Clarksons Research.

Notes: Propelled seagoing merchant vessels of 100 gross tons and above, beginning-of-year figures.

Table 3.8 Environmental indicators by ownership origin and top 50 economies by number of ships, 2019

Ranking by number of ships	Ownership origin	Percentage of vessels fitted with ballast water treatment systems	Percentage of vessels fitted with scrubbers	Percentage of vessels compliant with tier III regulations to reduce nitrogen-oxide emissions
1	Indonesia	0.25	0.02	0.00
2	Japan	13.13	0.14	0.16
3	China	8.05	0.43	0.13
4	Greece	17.07	7.94	0.29
5	United States	6.98	3.64	0.76
6	Singapore	12.00	1.53	0.09
7	Germany	9.91	1.97	0.68
8	Russian Federation	2.78	0.00	0.22
9	Republic of Korea	12.46	1.13	0.04
10	Norway	16.53	2.36	7.79
11	Turkey	3.95	1.35	0.35
12	Hong Kong, China	18.47	0.76	0.14
13	United Arab Emirates	3.52	0.20	0.30
14	Viet Nam	0.21	0.00	0.00
15	United Kingdom	15.40	2.01	0.85
16	Netherlands	8.25	2.04	0.55
17	India	2.17	0.67	0.44
18	Malaysia	1.43	0.00	0.34
19	Philippines	0.36	0.00	0.00
20	Italy	4.63	1.48	0.07
21	Taiwan Province of China	21.41	6.01	0.00
22	Denmark	17.20	4.50	1.85
23	Brazil	2.05	0.11	0.11
24	Thailand	2.73	0.23	0.11
25	Canada	5.76	1.28	0.26
26	France	8.39	1.31	0.00
27	Islamic Republic of Iran	1.72	0.00	0.00
28	Nigeria	1.29	0.00	0.29
29	Ukraine	1.05	0.00	0.15
30	Australia	3.33	0.48	0.79
31	Saudi Arabia	3.54	0.00	0.00
32	Spain	1.71	1.02	0.17
33	Mexico	0.69	0.00	0.00
34	Sweden	8.80	4.58	5.99
35	Egypt	1.45	0.00	1.08
36	Bermuda	40.99	5.88	0.92
37	Switzerland	17.76	18.20	1.54
38	Monaco	30.77	30.09	0.45
39	Belgium	19.31	1.24	1.73
40	Panama	0.53	0.00	0.00
41	Bangladesh	0.57	0.00	0.00
42	Cyprus	8.12	0.00	0.58
43	Croatia	2.41	0.00	0.30
44	Azerbaijan	1.01	0.00	0.00
45	Finland	4.75	10.51	5.42
46	Chile	1.10	0.00	0.00
47	Poland	20.46	0.00	0.00
48	Bolivarian Republic of Venezuela	0.00	0.00	0.00
49	Lebanon	0.00	0.00	0.00
50	Democratic People's Republic of Korea	0.00	0.00	0.00
	Subtotal top 50 shipowning economies	**8.30**	**1.74**	**0.57**
	Rest of world and unknown ownership origin	*1.95*	*0.21*	*0.15*
	World total	**7.66**	**1.58**	**0.53**

Source: UNCTAD secretariat calculations, based on data provided by Clarksons Research.

Notes: Propelled seagoing merchant vessels of 100 gross tons and above, beginning-of-year figures.

Figure 3.7 Port Management Programme coverage

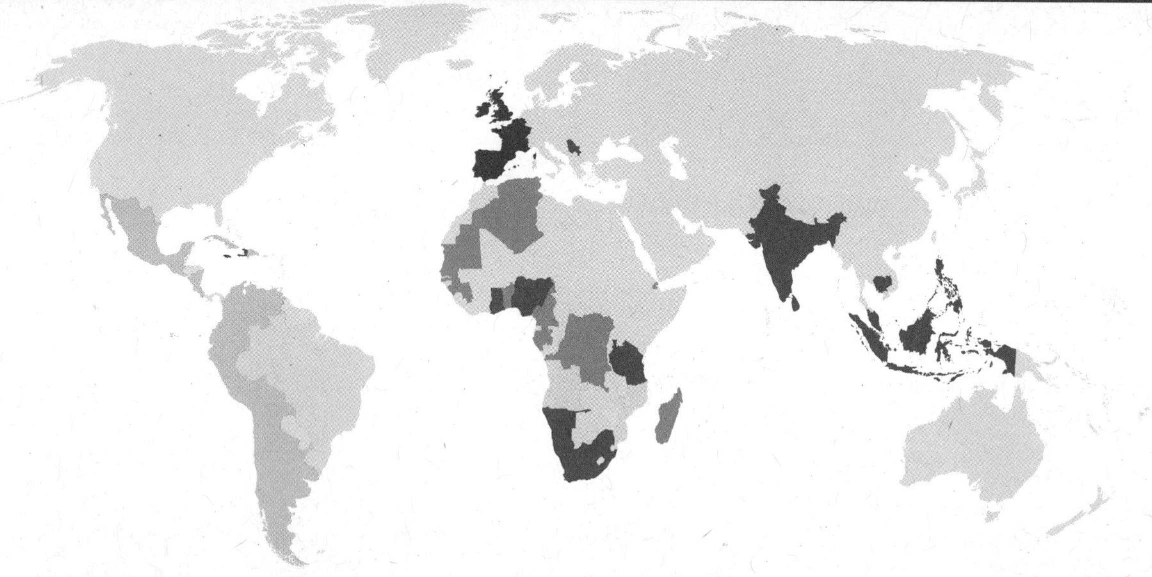

SPANISH(15)	ENGLISH (16)	FRENCH (16)	PORTUGUESE (7)	PARTNERS (6)
Argentina	Bangladesh	Algeria	Angola	Belgium
Plurinational State of Bolivia	Cambodia	Benin	Brazil	France
Chile	Ghana	Cameroon	Cabo Verde	Ireland
Colombia	India	Comoros	Timor-Leste	Portugal
Costa Rica	Indonesia	Congo	Guinea-Bissau	Spain
Cuba	Jamaica	Côte d'Ivoire	Mozambique	United Kingdom
Dominican Republic	Kenya	Djibouti	Sao Tome and Principe	
Ecuador	Malaysia	Gabon		
El Salvador	Maldives	Guinea		
Guatemala	Namibia	Haiti		
Mexico	Nigeria	Madagascar		
Nicaragua	Philippines	Mauritania		
Peru	Serbia	Senegal		
Uruguay	South Africa	Seychelles		
Bolivarian Republic of Venezuela	Sri Lanka	Togo		
	United Republic of Tanzania	Tunisia		

Source: UNCTAD secretariat calculations, based on data from port entities members of the Port Management Programme network.

Among the top 50 economies of ownership, the fleets with the largest share of ballast water treatment systems are those owned by companies in Bermuda (40.99 per cent), Monaco (30.77 per cent) and Taiwan Province of China (21.41 per cent) (table 3.8). With regard to scrubbers, the fleets owned in Monaco (30.09 per cent), Switzerland (18.20 per cent) and Finland (10.51 per cent) have the largest share of ships equipped with such systems. As regards systems to reduce nitrogen-oxide emissions, Norway (7.79 per cent), Sweden (5.99 per cent) and Finland (5.42 per cent) record the best indicators. None of the ships controlled by owners from the Democratic People's Republic of Korea, Lebanon and the Bolivarian Republic of Venezuela are reported to have installed any ballast water treatment systems or systems to reduce emissions of sulphur oxide or nitrogen oxide.

E. TRAIN FOR TRADE PORT MANAGEMENT PROGRAMME: LESSONS LEARNED

Since 2013, the Train for Trade Port Management Programme has been implementing knowledge networks covering Africa, Asia, Europe, Latin America and the Caribbean, and capacity-building activities covering 60 countries since 1996 (figure 3.7).[9] As a way to monitor and measure the performance of its member ports over time, the Programme has developed a port performance scorecard. The main objective is to provide members of the Programme with a useful tool that would benchmark performance and carry out port and regional comparisons.

9 A pool of over 3,635 port managers has been certified under the Modern Port Management lead course of UNCTAD in four language networks: English, French, Portuguese and Spanish.

Table 3.9 Port performance scorecard indicators, 2014–2018

Section		Indicator	Mean (2014–2018)	Number of values (2014–2018)
Finance	1	EBITDA/revenue (operating margin)	35.80%	90
	2	Vessel dues/revenue	16.40%	91
	3	Cargo dues/revenue	37.00%	86
	4	Rents/revenue	9.40%	83
	5	Labour/revenue	22.20%	80
	6	Fees and the like/revenue	12.40%	83
Human resources	7	Tons per employee	52 034	92
	8	Revenue per employee	$233 564	90
	9	EBITDA per employee	$117 776	79
	10	Labour cost per employee	$36 633	73
	11	Training cost/wages	1.40%	75
Gender	12	Female participation rate (global)	16.80%	76
	12.1	Female participation rate (management)	34.30%	75
	12.2	Female participation rate (operations)	12.10%	60
	12.3	Female participation rate (cargo handling)	5.10%	44
	12.4	Female participation rate (other employees)	30.60%	18
	12.5	Female participation rate (management + operations)	21.90%	96
Vessel operations	13	Average waiting time (hours)	15	83
	14	Average gross tonnage per vessel	17 315	98
	15.1	Oil tanker arrival average	10.90%	51
	15.2	Bulk carrier arrival average	10.70%	51
	15.3	Container ship arrival average	32.70%	53
	15.4	Cruise ship arrival average	1.60%	54
	15.5	General cargo ship arrival average	22.40%	52
	15.6	Other ships arrival average	20.20%	51
Cargo operations	16	Average tonnage per arrival (all)	6 918	105
	17	Tons per working hour, dry or solid bulk	416	61
	18	Boxes per ship hour at berth	24	23
	19	TEU dwell time (days)	6	54
	20	Tons per hour, liquid bulk	436	28
	21	Tons per hectare (all)	140 220	84
	22	Tons per berth metre (all)	4 077	93
	23	Total passengers on ferries	1 058 762	36
	24	Total passengers on cruise ships	78 914	37
Environment	25	Investment in environmental projects/total CAPEX	1.30%	20
	26	Environmental expenditures/revenue	0.40%	31

Source: UNCTAD secretariat calculations, based on data from port entities members of the Port Management Programme network.
Abbreviations: CAPEX, capital expenditure; EBITDA, earnings before interest, taxes, depreciation and amortization.

Based on the balanced scorecard concept, 26 indicators were identified, collected and classified into six main categories since 2010: finance, human resources, gender, vessel operations, cargo operations and environment. The global average is calculated based on a five-year rolling back average.[10] Results covering the period 2014–2018 are summarized in table 3.9, with reported values ranging from 20 to 183.[11] This section will highlight some of the key outcomes.

Some of the port entities in the network are directly engaged in activities that are not covered by management, operations and cargo-handling groups. For example, some ports own and run hospitals and education facilities and manage estates where substantial non-port property, such as hotels, is a substantial and separate business operation.

[10] In 2018, the port performance scorecard introduced new features based on recommendations adopted by the representatives of the four port networks in Geneva, Switzerland, during Port Management Week in April 2018. A regional benchmark was created and is accessible on the pps.unctad.org platform to allow direct comparisons between ports in the same geographical range and similar environment and constraints. The regions are simplified for this purpose under the following categories: Africa, Asia, Europe and Latin America.

[11] The lowest number of values (datapoints) reported from 2014 to 2018 is 20 for the indicator "investment in environmental projects/total CAPEX [capital expenditure]", followed by the indicator "boxes per ship hour at berth" (23 datapoints). The maximum datapoint is 105 for the indicator "average tonnage per arrival (all)", closely followed by the indicator "average gross tonnage per vessel", with 98 datapoints.

1. Gender participation

One of the six categories of indicators from the port performance scorecard covers gender in relation to Sustainable Development Goal 5. It measures the level of women's participation in the port workforce. Port workers are traditionally regarded as a male-dominated group in most societies. In general, changes in working practices, technology and society have opened up the possibility for higher levels of women's participation in the port workforce.

Figure 3.8 Women's participation in the port workforce, 2014–2018

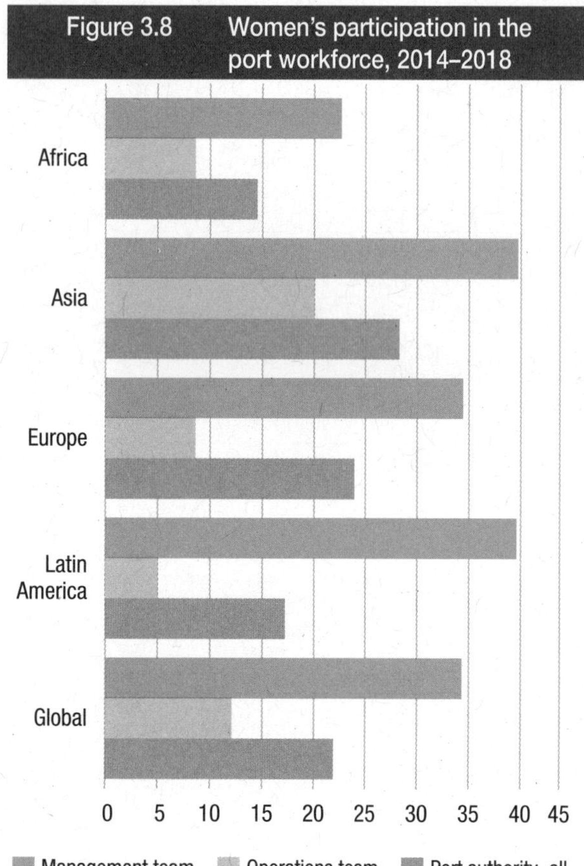

Source: UNCTAD secretariat calculations, based on data from port entities members of the Port Management Programme network.

Figure 3.9 Women's participation in cargo handling, 2014–2018

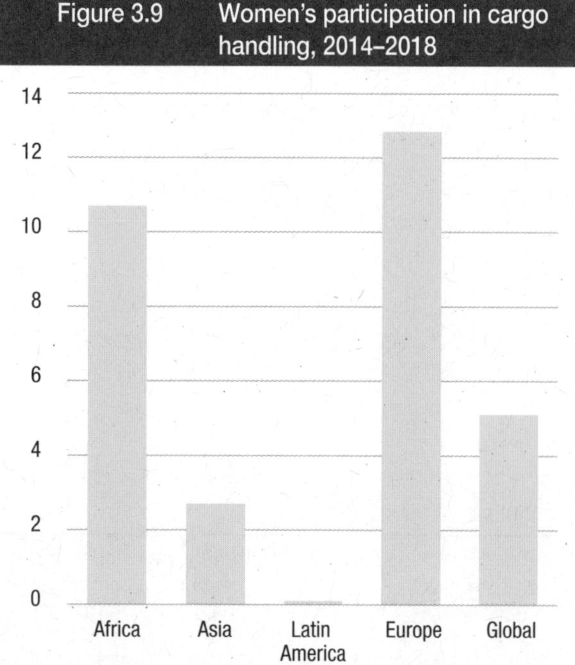

Source: UNCTAD secretariat calculations, based on data from port entities members of the Port Management Programme network.

Figure 3.8 examines the average rates of women's participation in the port workforce by region. General results show that overall participation is low, although participation at the management level is encouraging. The low level of women's participation in port operations suggests that their participation in activities such as engineering and service provision on the quays is also low.

Data on cargo-handling operations show a recurrent low level of women's participation in that area (figure 3.9). However, digitalization and the automation of activities in the shipping industry could lead to higher participation of women in this segment. It can also be argued that an increase in participation levels requires direct action by employers and society at large.

2. Finance, cost and revenues

Traditional revenue profiles in ports relied heavily on the dues charged to ship and cargo owners, usually through agents. This revenue stream is required to build and maintain port infrastructure for vessels and cargo-handling operations. Other revenue streams would consist of rent on storage sites and the provision of services such as tugs and pilots. Figure 3.10 shows that the port dues category is still the largest block of revenue. However, with privatization, a trend which began in the 1980s, has come a new and major source and category of revenue – concession fees.[12] The level of concessions is higher in the larger ports with significant container operations.

Another important indicator is earnings before interest, taxes, depreciation and amortization, which is the conventional accounting measure of annual financial performance (figure 3.11). It excludes items that vary across the regions and time such as depreciation, interest on debt and tax and allows for comparison. The value for Asia is an outlier, which may in part be explained by the State-supported capital funding structures for a number of ports in the sample.

A valuable port indicator is the cost of labour as a proportion of total revenue (figure 3.12). It is a high-level metric with a number of constituent parts. For example, as the level of automation or outsourcing increases, the average may be expected to fall. A shift to advanced technologies can also result in high skills recruitment and an increase in average wages. Port performance scorecard data show that the global average of labour

12 The port performance scorecard questionnaire defines this datapoint widely to capture the extent to which services, especially cargo handling, is now managed by the private sector. As this can be arranged in leases, operating contracts, joint venture agreements and concession agreements, the objective is to chart an expected rise in these levels. The variety of approaches is important to note and must be recognized in interpreting the data.

Figure 3.10 Revenue mix of ports by region, 2014–2018

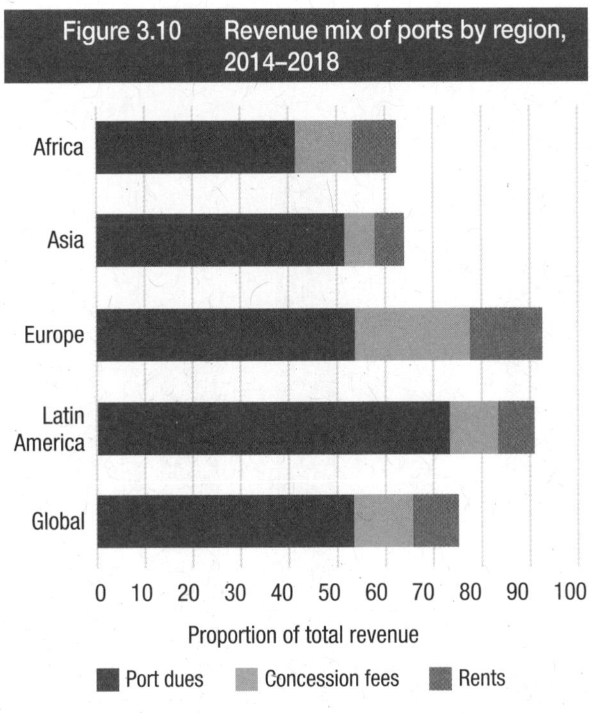

Source: UNCTAD secretariat calculations, based on data from port entities members of the Port Management Programme network.

Note: Financial comparisons of port performance are contingent on the use of the same currency and time periods. Accounting data are reported by ports in local currency, then converted by UNCTAD into United States dollars, using currency tables issued by the World Bank to facilitate comparison.

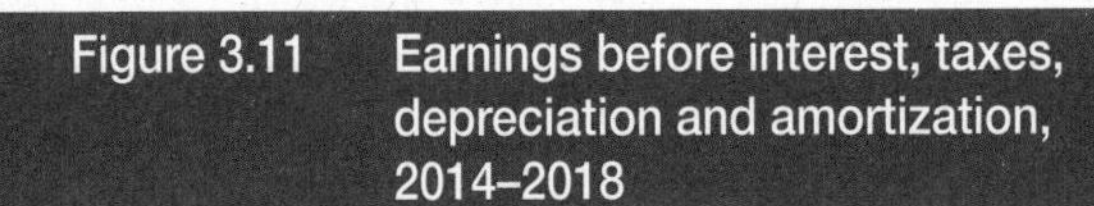

Figure 3.11 Earnings before interest, taxes, depreciation and amortization, 2014–2018

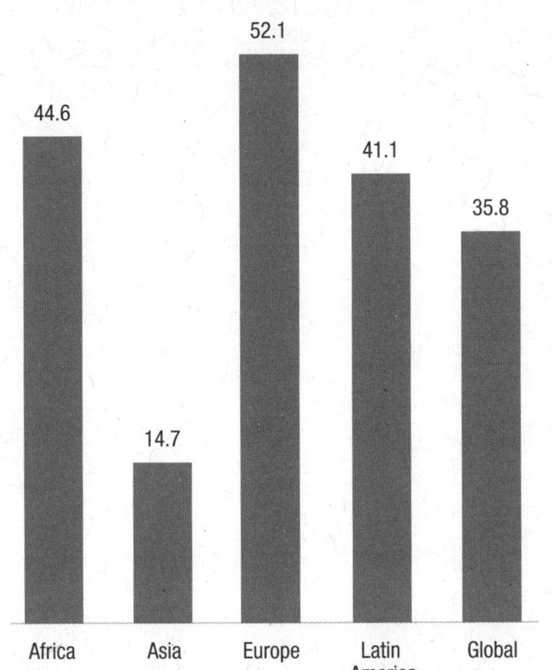

Source: UNCTAD secretariat calculations, based on data from port entities members of the Port Management Programme network.

Figure 3.12 Labour costs as a proportion of revenue, 2014–2018

Africa	Asia	Europe	Latin America	Global
31	22.1	21.1	15.2	22.2

Source: UNCTAD secretariat calculations, based on data from port entities members of the Port Management Programme network.

Figure 3.13 Employee contributions, 2014–2018

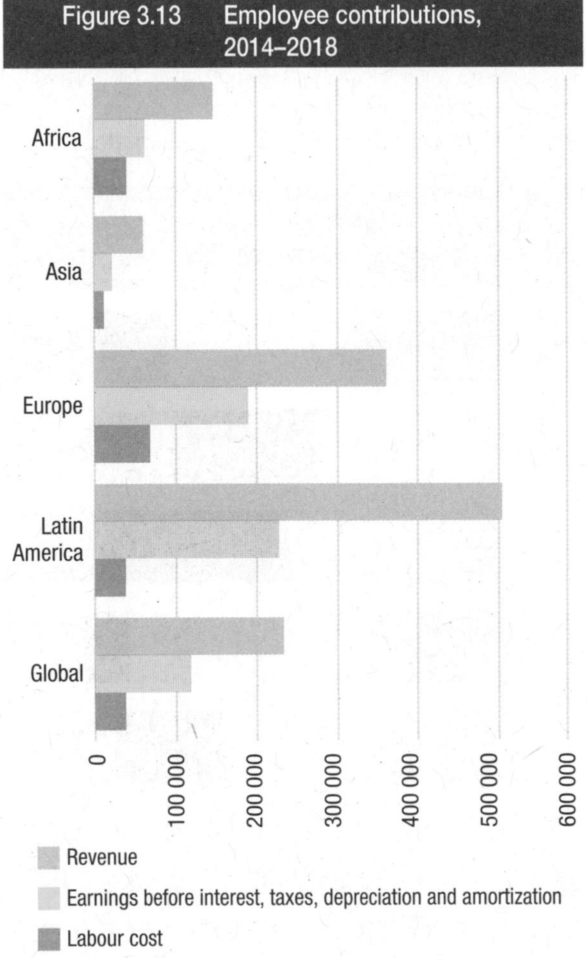

Source: UNCTAD secretariat calculations, based on data from port entities members of the Port Management Programme network.

cost as a proportion of total revenue was between 20 per cent and 25 per cent for the period 2014–2018.

The regional average for Asia and Europe falls within this range. The relative outliers are Africa and Latin America. Although there is insufficient detail in the data to be definitive, feedback from ports suggests that Latin America is below the range because of privatization and Africa is above the range because of higher numbers of employees. There are other possible explanations such as wage rates, revenue levels or differences in how ports classify employees. The relative contribution of each employee to the financial performance of a port is depicted in figure 3.13. The regional spread is noteworthy; however, it is unlikely that the explanations can be summed up in a single variable.

3. Port entity operations

The data on the variable mix of port configurations in terms of cargo and vessels reinforce industry wisdom that states "when you have seen one port, you have seen one port". Each has its own dynamic driven by geography and the local political economy.

The data in figure 3.14 provide a snapshot of the mix of vessels arriving in the member ports. The categorization of vessels is consistent with the definitions used in the *Review of Maritime Transport* for world fleet profiles. Member ports can compare their unique mix with the averages in their respective region and globally. The data are useful references when examining the revenue and profitability performance of individual ports.

Figure 3.14 Share of arrivals by vessel type, 2014–2018
(Percentage)

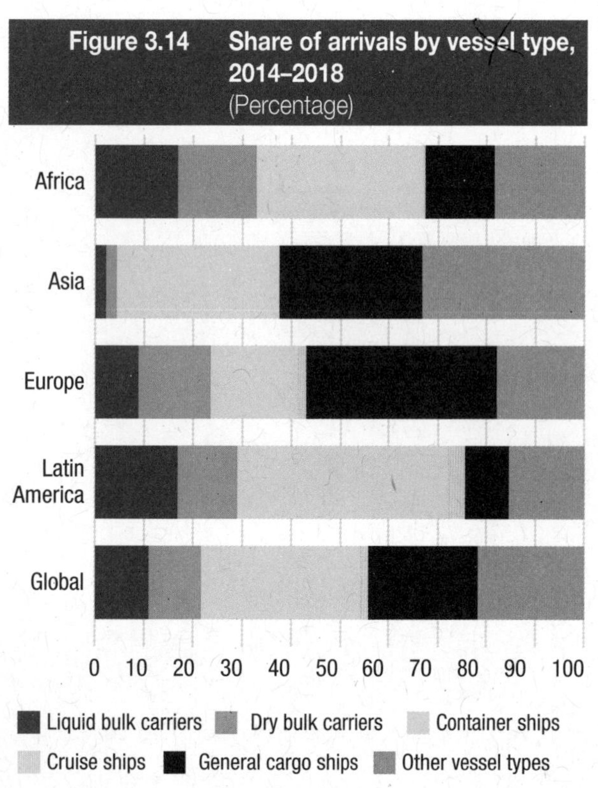

Source: UNCTAD secretariat calculations, based on data from port entities members of the Port Management Programme network.

Figure 3.15 Average cargo tons loaded or unloaded per arrival

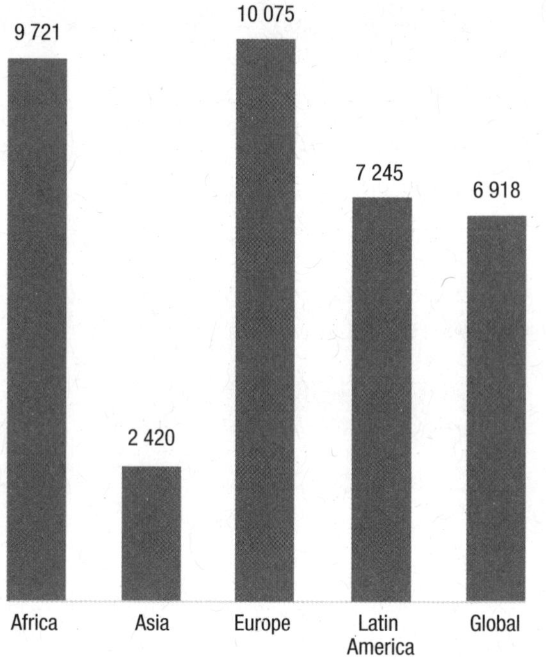

Africa 9 721
Asia 2 420
Europe 10 075
Latin America 7 245
Global 6 918

Source: UNCTAD secretariat calculations, based on data from port entities members of the Port Management Programme network.

Figure 3.15 illustrates the relative size of these vessels in terms or average cargo discharged or loaded per arrival. According to a port performance scorecard survey carried out in April 2019, some 65 per cent of all ports in a survey have annual cargo volumes of fewer than 10 million tons. Feedback from ports suggests that the relative low average for Asia is partly a function of inter-island traffic, including on ferry type vessels.

Figure 3.16 Environmental spending

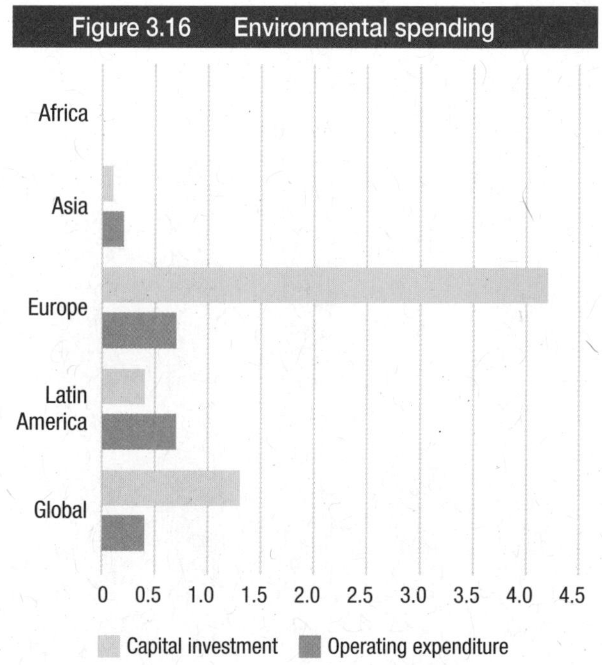

Source: UNCTAD secretariat calculations, based on data from port entities members of the Port Management Programme network.

The general profile of ports in the aforementioned survey is unchanged and the majority can be classified as small to medium in size, owned by an arm of the State, managed in some corporate form, with a broader recognition that functional models are less likely to be exclusively landlord in nature. The average volume of cargo discharged or loaded per arrival is marginally lower than last reported. This may reflect global and regional trade disruption.

4. Sustainability

One difficulty with data in this category is the variable way ports will account for their environmental spending (figure 3.16). Some will record specific costs, while for many, the environmental portion of a project is embedded in the overall costs. This applies to both capital and operating costs. The data suggest that the larger ports in Europe do indeed record such performance indicators. Feedback on environmental spending suggests that capital expenditures and operational costs are rarely classified as a single project. Therefore, such costs are included under many budget lines in other projects. This may in part explain the relatively low spending (1.7 per cent of capital expenditures) reported on the scorecard.

The data in this section provided a summary of the performance of Port Management Programme members between 2014 and 2018. Two points, which would require continued monitoring and reporting in the future, are worth highlighting. First, the levels of women's participation in the sector remain low. It is also necessary to bear in mind recent changes in working practices, technology and society that are opening up the possibility for greater participation of women in the sector. The advent of digitalization and the automation of activities in the shipping industry could lead to the increased participation of women in the future. Second, the growing trend towards privatization, which started in the 1980s, has brought a new and important category of revenue, concession fees.

REFERENCES

Benamara H, Hoffmann J, Rodríguez L and Youssef F (2019). Container ports: The fastest, the busiest and the best connected. 7 August. Available at https://unctad.org/en/pages/newsdetails.aspx?OriginalVersionID=2162 (accessed 17 September 2019).

Hoffmann J, Saeed N and Sødal S (2019). Liner shipping bilateral connectivity and its impact on South Africa's bilateral trade flows. *Maritime Economics and Logistics*. Pp. 1–27.

Humphreys M, Stokenberga A, Herrera Dappe M, Iimi A and Hartmann O (2019). *Port Development and Competition in East and Southern Africa: Prospects and Challenges*. International Development in Focus. World Bank. Washington, D.C.

Lind M, Watson RT, Ward R, Bergmann M, Bjørn-Andersen N, Rosemann M, Haraldson S and Andersen T (2018). Digital data sharing: The ignored opportunity for making global maritime transport chains more efficient. UNCTAD Transport and Trade Facilitation Newsletter No. 79. October. Available at https://unctad.org/en/pages/newsdetails.aspx?OriginalVersionID=1850 (accessed 7 July 2019).

Lind M, Ward R, Bergmann M, Bjørn-Andersen N, Watson R, Haraldson S, Andersen T and Michaelides M (2019). PortCDM [Port Collaborative Decision-making]: Validation of the concept and next steps. International PortCDM Council Concept Note 21.

Micco A, Pizzolitto G, Sánchez R, Hoffmann J, Sgut M and Wilmsmeier G (2003). Port efficiency and international trade: Port efficiency as a determinant of maritime transport costs. *Maritime Economics and Logistics*. 5(2):199–218.

UNCTAD (1998). Guidelines for Port Authorities and Governments on the Privatization of Port Facilities. UNCTAD/SDTE/TIB/1. Geneva.

UNCTAD (2014). Closing the Distance: Partnerships for Sustainable and Resilient Transport Systems in Small Island Developing States (United Nations publication. New York and Geneva).

UNCTAD (2016). Trade Facilitation and Development: Driving Trade Competitiveness, Border Agency Effectiveness and Strengthened Governance. Transport and Trade Facilitation Series No. 7 (United Nations publication. Geneva).

UNCTAD (2017a). *Review of Maritime Transport 2017* (United Nations publication. Sales No. E.17.II.D.10. New York and Geneva).

UNCTAD (2017b). *Rethinking Maritime Cabotage for Improved Connectivity*. Transport and Trade Facilitation Series No. 9 (United Nations publication. Geneva).

UNCTAD (2019a). Sustainable transport infrastructure in a world of growing trade and climate change, SDG [Sustainable Development Goal] pulse. Available at https://sdgpulse.unctad.org/transport-infrastructure/ (accessed 23 September 2019).

UNCTAD (2019b). Framework for Sustainable Freight Transport portal (https://unctadsftportal.org; accessed 24 September 2019).

UNCTAD (2019c). Digitalization in maritime transport: Ensuring opportunities for development. Policy Brief No. 75. UNCTAD/PRESS/PB/2019/4.

Wilmsmeier G and Hoffmann J (2008). Liner shipping connectivity and port infrastructure as determinants of freight rates in the Caribbean. *Maritime Economics and Logistics*. 10(1–2):130–151.

Wolde Woldearegay D, Sethi K, Hartmann O, Coste AHM and Isik G (2016). Making the most of ports in West Africa. Report No. ACS17308. World Bank.

World Bank (2007). *Port Reform Toolkit*. Washington, D.C.

This chapter provides a summary of important international legal and regulatory developments which took place during the period under review and presents some policy considerations. Some relevant technological developments, along with related work by UNCTAD, are also covered in context. Developments include an ongoing regulatory scoping exercise at IMO for the review of relevant legal instruments to ensure the safe design, construction and operation of autonomous ships and a legal framework that provides the same levels of protection as for operations with traditional ships.

Other regulatory developments relate to the reduction of greenhouse gas emissions from international shipping and other ship-source pollution control and environmental protection measures. Issues covered include air pollution, in particular sulphur emissions; marine litter; the protection of biodiversity in areas beyond national jurisdiction; shipping and climate change mitigation and adaptation; ballast water management; and the shipment of hazardous and noxious substances. Relevant developments – as they relate to environmentally sustainable shipping and the oceans – are highlighted and considered in the wider context of the implementation of the 2030 Agenda for Sustainable Development, the Paris Agreement under the United Nations Framework Convention on Climate Change and the Sendai Framework for Disaster Risk Reduction 2015–2030, which collectively provide the foundation for sustainable, low-carbon and resilient development in a changing climate.

In addition, developments covered in this chapter include a series of measures to prevent unlawful practices associated with the fraudulent registration of ships; discussion on the growing number of cases regarding the abandonment of seafarers, most of which come from developing countries; the importance of attaining and promoting equality between women and men working in the maritime industry; and international action needed to address these issues.

LEGAL ISSUES AND REGULATORY DEVELOPMENTS

Before autonomous ships start operating, the technology needs to be proven and appropriate institutional and regulatory safeguards and frameworks should be developed.

SO_2

The new **0.50%** limit on sulphur in ships' fuel oil (down from 3.50%) will be in force globally from 1 January 2020.

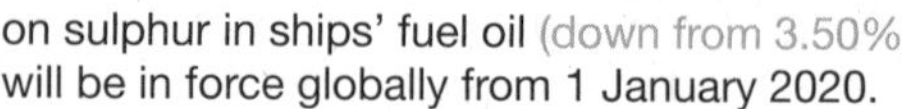

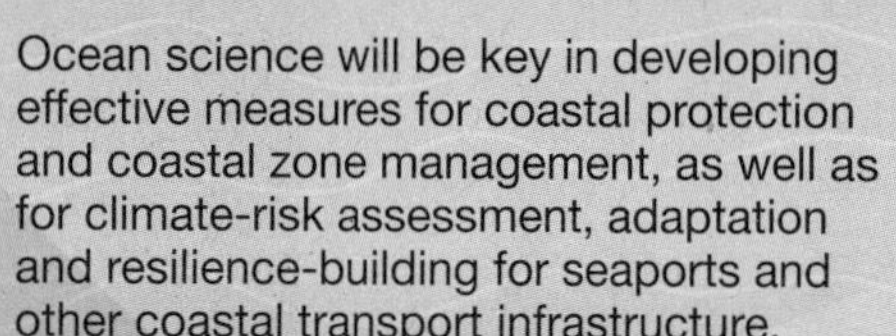

Ocean science will be key in developing effective measures for coastal protection and coastal zone management, as well as for climate-risk assessment, adaptation and resilience-building for seaports and other coastal transport infrastructure.

The fourth IMO greenhouse gas study, to be published in 2020, will include an inventory of current global emissions from ships of 100 gross tons and above engaged in international voyages, as well as scenarios for future international shipping emissions (2018–2050).

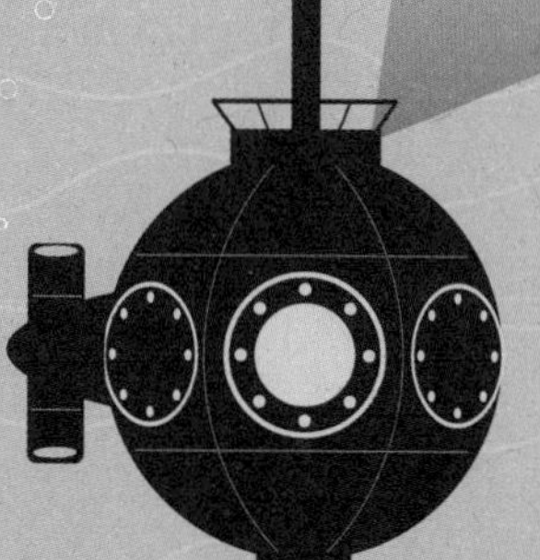

Ongoing negotiations for a legally binding international instrument under the United Nations Convention on the Law of the Sea on the conservation and sustainable use of marine biodiversity of areas beyond national jurisdiction seek to achieve consensus on complex substantive and procedural issues. The participation of all States, including developing countries, for which marine genetic resources are an important priority, will be essential.

A. TECHNOLOGICAL DEVELOPMENTS AND EMERGING ISSUES IN THE MARITIME INDUSTRY

Players in the shipping industry are increasingly taking advantage of digitalization and joint collaborative platforms and solutions enabled by new technologies and innovations, including blockchain, and are thus changing their business and partnership models. These aim to promote efficient and secure trade, including by offering greater supply chain visibility and the use of electronic documents, ultimately benefiting customers who rely on shipping industry services. Benefits include lower transaction costs and consumer prices, increased market access and competition, better use of underutilized resources and added flexibility for service providers. However, gains are not automatic, and there are growing concerns over the rising market power of certain platforms and its implications for competition, data protection and ownership, consumer protection, and taxation and employment policies (UNCTAD, 2019).

For instance, Trade Lens, a collaborative platform established by Maersk and IBM in 2018, has – after some initial concerns – attracted other major container shipping lines to its membership, including ZIM Integrated Shipping Services, Pacific International Lines, CMA CGM, Mediterranean Shipping Company, Hapag-Lloyd and ONE. In addition, four of the world's six largest carriers, namely Maersk, Mediterranean Shipping Company, Hapag-Lloyd and ONE, officially established the Digital Container Shipping Association in 2019, aiming to create common information technology standards that will improve the overall efficiency of the shipping sector. Five more carriers, namely CMA CGM, Evergreen, Hyundai Merchant Marine, Yang Ming and ZIM Integrated Shipping Services, joined subsequently (Port Technology, 2019; Splash 247, 2019).

Developments regarding ship automation and the related regulatory framework are highlighted below.

1. Maritime autonomous surface ships

Autonomous ships, or maritime autonomous surface ships – the general term for autonomous ships used at IMO – may soon become a reality, promising to provide enhanced safety and cost savings by removing the human element from certain operations. For instance, the safety and security of ship operations may benefit from the use of autonomous ships, since most marine accidents and liability insurance claims can be attributed to human error. Further, crew costs may decrease, and so may the risk of piracy and hostage-taking, and respective insurance premiums and costs. Vessel construction and other costs may also be reduced, with space required for seafarer accommodation being used for cargo storage instead. Vessel operations may also become more environmentally friendly because of the potential use of alternate fuels, zero-emission technologies, no ballast, and less garbage and sewage. However, while there are potential benefits, there are also a number of challenging concerns. These include cybersecurity; safety related to the lack of a crew on board; the undue impacts on the prospects of employment for seafarers, many of which come from developing countries; and regulatory issues, shipping rates and insurance (see UNCTAD, 2018a).

Considerations also depend on the degree of automation of a ship. For instance, should a fully autonomous ship suffer system failure caused by technical defects or hackers, there would be no scope for human intervention –no operators – on board to control the ship and prevent an incident. However, the human element would remain relevant, as shore-based operators and software programmers are needed to control autonomous ships. It appears that both autonomous and manned ships might coexist, and while shipmasters have the professional ability to make instant decisions, based on the circumstances – saving lives at sea, for example – it is still not clear whether and how shore-based operators acting remotely would be able to take similar decisions. Therefore, in view of past incidents where the use of autonomous vehicles has resulted in the loss of innocent lives, it is necessary that the technology be proven before autonomous ships start sailing and appropriate institutional and regulatory safeguards and frameworks be developed.

With regard to the effect of autonomous ships on the work of seafarers, a recent paper (IMO, 2018a) reflects the concern of seafarers about possible job losses owing to the advent of automation and their opposition to the technology. Further, if its introduction is motivated solely by cost-cutting considerations, livelihoods and safety may be adversely affected. The use of autonomous ships will require new skills from seafarers to ensure the safety and efficiency of operations. Seafarers and land-based personnel will need to improve their skills through continuous learning and training in order to keep abreast with changes in technology.

For instance, a study by the Hamburg School of Business Administration (2018), published by the International Chamber of Shipping, highlights the potential effects of autonomous ships on the global shipping industry and the role of seafarers. It suggests that automation will create new but different jobs, requiring higher skills, significant training and a redefinition of the role of personnel on board and ashore. Automation will require less physical strength and more information technology skills and knowledge.

A recent report found that, in many areas, automation in the transportation sector was likely to lead to a shift in the workforce, not in labour reduction (International Transport Workers' Federation, 2019). Thus, it is suggested that increased levels of technology and automation will contribute significantly to increasing efficiency. "In transportation, the highest potential for automation is in low-skilled jobs, which are intensive on predictable physical activities and data processing; therefore, those jobs face a high risk of being impacted by automation. At the same time, the further introduction of automation will also create a demand for new types of jobs, such as remote operators, worldwide operating maintenance crews and mobility-as-a-service providers. As a result, the demand for labour will not completely disappear, but the requirements and skills needed for individual jobs will change."

The report also notes that the introduction of automation in global transport will be "evolutionary, rather than revolutionary", and that despite high levels of automation, qualified human resources with the right skill sets would still be needed in the foreseeable future. It further notes that technological advances are inevitable, but that they will be gradual and will vary by region, and that workers will be affected in different ways, based on their skills levels and the varying degrees of preparedness of different countries.

2. Regulatory scoping exercise

Since the whole spectrum of applicable maritime laws and regulations operates on the presumption of having a master and crew on board, their traditional roles, as well as the role of artificial intelligence and the remote-control crew working ashore, will need to be assessed and (re)defined for autonomous shipping. In this context, recent international regulatory developments include an ongoing scoping exercise, initiated at the IMO in 2017, entailing the review of relevant legal instruments to ensure the safe design, construction and operation of autonomous ships, and to guarantee that the legal framework provides the same levels of protection in ship operation to autonomous ships as those afforded to traditional ships.

> The demand for labour will not completely disappear, but the requirements and skills needed for individual jobs will change.

IMO Maritime Safety Committee

The regulatory scoping exercise aimed at assessing the potential application of IMO instruments to ships with varying degrees of autonomy continued during the 100th session of the Maritime Safety Committee in December 2018. The Committee approved the framework for the regulatory scoping exercise on the use of maritime autonomous surface ships (IMO, 2018b, annex 2). The following degrees of autonomy were identified for the purpose of the exercise:

- Degree one: Ship with automated processes and decision support. Seafarers are on board to operate and control shipboard systems and functions. Some operations may be automated and may at times be unsupervised but with seafarers on board ready to take control.
- Degree two: Remotely controlled ship with seafarers on board. The ship is controlled and operated from another location. Seafarers are available on board to take control and operate shipboard systems and functions.
- Degree three: Remotely controlled ship without seafarers on board. The ship is controlled and operated from another location; there are no seafarers on board.
- Degree four: Fully autonomous ship. The operating system of the ship is able to make decisions and determine actions by itself.

The work methodology of the framework is divided into two steps. First, for each instrument related to maritime safety and security, and for each degree of autonomy, the methodology contains provisions applying to different cases: those that apply to autonomous ships and prevent their operations; those that apply to autonomous ships, do not prevent their operations and require no actions; those that apply to autonomous ships and do not prevent their operations but may need to be amended or clarified and/or may contain gaps; or those that have no application to the operations of autonomous ships.

Second, the most appropriate way of addressing the operations of autonomous ships will be analysed and determined, taking into account, inter alia, factors relating to the human element, technology and operations. The analysis will establish whether it is necessary to present equivalences as provided for by the instruments or developing interpretations; to amend existing instruments; to develop new instruments; or none of the aforementioned, depending on the result of the analysis.

The initial review of legal instruments under the purview of the Committee was to be conducted during the first half of 2019 by volunteering member States, with the support of interested international organizations, the ultimate goal being to complete the regulatory scoping exercise by 2020. The legal instruments related to maritime safety and security that will be covered in this exercise are as follows:

- Convention on the International Regulations for Preventing Collisions at Sea, 1972.
- International Convention for Safe Containers, 1972, as amended.
- International Convention on Load Lines, 1966.
- Protocol of 1988 relating to the International Convention on Load Lines, 1966.
- International Convention on Maritime Search and Rescue, 1979.

- International Convention for the Safety of Life at Sea, 1974, as amended.
- Agreement Concerning Specific Stability Requirements for Ro-ro Passenger Ships Undertaking Regular Scheduled International Voyages between, to or from Designated Ports in North West Europe and the Baltic Sea, 1996.
- 1978 Protocol relating to the International Convention for the Safety of Life at Sea, 1974, as amended.
- 1988 Protocol relating to the International Convention for the Safety of Life at Sea, 1974, as amended.
- 1973 Protocol on Space Requirements for Special Trade Passenger Ships.
- International Convention on Standards of Training, Certification and Watchkeeping for Seafarers, 1978, as amended.
- International Convention on Standards of Training, Certification and Watchkeeping for Fishing Vessel Personnel, 1995.
- Special Trade Passenger Ships Agreement, 1971.
- International Convention on Tonnage Measurement of Ships, 1969.

In addition, the Committee at its 100th and 101st sessions, noted the need to develop guidelines on autonomous ships trials. Such guidelines should be generic and goal-based; the trials should be in line with mandatory instruments, which would also include exemptions and equivalent arrangements; and the human element and training and certification requirements should be taken into account (IMO, 2019a).

IMO Legal Committee

At its 106th session in March 2019, the IMO Legal Committee began its work on the regulatory scoping exercise of international legal instruments under its purview. Its aim was to assess the degree to which the existing regulatory framework may need to be adjusted in order to address issues related to the operation of maritime autonomous surface ships.

Like the Maritime Safety Committee, a framework for the regulatory scoping exercise was agreed, including the list of instruments to be reviewed. A similar methodology was agreed to be used by the Legal Committee as well, with appropriate adjustments to accommodate the specificities of the conventions under its purview. It was also agreed that the differentiation between the four degrees of autonomy were not as relevant in the context of the Legal Committee's regulatory scoping exercise and that a simplified approach might be used, focusing on only two levels of autonomy. Volunteer member States, along with interested non-governmental and intergovernmental organizations, would work on the review and analysis (IMO, 2019b, annex 3; 2019c).

The international legal instruments under the purview of the IMO Legal Committee to be reviewed are as follows:

- International Convention on Civil Liability for Bunker Oil Pollution Damage, 2001.
- International Convention on Civil Liability for Oil Pollution Damage, 1969.
- 1976 Protocol to Amend the International Convention on Civil Liability for Oil Pollution Damage, 1969.
- 1992 Protocol to Amend the International Convention on Civil Liability for Oil Pollution Damage, 1969.
- 1992 Protocol to Amend the International Convention on the Establishment of an International Fund for Compensation for Oil Pollution Damage, 1971.
- 2003 Protocol to the International Convention on the Establishment of an International Fund for Compensation for Oil Pollution Damage, 1992.
- Convention relating to Civil Liability in the Field of Maritime Carriage of Nuclear Material, 1971.
- Athens Convention Relating to the Carriage of Passengers and Their Luggage by Sea, 1974.
- 1976 Protocol to the Athens Convention relating to the Carriage of Passengers and Their Luggage by Sea, 1974.
- 2002 Protocol to the Athens Convention relating to the Carriage of Passengers and Their Luggage by Sea, 1974.
- Convention on Limitation of Liability for Maritime Claims, 1976.
- 1996 Protocol to amend the Convention on Limitation of Liability for Maritime Claims, 1976.
- Convention for the Suppression of Unlawful Acts against the Safety of Maritime Navigation, 1988.
- 1988 Protocol for the Suppression of Unlawful Acts against the Safety of Fixed Platforms Located on the Continental Shelf.
- 2005 Protocol to the Convention for the Suppression of Unlawful Acts against the Safety of Maritime Navigation.
- 2005 Protocol to the Protocol for the Suppression of Unlawful Acts against the Safety of Fixed Platforms Located on the Continental Shelf.
- International Convention on Salvage, 1989.
- Nairobi International Convention on the Removal of Wrecks, 2007.

- 2010 Protocol to the International Convention on Liability and Compensation for Damage in Connection with the Carriage of Hazardous and Noxious Substances by Sea, 1996.

The following international legal instruments emanating from the IMO Legal Committee, with shared cognizance with other IMO committees, will also be reviewed:

- International Convention Relating to Intervention on the High Seas in Cases of Oil Pollution Casualties, 1969.
- 1973 Protocol relating to Intervention on the High Seas in Cases of Pollution by Substances other than Oil.

The following joint international legal instruments concluded between IMO and other United Nations bodies, emanating from the IMO Legal Committee, will be reviewed as well:

- International Convention on Maritime Liens and Mortgages, 1993 (with UNCTAD).
- International Convention on Arrest of Ships, 1999 (with UNCTAD).

Within the liability regime, the role of the remote operator would also have to be considered by the Legal Committee at some stage. However, it was agreed that this discussion was not within the scope of the regulatory scoping exercise. It was generally observed that autonomous shipping should not compromise safety, security and environmental protection and should be discussed in a comprehensive manner. In addition, considering the drastic effect the introduction of autonomous ships might have on seafarers, their concerns should also to be taken into consideration. The Legal Committee invited member States and observer organizations willing to volunteer to lead or support the initial review of specific instruments, to inform the IMO Secretariat by 30 April 2019 (IMO, 2019b).

B. REGULATORY DEVELOPMENTS RELATING TO THE REDUCTION OF GREENHOUSE GAS EMISSIONS FROM INTERNATIONAL SHIPPING AND OTHER ENVIRONMENTAL ISSUES

Recent regulatory developments relate to the reduction of greenhouse gas emissions from international shipping and other ship-source pollution control and environmental protection measures, including those concerning air pollution, marine litter, the protection of biodiversity in areas beyond national jurisdiction, oceans and climate change mitigation and adaptation, ballast water management and the shipment of hazardous and noxious substances.

This chapter discusses relevant regulatory developments as they relate to environmentally sustainable shipping and the oceans and in the wider context of the implementation of the 2030 Agenda for Sustainable Development, the Paris Agreement under the United Nations Framework Convention on Climate Change and the Sendai Framework for Disaster Risk Reduction 2015–2030. These collectively provide the foundation for sustainable, low-carbon and resilient development in a changing climate.

1. Paris Agreement under the United Nations Framework Convention on Climate Change

Since its adoption in 1992, the United Nations Framework Convention on Climate Change has progressively built a global response to climate change and its impacts, with the most recent multilateral response outlined in the 2015 Paris Agreement. Greenhouse gas emissions from international shipping are also addressed at the global level, although they are not covered under the 1997 Kyoto Protocol to the Convention. Article 2.2 of the Protocol specifies that parties shall pursue the limitation or reduction of emissions of greenhouse gases from marine bunker fuels by working through IMO. Work has been going on at IMO for many years; the Organization adopted a resolution on carbon-dioxide emissions from ships in September 1997 and an initial strategy in April 2018 aimed at setting emissions-reduction targets consistent with the Paris Agreement (see section 2 below).

The Paris Agreement was adopted in December 2015, entered into force in November 2016 and has been ratified to date by 186 States (see https://unfccc.int/process/the-paris-agreement/status-of-ratification). Under article 2 of the Agreement, parties commit to reducing emissions expeditiously to achieve the goal of "holding the increase in the global average temperature to well below 2°C above pre-industrial levels and to pursue efforts to limit the temperature increase to 1.5°C above pre-industrial levels".

A special report by the United Nations Intergovernmental Panel on Climate Change (2018), prepared by eminent climate scientists at the request of the parties to the Paris Agreement, warns that a global warming beyond 1.5°C will significantly worsen the risks of drought, floods, extreme heat and poverty for hundreds of millions of people. Urgent and unprecedented changes are needed to reach the target, which according to the report, is affordable and feasible, although it lies at the most ambitious end of the pledge of the Agreement to maintain temperatures between 1.5°C and 2°C. "Limiting warming to 1.5°C is possible but the window is narrowing" (*The Guardian*, 2018).

Twenty-fourth Conference of the Parties and the Katowice climate package

Coinciding with the third anniversary of the adoption of the Paris Agreement, the twenty-fourth session of the Conference of the Parties to the United Nations Framework Convention on Climate Change was held in Katowice, Poland, in December 2018. The participating States adopted the Katowice climate package (https://unfccc.int/process-and-meetings/the-paris-agreement/paris-agreement-work-programme/katowice-climate-package), designed to operationalize the climate change regime contained in the Paris Agreement.

The Katowice climate package aims to promote international cooperation and encourage greater ambition for implementing the Paris Agreement as of 2020. It indicates how countries will provide information about their nationally determined contributions, outlining their domestic climate actions, including mitigation and adaptation measures, as well as details of financial support for climate action in developing countries.

The package includes guidelines on the establishment of new finance targets from 2025 onwards to follow up on the current target of mobilizing $100 billion per year from 2020 to support developing countries (United Nations Framework Convention on Climate Change, 2016, paragraph 53). It also describes how to conduct a global stocktaking of climate action in 2023 and how to assess progress on the development and transfer of technology (United Nations Framework Convention on Climate Change, 2018).

Issues related to market and non-market cooperative approaches, as contained in article 6 of the Paris Agreement, including internationally transferable mitigation outcomes (article 6.2), as well as the sustainable development mechanism (article 6.4), will continue to be discussed at the twenty-fifth Conference of the Parties.

In order to boost political and economic efforts to strengthen climate action and ambition globally, the Secretary-General of the United Nations convened the Climate Action Summit in New York, United States, in September 2019.[13] In advance of the 2020 deadline for countries to raise their commitments in their national climate plans, the Summit focused on practical initiatives to limit emissions and build climate resilience, emphasizing six key areas: energy transition, climate finance and carbon pricing, industry transition, nature-based solutions, cities and local action, and resilience.

Climate finance

In the decision adopting the Paris Agreement (United Nations Framework Convention on Climate Change, 2016), States agreed to set by 2025 a "collective quantified goal from a floor of $100 billion per year, taking into account the needs and priorities of developing countries" (paragraph 53). In this context, the Green Climate Fund is the world's largest dedicated fund, aiming to help developing countries reduce their greenhouse gas emissions and enhance their ability to respond to climate change. The Fund has a crucial role in serving the Paris Agreement by channelling climate finance to developing countries, which have joined other nations in committing to climate action. With $5 billion of the Fund committed to projects and more than $17 billion in the pipeline, there is a real demand for climate finance (www.greenclimate.fund/home). However, whether adequate financing will be available on the ground remains to be seen.

As an expression of global solidarity and partnership with countries and communities most affected by climate change, and in order to accelerate and scale up global action to match the ambition and urgency needed to meet the climate challenge, the Fund's first replenishment was launched in October 2018 (www.greenclimate.fund/how-we-work/resource-mobilization/replenishment). This followed pledges for the 2015–2018 period of $10.2 billion, nearly $7 billion of which had been received at the time. The replenishment process involves organizational and consultation meetings with potential contributors and was set to conclude with a pledging conference in October 2019. In addition, the World Bank has pledged $200 billion in climate action funding for the period 2021–2025 (World Bank, 2018a). Multilateral development and other leading banks have committed to aligning their activities and exploring ways to steer financial streams towards the goals of the Paris Agreement (World Bank, 2018b).

2. Developments at the International Maritime Organization related to the reduction of greenhouse gas emissions from ships

Various relevant regulatory activities are carried out at IMO. These include complementing international efforts to address greenhouse gas emissions[14] and an initial strategy on reduction of greenhouse gas emissions from ships, adopted in April 2018. In particular, the strategy sets out a vision and levels of ambition for international shipping (IMO, 2018c, annex 1). The vision states that IMO remains committed to reducing greenhouse gas emissions from international shipping and, as a matter of urgency, aims to phase them out as soon as possible in the present century.

The IMO initial strategy envisages a reduction of carbon-dioxide emissions per transport work (carbon intensity), as an average across international shipping, by at

[13] As information related to the twenty-fourth Conference of the Parties suggests, "even if all the commitments made by countries for the Paris Agreement are achieved, the world will still be on a course to warm by more than 3°C this century"(www.un.org/en/climatechange/cop24.shtml).

[14] For example, the Paris Agreement and the 2030 Agenda for Sustainable Development (Sustainable Development Goal 13, take urgent action to combat climate change and its impacts).

least 40 per cent by 2030, pursuing efforts to achieve 70 per cent by 2050, compared with 2008. Importantly, for the first time, the strategy aims to reduce total annual greenhouse gas emissions by at least 50 per cent by 2050, compared with 2008, while, at the same time, pursuing efforts towards phasing them out in accordance with the vision, for achieving carbon-dioxide emissions reduction consistent with the Paris Agreement goals.

Technical and operational energy efficiency measures for both new and existing ships, such as speed optimization and reduction, the development of robust lifecycle greenhouse gas and carbon intensity guidelines for all types of fuels to prepare for the use of alternative low-carbon and zero-carbon fuels, port activities and incentives for first movers, were included, inter alia, under candidate short-term measures to be further developed and agreed upon by member States between 2018 and 2023.

Innovative emissions-reduction mechanisms, possibly including market-based measures, to incentivize greenhouse gas emission reduction, were included among candidate midterm measures to be agreed and decided upon between 2023 and 2030, along with possible long-term measures to be undertaken beyond 2030 that would ultimately lead to zero-carbon or fossil-free fuels to enable the potential decarbonization of the shipping sector in the second half of the century (for more information, see UNCTAD, 2018a).

Another regulatory development is the approval in October 2018 of a programme of follow-up actions of the initial IMO strategy on reduction of greenhouse gas emissions from ships up to 2023, including the consideration of concrete proposals on candidate short-term measures and the finalization of the procedure for assessing the impacts on States, starting from 2019 (IMO, 2018d, annex 9).

Further developments include the implementation in phases of IMO energy efficiency requirements, which have been legally binding and applicable to the maritime industry since 2013. For example, the energy efficiency design index sets standards for new ships and associated operational energy efficiency measures for existing ships (UNCTAD, 2011a, pp. 113–116; 2012a, pp. 96–98). At its seventy-fourth session in May 2019, the Marine Environment Protection Committee of IMO agreed to bring forward the phase III requirement from 2025 to 2022 for some ship types and approved phase III reduction rates for containerships that are based on different size categories (up to a 50 per cent reduction by 2022 for the largest ships). (For information on policy measures to reduce greenhouse gas emissions from ships, see also chapter 2.)

In addition to technical and operational measures, IMO has for a number of years been discussing in parallel market-based measures to reduce emissions from international shipping. However, no agreement has been reached so far (for earlier discussions, see UNCTAD, 2011a, pp. 118–119; 2012a, pp. 99–101). In 2014, prompted by controversies, formal discussion on market-based measures by the Marine Environment Protection Committee was suspended (IMO, 2014, p. 44). The topic was reconsidered at meetings of the Intersessional Working Group on Reduction of Greenhouse Gas Emissions from Ships in June and October 2017 (IMO, 2017a, 2017b), for possible inclusion in the future comprehensive IMO strategy on reduction of greenhouse gas emissions from ships, as candidate midterm measures, to help incentivize the uptake of alternative fuels. Indeed, the IMO initial strategy lists "new/innovative emission reduction mechanisms, possibly including market-based measures, to incentivize greenhouse gas emission reduction" among candidate midterm measures (IMO, 2018c, p. 8). (For a summary of various potential market-based measures under consideration, see UNCTAD 2018a, chapter 3).

In addition, during its seventy-fourth session, the Committee took the following actions:

- Decided to initiate a fourth IMO greenhouse gas study, expected to be published in autumn 2020, which will include an inventory of current global emissions of greenhouse gas and relevant substances emitted from ships of 100 gross tons and above engaged in international voyages, as well as business-as-usual scenarios for future international shipping emissions (2018–2050).
- Adopted resolution MEPC.323(74), encouraging voluntary cooperation between the port and the shipping sectors to contribute to the reduction of greenhouse gas emissions from ships. This could include regulatory, technical, operational and economic measures in key areas such as the provision of onshore power supply (preferably from renewable sources); safe and efficient bunkering of alternative low-carbon and zero-carbon fuels; incentive schemes that address greenhouse gas emissions and sustainability; and support for the optimization of port calls, including the facilitation of just-in-time arrival of ships.
- Approved a four-step procedure for assessing the impacts on States of candidate measures for the reduction of greenhouse gas emissions from ships.
- Agreed to establish a voluntary multi-donor trust fund to provide a dedicated source of financial support for technical cooperation and capacity-building activities as support for the implementation of the initial IMO strategy on reduction of greenhouse gas emissions from ships (IMO, 2019d).

3. Interlinkages between ocean issues, climate change mitigation and adaptation, and sustainable development

Related processes under the United Nations Framework Convention on Climate Change

For people living on the coasts, the link between climate change and the ocean is clearly present, including in terms of sea-level rise and extreme weather events, changing weather patterns, rising ocean temperatures and related impacts on fisheries, tourism and coastal infrastructure. An important development in this context, highlighting the close nexus between ocean and climate-related issues, was the launch of the Ocean Pathway (https://cop23.com.fj/the-ocean-pathway/) at the twenty-third session of the Conference of the Parties to the United Nations Framework Convention on Climate Change, in Bonn, Germany in 2017, followed by the holding of Oceans Action Days at the twenty-third and twenty-fourth sessions of the Conference of the Parties, and the launch of various ocean-related initiatives, alliances and action agendas. The Ocean Pathway introduced a two-tracked strategy for 2020 supporting the goals of the Paris Agreement. The strategy aims to increase the role of ocean considerations in the United Nations Framework Convention on Climate Change process, as well as further action and activities in priority areas relevant to ocean and climate change. These would include cooperation with coastal cities and settlements and islands States, which are on the frontline of ocean and climate change impacts – particularly in the areas of emissions reduction, adaptation, and ocean health; reducing emissions from transportation, including maritime transportation; ocean acidification; blue and resilient economies; coastal habitats and ecosystems; ocean law and policy; and nationally determined contributions.

The latest Oceans Action Day was held as part of the Marrakech Partnership for Global Climate Action (https://unfccc.int/climate-action/marrakech-partnership/events/gca-at-cop24) on 8 December 2018 during the twenty-fourth session of the Conference of the Parties. Panel discussions focused on new scientific findings, adaptation and displacement, ocean content of nationally determined contributions and ocean financing, and ocean acidification. It was said among others, that the second United Nations Ocean Conference in 2020 should focus on action and funding needed to address risks to the ocean as they relate to climate change (www.oceanactionhub.org/ocean-action-day-held-climate-change-cop-24-poland).

The inclusion of ocean matters in nationally determined contributions as they are implemented and enhanced, has been increasingly encouraged. Under the Paris Agreement, States are required to commit to climate mitigation goals by submitting and implementing increasingly ambitious nationally determined contributions in five-year cycles (article 4). Also, under the Paris Agreement, each Party should, as appropriate, submit and update periodically an adaptation communication, which may include its priorities, implementation and support needs, plans and actions, without creating any additional burden for developing country Parties (article 7.10).

Therefore, as the call to global climate action of civil society and industry leaders at the Global Climate Action Summit 2018 suggests, one action by countries could be to increase specific and meaningful ocean-related content in their 2020 nationally determined contributions submissions. Another action could be to increase specific and meaningful ocean-related adaptation measures in their adaptation communications, which include their priorities, plans, and actions to enhance adaptive capacity, strengthen resilience, and reduce vulnerability to climate change.

UNCTAD work on climate change impacts and adaptation for ports and coastal transport infrastructure

With an estimated 80 per cent of the volume of world trade carried by sea, international shipping and ports provide crucial linkages in global supply chains and are essential to enable all countries, including those that are landlocked, to access global markets. Ports are likely to be affected directly and indirectly by climatic changes, such as rising sea levels, extreme weather events and rising temperatures, with broader implications for international trade and for the development prospects of the most vulnerable nations, in particular the least developed countries and small island developing States. Given the strategic role of seaports and of other key transport infrastructure as part of the global trading system and the potential for climate-related delays and disruptions across global supply chains, enhancing the climate resilience of key transport infrastructure is a matter of strategic economic importance and one in respect of which UNCTAD research and technical assistance work, as well as the outcomes of a series of UNCTAD expert meetings since 2008, have helped to raise awareness and advance the international debate (For further information, see https://unctad.org/ttl/legal).

Recent UNCTAD work in support of climate change adaptation for coastal transport infrastructure has included technical assistance and capacity-building with a focus on key coastal transport infrastructure in Caribbean small island developing States, using innovative methodological approaches (for further information and full documentation, see https://SIDSport-ClimateAdapt.unctad.org; see also chapter 2, box 2.1). Key project outcomes include the assessment of potential operational disruptions and marine inundation risk to eight coastal international airports and seaports of Jamaica and Saint Lucia under different climate scenarios, as well as a transferable methodology to assist in adaptation planning for small island developing States in the Caribbean and beyond.

Some of the main substantive findings and technical details of the methodology developed under the project were presented and discussed in a peer-reviewed scientific paper (Monioudi et. al, 2018) and have helped inform the Panel 1.5 degrees report (Intergovernmental Panel on Climate Change, 2018), highlighting substantial increases in risk to small island developing States' critical coastal transportation infrastructure from climate changed-induced marine inundation as early as in the 2030s, unless further climate change adaptation is undertaken. Relevant substantive findings are also reflected as part of the United Nations report World Economic Situation and Prospects (United Nations, 2019a, chapter 2, pp.75–76; see also UNCTAD, 2018b).

UNCTAD has also published the findings of a port industry survey on climate change impacts and adaptation (Asariotis et al., 2017), designed in collaboration with global port industry associations and other experts. The survey aimed to improve the understanding of weather- and climate-related impacts on ports, identify data availability and information needs, and determine current levels of resilience and preparedness among ports. Although the majority of respondents had been affected by weather- or climate-related events, including by extremes, the study revealed important gaps in terms of relevant information available to seaports of all sizes and across regions, with implications for effective climate risk assessment and adaptation planning.

The important trade-related implications of weather- and climate-related extreme events were also highlighted by UNCTAD at the twenty-fourth session of the Conference of the Parties (UNCTAD, 2018b), in an online article (UNCTAD, 2018c) and as part of an interactive discussion that was co-organized with the International Trade Centre and the United Nations Office for Disaster Risk Reduction as part of the International Day for Disaster Reduction 2018 (see UNCTAD, 2018d), focusing on the need to reduce economic losses from disasters. Most recently, relevant UNCTAD work included an ad hoc expert meeting on climate change adaptation for international transport in preparing for the future, held in Geneva, Switzerland, on 16 and 17 April 2019. The meeting brought together technical experts, key industry stakeholders and a number of international organizations, with an aim to identify effective ways to support climate change adaptation action, resilience- and capacity-building across closely interlinked transport modes and global supply chains, and to develop policy recommendations to help inform the United Nations Climate Action Summit of September 2019. It also aimed to contribute towards progress in advancing the 2030 Agenda for Sustainable Development and explore options for an informal international transport adaptation forum (for more information and material relating to the meeting, see https://unctad.org/en/pages/MeetingDetails.aspx?meetingid=2092).

UNCTAD work on climate change mitigation and related aspects of sustainable freight transport

Since its inception, UNCTAD has been contributing to the advancement of the sustainable transport agenda, including maritime transport. Relevant areas of intervention include promoting blue growth, sustainability in ports, and low-carbon and clean shipping. More recently, building on the growing international momentum on global sustainability and climate action, UNCTAD intensified its efforts to ensure that maritime transport effectively integrates the triple bottom-line principle aimed at striking the right balance between the economic, social and environmental objectives of the sector.

A key development in 2018 was the agreement with other United Nations agencies with a mandate in the field of transport for UNCTAD to act as the lead organization representing the United Nations system at relevant deliberations under the global Sustainable Mobility for All Initiative. This reflects a recognition of the role of UNCTAD in promoting the sustainable transport and shipping portfolio, as well as its ability to leverage its extensive network of transport sustainability-minded partners.

Recent work in the field include the UNCTAD Multi-year Expert Meeting on Transport, Trade Logistics and Trade Facilitation held in Geneva in November 2018 under the theme "Sustainable freight transport in support of the 2030 Agenda for Sustainable Development". The meeting provided a platform for policy dialogue and expert discussions that clarified the strategic importance of sustainable freight transportation, including maritime transport, in achieving the 2030 Agenda. It also provided an opportunity to collaborate with the World Bank and other partners driving the Carbon Pricing Leadership Coalition, whose main objective is to help the shipping sector in its transition to energy-efficient, clean and low-carbon shipping.

Under the overall theme "Challenges and opportunities of global climate policy, including potential market-based mechanisms applied to international shipping", the panel discussions of the meeting brought together experts and executives from industry, academia, development banks, civil society and government, including from small island developing States. Discussions helped inform the state of play of climate discussions at IMO and outline a possible way forward to decarbonizing the maritime transport sector. The meeting underscored the importance of international shipping for world trade; the shipping and climate change nexus, the need to decarbonize international shipping and the IMO plan; and operational, technical and policy aspects of decarbonization in international shipping. Importantly, the meeting emphasized the perspective of developing countries and the potential implications of some market-based measures on the transport and trade of these countries, in particular small island developing States.

In parallel, UNCTAD disseminated and, in some cases, applied, various tools and instruments that had been developed under a technical assistance project on building capacities of developing countries to shift towards sustainable freight transport. These include a methodology to assess gaps and strengthen the capacity to design, develop, and implement sustainable freight transport and finance strategies (UNCTAD Sustainable Freight Transport Framework); a training and capacity-building package consisting of training modules, case studies, a compilation of good practices and useful knowledge products and resources; and a web portal that facilitates information sharing and partnership-building.

Concrete examples of UNCTAD assistance being deployed and resulting in tangible outcomes include capacity-building activities delivered in small island developing States of the Caribbean. These activities and the supporting planning and decision-making tools made available to the beneficiaries have helped enhance the capacities of transport stakeholders in these regions and enable them to develop and implement sustainable freight transport strategies.

This work continues and complements the long-standing support of UNCTAD to small island developing States that seeks to address the unique sustainability challenges arising from their heightened economic, social and environmental vulnerability. This is also illustrated by the active contribution of the Organization to the 2014 Third International Conference on Small Island Developing States, including through a substantive report entitled "Closing the Distance: Partnerships for Sustainable and Resilient Transport Systems in Small Island Developing States" (UNCTAD, 2014), as well as the UNCTAD special programme on small island developing States.

United Nations Decade of Ocean Science for Sustainable Development, 2021–2030

To enhance the knowledge and understanding of the linkages between the ocean and climate, more investment in ocean research, monitoring and observation will be needed. The upcoming Decade of Ocean Science for Sustainable Development, 2021–2030 proclaimed by the United Nations General Assembly (https://en.unesco.org/ocean-decade/resources), which was also the subject of the twentieth meeting of the United Nations Open-ended Informal Consultative Process on Oceans and the Law of the Sea, on 10–14 June 2019 (www.un.org/depts/los/consultative_process/consultative_process.htm), could help in this respect, and also mobilize action and support by Governments. Its implementation will be coordinated by the Intergovernmental Oceanographic Commission of the United Nations Educational, Scientific and Cultural Organization (www.ioc-unesco.org/). In September 2019, the Intergovernmental Panel on Climate Change is expected to finalize the Special Report on the Ocean and Cryosphere in a Changing Climate. Yet, much more needs to be done to strengthen the linkages between ocean-related action and climate-related processes.

With respect to international maritime transport which, as already noted, accounts for over 80 per cent of global merchandise trade (by volume), ocean science plays an import role in providing data and information required to ensure the safety of navigation, effectively monitor compliance with environmental regulations and respond to ship-source marine pollution incidents, among others. In addition, ocean science will be key in developing effective measures for the purposes of coastal protection and coastal zone management, as well as for climate-risk assessment, adaptation and resilience-building for seaports and other coastal transport infrastructure.

> Ocean science will be key in developing effective measures for the purposes of coastal protection and coastal zone management, as well as for climate-risk assessment, adaptation and resilience-building for seaports and other coastal transport infrastructure.

UNCTAD has been highlighting the importance of scientific data and evidence-based information in the context of climate change impacts and adaptation for critical coastal transport infrastructure, as well as in the context of disaster risk reduction and response (see above). Among others, ocean science and related human capacity-building, in particular at the local level, have an important role to play in adapting critical transport infrastructure and services to the impacts of climate variability and change and in enhancing their overall climate and disaster-risk resilience. Relevant scientific data are necessary, in particular, for monitoring and early warning systems for effective disaster risk reduction and management and effective emergency response; as well as forecasting and effective risk- and vulnerability assessment, to improve levels of preparedness and help take appropriate adaptation response measures.

4. Sendai Framework for Disaster Risk Reduction 2015–2030

The Sendai Framework for Disaster Risk Reduction 2015–2030 is an important agreement, adopted in 2015, in the context of the post-2015 sustainable development agenda. It is a 15-year voluntary agreement that recognizes that the State has the lead role in reducing disaster risk but that responsibility should be shared among other stakeholders, including local government and the private sector.

With regard to its scope, the Framework applies to the risk of small-scale and large-scale, frequent and infrequent, sudden and slow-onset disasters, caused by natural or human-made hazards, as well as related environmental, technological and biological hazards and risks. It aims to guide the multi-hazard management of disaster risk in development at all levels, within and across all sectors.

The aim of the Framework is to achieve the substantial reduction of disaster risk and losses in lives, livelihoods and health and in the economic, physical, social, cultural and environmental assets of people, businesses, communities and countries over the next 15 years. The goal of the Framework is to "prevent new and reduce existing disaster risk through the implementation of integrated and inclusive economic, structural, legal, social, health, cultural, educational, environmental, technological, political and institutional measures that prevent and reduce hazard exposure and vulnerability to disaster, increase preparedness for response and recovery, and thus strengthen resilience" (paragraph 17).

The Framework outlines seven targets and four priorities for action to prevent new disaster risks and reduce existing ones. The seven global targets (paragraph 18), are as follows:

- Substantially reduce global disaster mortality by 2030, aiming to lower the average per 100,000 global mortality rate in the decade 2020–2030, compared with the period 2005–2015.
- Significantly decrease the number of affected people globally by 2030, aiming to lower the average global figure per 100,000 in the decade 2020–2030, compared with the period 2005–2015.
- Diminish direct economic loss caused by disasters in relation to global GDP by 2030.
- Greatly reduce disaster damage to critical infrastructure and the disruption of basic services such as health and educational facilities, including by developing their resilience by 2030.
- Substantially increase the number of countries with national and local disaster risk reduction strategies by 2020.
- Considerably enhance international cooperation with developing countries through adequate and sustainable support to complement their national actions for implementation of the Framework by 2030.
- Significantly improve the availability of, and access to multi-hazard early warning systems and disaster risk information and assessments to people by 2030.

The four priorities for action (paragraph 20) are as follows: understanding disaster risk; strengthening disaster risk governance to manage disaster risk; investing in disaster reduction for resilience; and enhancing disaster preparedness for effective response to "build back better" through recovery, rehabilitation and reconstruction.

The United Nations Office for Disaster Risk Reduction has been tasked with supporting the implementation, follow-up and review of the Sendai Framework.[15] As noted previously, UNCTAD in 2018 highlighted the important trade-related implications of extreme weather- and climate-related events as part of an interactive discussion (UNCTAD, 2018d), co-organized with the United Nations Office for Disaster Risk Reduction and the International Trade Centre in connection with the International Day for Disaster Reduction 2018, focusing on the need to reduce economic losses caused by disasters.

5. Tackling ship-source pollution

The role of the ocean as a prominent factor in stabilizing climate and supporting life and human well-being, and as a resource that needs to be protected and supported, cannot be overemphasized. However, the first world ocean assessment found that much of the ocean is now seriously degraded, with changes and losses in the structure, function and benefits from marine systems (UNEP, 2016a). In addition, as the human population grows towards the expected 9.7 billion by 2050 (United Nations, 2019b), the impact of multiple stressors on the ocean is projected to increase.

Particularly relevant in the context of sustainable maritime transport, ship-source pollution control and coastal zone management, is Sustainable Development Goal 14, Conserve and sustainably use the oceans, seas and marine resources for sustainable development. Since the adoption of the 2030 Agenda, action for the implementation of this goal has been taken in various areas of ocean governance, although much remains to be done. In addition to sustainable fisheries management, which will not be the subject of analysis here, some relevant areas where action has recently been taken or is under way are as follows: the reduction of ship-source pollution and protection of the environment by implementing the new IMO 2020 sulphur limit; ballast water management; means of dealing with liability for the shipment of hazardous and noxious substances; pollution from plastics and microplastics; and the conservation of coastal and marine areas, including in areas beyond national jurisdiction.

It is worthwhile recalling that sustainable and resilient transport is key to sustainable development and, therefore, is among the cross-cutting issues of relevance to progress in achieving several Sustainable Development Goals and targets. These include not only Goal 14, but also, for instance, Goal 1, End poverty in all its forms everywhere, in particular target 1.5, Build the resilience of the poor and those in vulnerable situations and reduce their exposure and vulnerability

15 For progress in implementation by global target and country, see https://sendaimonitor.unisdr.org.

to climate-related extreme events and other economic, social and environmental shocks and disasters; Goal 9, Build resilient infrastructure, promote inclusive and sustainable industrialization and foster innovation; and Goal 13, Take urgent action to combat climate change and its impacts.

Implementing the new 2020 sulphur limit of the International Maritime Organization

The new 0.50 per cent limit on sulphur ships' fuel oil, down from 3.50 per cent, will be in force from 1 January 2020. Yet, in designated emission control areas,[16] the limit will remain even lower, at 0.10 per cent. With shipping emissions associated with hundreds of thousands of fatalities and millions of cases of illness at the global level (*Independent*, 2018), the consistent implementation of the global sulphur limit for all ships is expected to bring positive results for human health and the environment, particularly for populations living close to ports and major shipping routes.

In order to support consistent implementation and compliance and provide a means for effective enforcement by States, particularly port State control, IMO in October 2018 adopted an additional amendment to MARPOL 73/78 that will prohibit not just the use, but also the carriage of non-compliant fuel oil for combustion purposes for propulsion or operation on board a ship, unless the ship is fitted with a scrubber, which is an exhaust gas cleaning system. This amendment is expected to enter into force on 1 March 2020, but it does affect the date of entry into force of the 0.50 per cent limit from 1 January 2020. Also, a comprehensive set of guidelines to support the consistent implementation of the lower 0.50 per cent limit on sulphur in ships' fuel oil, and related MARPOL amendments were approved (IMO, 2019d). (For more information about the effects of the IMO sulphur 2020 limit on the shipping industry, see chapter 2, section D).

Enforcement, compliance with and monitoring of the new sulphur limit is the responsibility of States party to MARPOL 73/78, annex VI. Ships found not to be in compliance may be detained by port State control inspectors, and/or be imposed sanctions for violations, including fines determined by local law where the violation occurs, or the law of the flag State. In the light of the implications for the required fuel oil quality, relevant industry associations have recommended that shipowners consider the relevant charter-party terms to protect their position with respect to potential fines and/or charter-party disputes. Both BIMCO and the International Association of Independent Tanker Owners have drafted relevant bunker 2020 clauses (www.standard-club.com/media/2767972/bimco-2020-marine-fuel-sulphur-content-clause-for-time-charter-parties-1.pdf; www.intertanko.com/info-centre/model-clauses-library/templateclausearticle/intertanko-bunker-compliance-clause-for-time-charterparties) that deal with these MARPOL 73/78 regulations compliance, both equally valid and ready for use in time charters being negotiated now. (For more information, see www.bimco.org/ships-ports-and-voyage-planning/environment-protection/2020-sulphur-cap/contractual-issues-for-scrubbers/time-charter-issues/additional-clauses.)

[16] The four emission control areas are as follows: the Baltic Sea area; the North Sea area; the North American area (covering designated coastal areas of Canada and the United States); and the United States Caribbean Sea area (around Puerto Rico and the United States Virgin Islands).

Ballast water management

The Ballast Water Management Convention, 2004 (as of 31 July 2019: 81 State parties, representing 80.76 per cent of the gross tonnage of the world's merchant fleet), has been in force since September 2017. The Convention aims to prevent the risk of the introduction and proliferation of non-native species following the discharge of untreated ballast water from ships. This is considered one of the four greatest threats to the world's oceans and a major threat to biodiversity, which, if not addressed, can have extremely severe public health-related and environmental and economic impacts (http://globallast.imo.org; UNCTAD, 2011b, 2015). From the date of entry into force, ships have been required to manage their ballast water to meet standards referred to as D-1 and D-2; the former requires ships to exchange and release at least 95 per cent of ballast water by volume far away from a coast; the latter raises the restriction to a specified maximum amount of viable organisms allowed to be discharged, limiting the discharge of specified microbes harmful to human health.

Currently, the regulatory focus is on the effective and uniform implementation of the Ballast Water Management Convention, 2004, and on an experience-building phase associated with it, with a focus on gathering data on its application (see IMO, 2018d, 2019d).

Hazardous and noxious substances

The International Convention on Liability and Compensation for Damage in Connection with the Carriage of Hazardous and Noxious Substances by Sea, 1996, as amended by its 2010 Protocol, requires accession by at least 12 States, representing at least 40 million tons of contributing cargo to enter into force. Until 31 July 2019, the 2010 Convention had been ratified by only five States (Canada, Denmark, Norway, South Africa and Turkey), bringing the Convention closer to its entry into force. The Convention covers liability and compensation in the event of an incident involving hazardous goods. With the number of ships carrying cargoes of hazardous and noxious substances growing steadily and more than 200 million tons of chemicals traded annually, other States are encouraged to consider becoming parties to the Convention as well.

The Convention will help cover a broad gap in the global liability and compensation framework: while a comprehensive and robust international liability and compensation regime is in place with respect to oil pollution from tankers (International Oil Pollution Compensation Fund regime),[17] as well as with respect to bunker oil pollution from ships other than tankers (International Convention on Civil Liability for Bunker Oil Pollution Damage, 2001), this is presently not the case for hazardous and noxious substances, which may cause marine pollution, as well as significant personal injury (UNCTAD, 2012b; 2013, pp.110–111). Administrative preparations for the setting up of the hazardous and noxious substances Fund, required under the International Convention on Liability and Compensation for Damage in Connection with the Carriage of Hazardous and Noxious Substances by Sea, as amended by the 2010 Protocol thereto, are under way. Preliminary preparations have also been made for the first session of the Assembly on Hazardous and Noxious Substances, which will be convened in accordance with article 43 of the Convention, when all entry-into-force criteria of the 2010 Protocol to the Convention have been met (IMO, 2019b).

Marine pollution from plastics and microplastics

The plastic pollution crisis, including microplastics, in the oceans is already known, and has been receiving increased public attention (see https://www.cleanseas.org/). It was also the topic of the seventeenth session of the United Nations Open-ended Informal Consultative Process on Oceans and the Law of the Sea in 2016 (www.un.org/depts/los/consultative_process/consultative_process.htm). It has been recognized that marine debris in general, and plastics and microplastics in particular, give rise to some of the greatest environmental concerns of all times, along with climate change, ocean acidification and loss of biodiversity. These directly affect the sustainable development aspirations of developing countries and small island developing States in particular, which, as custodians of vast areas of oceans and seas, are disproportionately affected by the effects of such pollution.

Marine plastic debris and microplastics are already harming many marine species by ingestion and entanglement and are likely to have an impact on human health in ways not yet fully understood. The recognition of these threats has finally brought the topic onto the international agenda (Finska, 2018). For many States, such pollution is also having a direct economic impact, and pollution from land-based activities is the biggest source of the problem. This trend is linked to a global increase of production and consumption of plastic in recent decades, combined with insufficient waste management infrastructure and lack of political urgency about the problem, which has caused a severe deficiency in the capacity to collect and safely manage all plastic waste (Norwegian Academy of International Law, 2018).

Target 14.1 of the 2030 Sustainable Development Agenda calls for the prevention and significant reduction of marine pollution of all kinds, in particular from land-based activities, including marine debris and nutrient pollution, by 2025, while target 14.2 calls for sustainably managing and protecting marine and coastal ecosystems, by 2020, to avoid significant adverse impacts, including by strengthening their resilience. Given the cross-cutting nature of the problem, other related targets include 11.6 (reduce the adverse per capita environmental impact of cities including through municipal and other waste management), 12.4 (by 2020 achieve the environmentally sound management of chemicals and all wastes throughout their life cycle), and 12.5 (substantially reduce waste generation through prevention, reduction, recycling and reuse).

Plastic pollution management is a global transboundary environmental issue that needs to be regulated internationally. Several conventions and other instruments have already or could potentially be taking steps to address certain aspects of plastic pollution. However, none of these is specifically designed to prevent increasing plastic pollution, or to comprehensively manage the current degree of plastic pollution. Relevant legal instruments worth noting include the following: globally binding conventions dealing with sea-based sources of marine litter; multilateral environmental conventions addressing trade in hazardous waste and persistent organic pollutants; and other programmes and partnerships.

Globally binding conventions dealing with sea-based sources of marine litter

With regard to sea-based sources of maritime litter, four globally binding conventions are of particular relevance. These are the United Nations Convention on the Law of the Sea, 1982; the International Convention for the Prevention of Pollution from Ships, 1973, as modified by the Protocol of 1978 (MARPOL 73/78); the Convention on the Prevention of Marine Pollution by Dumping of Wastes and Other Matter, 1972 and the 1996 Protocol thereto; and the Convention on Biological Diversity, 1992.

The United Nations Convention on the Law of the Sea, 1982 is the framework convention governing the use of the world's oceans.[18] While it does not specifically address pollution of the marine environment by plastic waste, the Convention contains several provisions applicable to marine plastic pollution. Thus, for instance, article 194.1 requires States to "prevent, reduce and control pollution of the marine environment from any

[17] International Convention on Civil Liability for Oil Pollution Damage, 1969, and its 1992 Protocol and International Convention on the Establishment of an International Fund for Compensation for Oil Pollution Damage, 1971 and its 1992 and 2003 Protocols.

[18] The status of ratification of the Convention can be found at https://treaties.un.org/Pages/ViewDetailsIII.aspx?src=TREATY&mtdsg_no=XXI-6&chapter=21&Temp=mtdsg3&clang=_en.

source, using for this purpose the best practicable means at their disposal and in accordance with their capabilities". Article 207 requires States to "adopt laws and regulations to prevent, reduce and control pollution of the marine environment from land-based sources" and specifies that "States, acting especially through competent international organizations or diplomatic conference [sic], shall endeavour to establish global and regional rules, standards and recommended practices and procedures to prevent, reduce and control pollution of the marine environment from land-based sources".

MARPOL 73/78 is one of the most important international marine environmental conventions adopted by IMO, aiming to minimize pollution of the oceans and seas, including dumping, oil and air pollution.[19] Annex V to the Convention, entitled Regulations for the Prevention of Pollution by Garbage from Ships, specifically prohibits the discharge of plastics from ships.

In October 2018, the Marine Environment Protection Committee adopted an action plan to address marine plastic litter from ships, intended to contribute to the global solution for preventing marine plastic litter entering the oceans by means of ship-based activities. Areas of action include the following: reducing marine plastic litter generated from, and retrieved by, fishing vessels; lessening shipping's contribution to marine plastic litter; improving the effectiveness of port reception and facilities and treatment in the reduction of marine plastic litter; enhancing public awareness, education and seafarer training; broadening the understanding of the contribution of ships to marine plastic litter; strengthening international cooperation; and targeting technical cooperation and capacity-building activities (IMO, 2018d, annex 10). In May 2019, the Committee approved the terms of reference for an IMO study on marine plastic litter from ships to focus on information on the contribution of all ships to marine plastic litter and on the storage, delivery and reception of plastic waste from and collected by ships (IMO, 2019d). An earlier IMO resolution adopted in 2017, had recommended that "all shipowners and operators should minimize taking on board material that could become garbage" (IMO, 2017c).

The 1996 Protocol to the Convention on the Prevention of Marine Pollution by Dumping of Wastes and Other Matter, 1972 prohibits the dumping and incineration at sea of wastes, including plastics. It establishes reporting requirements and compliance procedures and mechanisms for its Parties.[20] Recent efforts include the investigation of permit requirements to address plastics in sewage waste and dredged material dumped at sea (IMO, 2016).

The Convention on Biological Diversity, 1992 has as its objective the conservation of biological diversity, the sustainable use of its components and the fair and equitable sharing of the benefits arising from the utilization of genetic resources.[21] The Conference of the Parties to the Convention issued a decision on addressing the impacts of marine debris on marine and coastal biodiversity, urging parties "to develop and implement measures, policies and instruments to prevent the discard, disposal, loss or abandonment of any persistent, manufactured or processed solid material in the marine and coastal environment" (United Nations Environment Programme (UNEP), 2016b, paragraph 8).

Multilateral environmental conventions addressing trade in hazardous waste and persistent organic pollutants

Two multilateral environmental conventions focus specifically on trade in hazardous waste and persistent organic pollutants: the Basel Convention on the Control of Transboundary Movements of Hazardous Wastes and Their Disposal, 1989 and the Stockholm Convention on Persistent Organic Pollutants, 2001.

The main objective of the Basel Convention is to protect human health and the environment against the adverse effects of hazardous wastes.[22] According to the definition in article 2.1 of the Convention, "wastes" are "substances or objects which are disposed of or are intended to be disposed of or are required to be disposed of by the provisions of national law". Article 2.3 of the Convention defines "transboundary movement", while article 1 provides for certain categories of wastes which are considered to be "hazardous wastes" for the purposes of the Convention. Plastic waste would not appear to fall under the category of "hazardous waste" or "other wastes" under this Convention.

However, in their recent decision 13/17, the parties to the Basel Convention agreed to consider relevant options available to further address marine plastic pollution and develop a proposal for further action within the scope of the Basel Convention for its Conference of the Parties (see UNEP, 2018a). Among these were two amendments aimed at reclassifying solid plastic waste to remove the presumption that it is non-hazardous (annex IX) and to list it among the wastes requiring prior informed consent (annex II), which in turn would provide transparency on transboundary shipments of scrap plastic. Parties are also considering the establishment of a partnership on plastic wastes, which would produce non-binding guidelines on plastic waste management.

The Stockholm Convention on Persistent Organic Pollutants, 2001 aims to protect human health and

[19] The status of ratification of the Convention can be found at www.imo.org/en/About/Conventions/StatusOfConventions/Pages/Default.aspx.

[20] The status of ratification of the Convention can be found at www.imo.org/en/About/Conventions/StatusOfConventions/Pages/Default.aspx.

[21] The status of ratification of the Convention can be found at https://www.cbd.int/information/parties.shtml.

[22] The status of ratification of the Convention can be found at www.basel.int/Countries/StatusofRatifications/PartiesSignatories/tabid/4499/Default.aspx.

the environment from such pollutants.[23] It can have the potential to regulate the production, use and disposal of additives used in the manufacture of plastics, to the extent that they are persistent organic pollutants. However, its role would be limited to such pollutants in greening the lifecycle of a range of plastic polymers to promote safer design and increase rates of recycling and reuse (UNEP, 2017, pp.17, 32–22, 64–65). Along with the Basel Convention, it also addresses the re-entry of regulated chemicals onto the market through the recycling of products that contain such pollutants.

Regional Seas programmes

The 18 Regional Seas programmes[24] dealing with land-based sources of pollution vary in scope and effectiveness. In general, they are fragmented in their legal structure, and in some cases, rely solely on non-binding instruments. Nevertheless, they serve as important regional tools to strengthen regional cooperation and address region-specific issues. To some extent, some of the gaps regarding plastic pollution have been narrowed with the introduction of action plans but again these are varied in their approaches and methodologies (UNEP, 2017, pp. 49–62).

Addressing gaps in the existing regulatory framework

Despite the existence of the above-mentioned instruments, significant gaps remain in the governance structure of marine plastic pollution. The global regulatory framework is based on the United Nations Convention on the Law of the Sea, 1982; MARPOL 73/78; and the Convention on the Prevention of Marine Pollution by Dumping of Wastes and Other Matter, 1972 and the 1996 Protocol thereto. Although the framework should in principle be capable of preventing marine litter, including the discharge of plastic waste into the marine environment, there are challenges in implementation and compliance that need to be urgently addressed (UNEP, 2017). For instance, MARPOL 73/78, annex V, contains exemptions based on vessel size, excluding most fishing vessels, that are responsible for abandoned, lost or otherwise discarded fishing gear (UNEP, 2018b).

There are no global agreements that specifically prevent marine plastic litter and microplastics or provide a comprehensive approach to managing the lifecycle of plastics. Further, the regional framework is fragmented in its legal structure in general and in addressing land-based sources of pollution in particular. The Convention on Biological Diversity, 1992 principally applies to the conservation of biological diversity and does not directly address pollution of the marine environment. The Basel Convention, 1989 focuses on plastics in the waste phase, mainly regulating the transboundary movement of plastic waste. However, it establishes a general duty for the parties to the Convention to reduce the generation of plastic waste, providing non-binding guidelines in this regard. The Stockholm Convention, 2001 does not regulate all chemical additives used in plastic products. It provides protection for a limited number of persistent organic pollutants used in the manufacture of plastics; however, the rapid innovation of plastics, particularly in the application of packaging, and the length of time it takes to amend the Convention, make this an unsuitable instrument to keep up with industry trends (UNEP, 2017). In addition, none of the instruments is specifically designed to prevent and minimize marine plastic pollution, particularly from land-based sources. As a result, most sources of plastic pollution in the ocean remain unregulated. For instance, only 9 out of 18 regional seas conventions and action plans have adopted protocols related to land-based sources and activities; this is problematic, since most marine plastic litter originates on land (UNEP, 2018b).

Further, national legal frameworks do not comprehensively address the issue. At times, it has even been observed that more creative and effective measures have been taken at the domestic level by local governments and non-State actors, rather than by central governments. A recent article focusing on the case studies of two countries in Asia suggests that there is a need to create specific marine plastic pollution laws or strengthen existing national laws, in particular waste management and recycling laws; build awareness and educate consumers on plastic consumption habits, reduce plastic pollution as part of corporations' business practices and forge multi-stakeholder and cross-border partnerships to combat plastic pollution. If taken altogether, such governance efforts are likely to be more effective (García et al., 2019).

With regard to the way forward, an assessment by UNEP (2017) suggests that one possible approach would be to strengthen current efforts and focus on each aspect of the lifecycle of plastics and combine voluntary and binding measures to address the issue.

Conservation and sustainable use of marine biodiversity of areas beyond national jurisdiction: Legally binding instrument under the United Nations Convention on the Law of the Sea, 1982

The use of the marine environment and its resources, including in areas beyond national jurisdiction is increasingly expanding.[25] For instance, shipping activity has increased and so have its environmental

[23] The status of ratification of the Convention can be found at www.pops.int/Countries/StatusofRatifications/PartiesandSignatoires/tabid/4500/Default.aspx.

[24] See www.unenvironment.org/explore-topics/oceans-seas/what-we-do/working-regional-seas/regional-seas-programmes.

[25] Maritime zones under the United Nations Convention on the Law of the Sea, 1982 include the following: the territorial sea, extending up to 12 nautical miles from the baselines (part II, section 2, article 3); exclusive economic zones, extending from the edge of the territorial sea to 200 nautical miles from the baseline (part V. article 57); the continental shelf, the natural prolongation of land territory to the outer edge of the continental margin, or 200 nautical miles from the baselines, whichever is greater (part VI, article 76); and areas beyond

impacts, including marine and air pollution, litter and the introduction of invasive species. In addition, other marine activities, such as high-seas fishing, seabed mining, submarine cables, marine scientific research, bioprospecting[26] and the development of commercial products, could all have significant environmental impacts, including on marine ecosystems. Moreover, greenhouse gas emissions, climate change and ocean acidification are placing further pressure on marine ecosystems, reducing their resilience and compounding existing impacts (The National Academies Press, 2010). Areas beyond national jurisdiction hold unique oceanographic and biological features and play a role in climate regulation. They provide seafood, raw materials, and genetic and medicinal resources, which are of increasing commercial interest and hold promise for the development of new drugs to treat infectious diseases that are a major threat to human health. From the perspective of developing countries, access and benefit sharing, as well as the conservation of marine genetic resources, are of particular importance in this context (UNCTAD, 2018e).

Sustainable Development Goal target 14.5 sets the deadline for conserving at least 10 per cent of coastal and marine areas by 2020. Prior to the expiry of the deadline, this target should be enhanced by international consensus to conserve at least 30 per cent of coastal and marine areas by 2030 through well monitored and managed ecologically representative and well-connected systems of marine protected areas and other effective area-based conservation measures (The Pew Charitable Trusts, 2018).

The United Nations Convention on the Law of the Sea, 1982 sets forth the rights and obligations of States regarding the use of the oceans, their resources and the protection of the marine and coastal environment; however, it does not expressly refer to marine biodiversity or to exploration and exploitation of resources within the water column in areas beyond national jurisdiction. In the absence of a specific international legal framework regulating related issues, negotiations have been taking place under the auspices of the United Nations towards the establishment of an international legally binding instrument under the United Nations Convention on the Law of the Sea on the conservation and sustainable use of marine biological diversity of areas beyond national jurisdiction. Three sessions of the intergovernmental conference on the issue have taken place, the most recent being in August 2019.

Marine genetic resources in areas beyond national jurisdiction are an important priority, including for developing countries, given the economic value that can be generated from their exploitation and the potential expansion of economic activities in coastal and offshore areas, sustainably and in line with the Sustainable Development Goals. However, differences currently exist between developed and developing countries. According to a recent study, players located or headquartered in 10 developed countries registered 98 per cent of the patents related to genes of marine origin, making possible their economic exploitation, and 165 countries were unrepresented (Blasiak et al., 2018). These findings highlight the importance of inclusive participation by all States in international negotiations and the urgency of clarifying the legal regime around access and benefit sharing of marine genetic resources. Therefore, in addition to aiming to achieve consensus on relevant complex substantive and procedural issues, negotiations for the new legal instrument will need to ensure a wide participation of all States, especially developing countries.

At the three sessions of the intergovernmental conference held so far, discussions reflected the elements of a package agreed in 2011, namely, marine genetic resources; area-based management tools, including marine protected areas; environmental impact assessments; and capacity-building and marine technology transfer. During the first session of the conference, discussions on the main issues largely reiterated familiar positions that had been presented during earlier sessions of a preparatory committee established by General Assembly resolution 69/292. Work was still needed on finding common solutions, particularly among options based on common heritage versus the high seas, and global versus regional approaches.

During the second session of the conference, participants continued their deliberations on the basis of the conference President's aid to discussions, structured along the lines of the elements of the 2011 package. Convergence was achieved in a few areas, such as the need to promote coherence, complementarity and synergies with other frameworks and bodies; benefit sharing as part of conservation and sustainable use; and environmental impact assessments being mutually supportive with other instruments. However, there is still no agreement about other important issues, including the scope of the instrument; whether benefit sharing would be carried out on a monetary or non-monetary basis; and the overarching principles governing the future instrument, particularly the common heritage of humankind and the principle of the high seas (International Institute for Sustainable Development Reporting Services, 2019a).

During the third session of the conference, held in August 2019, participants held textual negotiations for the first time on the basis of a zero draft containing treaty language developed by the President of the conference. The draft contained 12 parts, which in addition to the dedicated parts addressing the elements of the package agreed in 2011, included a preamble and general provisions, such as on the use of terms, institutional

national jurisdiction, composed of the "Area" (part I, article 1) and the high seas (part VII, article 86).

26 Bioprospecting is the search for genes in organisms living in extreme environments in areas beyond national jurisdiction.

arrangements and the settlement of disputes (United Nations, 2019c). Negotiating on a zero draft allowed delegations to move away from restating general views towards making concrete textual proposals. However, divergence still remained on the substance of certain provisions, as well as on the scope of the new convention. Discussions are expected to continue during the fourth session of the conference, to be held from 23 March to 3 April 2020, at United Nations Headquarters in New York, United States (International Institute for Sustainable Development Reporting Services, 2019b; United Nations, 2019d).

C. OTHER LEGAL AND REGULATORY DEVELOPMENTS AFFECTING TRANSPORTATION

1. Seafarers' issues

According to the International Chamber of Shipping, the worldwide population of seafarers serving on internationally trading merchant ships is estimated at 1,647,500. Most seafarers come from developing countries, with China, the Philippines, Indonesia, the Russian Federation and Ukraine estimated to be the five largest supply countries for all seafarers (www.ics-shipping.org/shipping-facts/shipping-and-world-trade/global-supply-and-demand-for-seafarers).

At its 106th session in March 2019, the IMO Legal Committee expressed concern about the growing number of cases of abandonment of seafarers and action needed to address this issue. An update on the latest cases was provided, including those which had been successfully resolved, following intervention by the IMO Secretariat, relevant flag States, port States, seafarers' States, the International Labour Organization and others. As at 31 December 2018, 366 abandonment incidents were listed in the database since its establishment in 2004, affecting 4,866 seafarers. Of those incidents, 175 cases had been resolved, 77 cases had been disputed, and 52 cases were inactive. There are still 52 unresolved cases. From 2011 to 2016, the number of cases per year ranged from 12 to 19 (IMO, 2019b). At times, shipowners who do not take their responsibilities seriously and find themselves in financial difficulty abandon seafarers in ports far from home, leaving them without fuel, food, water or medical care and without pay for months. The 2014 amendments to the International Labour Organization Maritime Labour Convention, 2006, which entered into force in January 2017, require shipowners to put in place a financial security system to ensure compensation for seafarers and their families in the event of abandonment, as well as in respect of claims for death or long-term disability due to an occupational injury, illness or hazard. This requirement will help prevent the unfortunate situation of seafarers being stranded in port for long periods when shipowners abandon their crews without paying their wages or repatriating them to their home countries.

The IMO Legal Committee also addressed the fair treatment of seafarers on suspicion of committing maritime crimes. The inadequacy of the current guidelines on fair treatment of seafarers in the event of a maritime accident, adopted in 2006, was highlighted, as the guidelines are limited to the fair treatment of seafarers in the case of a maritime accident and do not adequately address the fair treatment of seafarers detained on suspicion of committing maritime crimes. The establishment of a joint working group consisting of representatives of IMO, the International Labour Organization and the International Transport Workers' Federation to look into the issue was suggested.

2. Fraudulent registration of ships

Following recent reports by several member States on cases concerning the fraudulent use of their flag, the IMO Legal Committee, at its 106th session in March 2019, agreed on a series of measures to prevent unlawful practices associated with the fraudulent registration and fraudulent registries of ships.

Information compiled by the IMO Secretariat on the cases received included the following:

- The registration of ships without the knowledge or approval of the relevant national maritime administration.
- The continuous operation of a ship registry after the contact with the registration company had expired or had otherwise been terminated.
- The submission of fraudulent documentation to IMO, without the knowledge of the cognizant flag State authority, in order to obtain IMO documentation and ship identification numbers.
- The intentional manipulation of automatic identification system data to materially alter a ship's identifying information or to reflect such data pertaining to an entirely different ship.
- The operation of an illegal international ship registry.

Participating in the session, UNCTAD recalled the long-standing history of its fruitful collaboration with IMO, in line with the respective mandates of the two bodies, including the joint negotiation and adoption of the International Convention on Maritime Liens and Mortgages, 1993 and the International Convention on Arrest of Ships, 1999. UNCTAD joined others in expressing concern regarding the growing problem of fraudulent ship registries and noted that addressing fraudulent practices effectively was vital to promoting maritime safety, security and environmental protection. UNCTAD also highlighted that this issue was closely related to the achievement of the Sustainable Development Goals, notably Goals 14 and 16, and reiterated its support for combating unlawful practices associated with fraudulent registration and

registries. UNCTAD further noted that in the interest of achieving relevant public policy objectives, stakeholders, including shippers and charterers, should also have access to information concerning registration and registries (IMO, 2019b).

The Committee supported the development of a comprehensive database of registries in the publicly available contact points module of the IMO Global Integrated Shipping Information System that would contain the names and contact details of the national governmental bodies or authorized/delegated entities in charge of registration of ships, as well as other relevant information.

The Legal Committee also approved recommended best practices to help combat fraudulent registration and registries of ships. Such practices include the following:

- Verifying IMO numbers of vessels when receiving an application for registration.
- Making sure that flag State administration contact point information is up to date.
- Ensuring the application of the requirement for the continuous synopsis record, which is intended to provide an onboard record of a ship's history.
- Recommending that prospective flag States review the United Nations Security Council Sanctions List Search webpage (https://scsanctions.un.org/search).
- Checking the relevant information pertaining to registries of ships in the contact points module of the Global Integrated Shipping Information System.

An intersessional correspondence group was established to further discuss some issues and consider various proposals in more detail. These issues included enhancing capabilities for the detection and reporting of fraudulent registration documentation and working with the IMO Secretariat, member States, port State control authorities, vessel owners and operators, non-governmental organizations and the private sector, including the maritime insurance industry ship brokers and relevant maritime stakeholders.

The Committee also agreed that IMO should work with the United Nations Security Council to establish an easily searchable database by IMO number and name of vessel currently the subject of, or designated pursuant to, Security Council resolutions (IMO, 2019b).

3. Women in shipping: Achieving gender equality

The attainment of equality between women and men, and the elimination of all forms of discrimination against women are fundamental human rights and United Nations values. At the global level, the United Nations has emphasized gender equality over the years, through various instruments, including the 1995 Beijing Declaration, the Millennium Development Goals and the Sustainable Development Goals. With the adoption of the 2030 Agenda for Sustainable Development, world leaders committed "to achieve full and productive employment and decent work for all women and men, including for young people and persons with disabilities, and equal pay for work of equal value" (Goal 8, target 8.5) and "to achieve gender equality and empower all women and girls" (Goal 5) by 2030.

Despite some progress and ongoing efforts to address gender inequality, the global labour force participation rate for women remains low overall – women continue to have fewer career opportunities and earn less than men. Reducing the gender gap in labour force participation could also lead to additional economic gains and increased growth.

With regard to the maritime industry, women still make up a small percentage of the seagoing workforce and are faced with challenges that could hinder their participation in the sector, ranging from overt abuse, to covert discrimination and fundamental barriers. To close the gender gap in the maritime industry and foster gender equality, it is necessary to combat the traditional perceptions of having women at sea, promote career opportunities and ensure appropriate living and working conditions for women in the sector. This requires political and legal action at the international level, accompanied by corresponding action at the national level by all key stakeholders.

Economic benefits of achieving gender equality

According to the International Labour Organization report, World Employment and Social Outlook: Trends 2019 (International Labour Organization, 2019a), gender gaps still remain a pressing challenge facing the world of work. On average, women remain much less likely to participate in the labour market than men. The much lower labour force participation rate of women, which stood at 48 per cent in 2018, compared with 75 per cent for men, means that about three in five of the 3.5 billion people in the global labour force in 2018 were men. An earlier report (International Labour Organization, 2017) estimated that if a goal to reduce the gap in participation rates between men and women by 25 per cent by the year 2025 was realized at the global level, it had the potential to add $5.8 trillion to the global economy, which could also unlock large potential tax revenues. Northern Africa, the Arab States and Southern Asia would see the greatest benefits, given that in these regions the gaps in participation rates between men and women exceed 50 per cent.

According to the United Nations Industrial Development Organization, targeting gender equality and women's economic empowerment is not only important from the perspective of realizing women's rights but is also smart economics. Women are key agents of change, and when women and men are equal, economies grow faster, less people remain in poverty and the overall well-being of people increases. Harnessing women's potential as economic actors, leaders and consumers results in higher levels of industrialization and more sustained growth rates. Global GDP could increase by more than 25 per cent by 2025 if women played the same role in labour markets as men (www.unido.org/our-focus-cross-cutting-services/gender-equality-and-empowerment-women).

Ostry et al. (2018) found that while progress has been made in increasing women's labour force participation in the past 20 years, the pace has been uneven and large gaps remain. Narrowing participation gaps between women and men is likely to bring large economic gains. In addition, reducing female underemployment should yield greater gains than an equivalent increase in male employment: gender diversity brings benefits all its own. The paper supports the view that women bring different skills and ideas to the workplace, which are economically valuable, and women and men complement each other in the production process. Narrowing gender gaps can bring benefits, including a bigger boost to growth. Closing the gender gap could increase GDP by between 10 and 80 per cent, depending on the initial value of women's labour force participation. Men stand to gain from this as well, with higher wages for males, because gender complementarity raises productivity. In turn, as the demand for services rises, driven by economic development and income growth, more women are brought into the labour force. In addition, the growth of the services sector in developing economies should contribute to smaller gender gaps over time.

The World Economic Forum (2017) estimated that if the global gender gap in labour market participation was closed by 25 per cent by 2025, an additional $5.3 trillion would be added to GDP globally. More recently, an International Labour Organization survey of almost 13,000 enterprises in 70 countries found that, at the national level, an increase in female employment is positively associated with GDP growth (International Labour Organization, 2019b).

Gender equality in the maritime industry

Facts and figures

Attention to women in the shipping industry began to increase in conjunction with discussion on the shortage of seafarers and the publication in 1995 of the first Manpower Report by BIMCO and the International Chamber of Shipping. These reports, issued every five years, provide a comprehensive assessment of the global supply of and demand for seafarers, and make predictions for developments in the industry for the next 5 to 10 years. The latest one, issued in 2016, forecasts a serious shortage in the supply of seafarers. According to the report, a combination of factors, including an ageing workforce, lack of skills diversity and the industry's inability to attract young new talent, has led to a labour shortage of about 16,500 officers (2.1 per cent), and by 2025, the world merchant fleet would be needing an additional 147,500 officers (BIMCO, 2016).

It has been recognized that there is a gender gap in the maritime and related industries, including for seafarers, fishers, port operators, port State control officers and government officials, particularly in senior roles, which remain mostly male dominated. It appears that the underrepresentation of women in the maritime industry has not changed much over the past decades. According to the International Transport Workers' Federation (www.itfseafarers.org/en/issues/women-seafarers), only 2 per cent of the world's maritime workforce are women. Women seafarers work mainly in the cruise and ferries sector, often for flags of convenience vessels, which are among the most underpaid and least protected of jobs at sea. Women also tend to be younger, and fewer are officers or in other leadership roles, compared with their male crew mates (Fjærli et al., 2017). Their low number means that women can be subject to discrimination and harassment.

A joint industry survey conducted in 2015 indicates that 40 per cent of women are employed within the cruise sector, whereas the rest work on cargo ships, ferry services, tankers and other vessels (International Maritime Health Association et al., 2015, p. 9). According to 2018 data on global workforce positions in organizations belonging to the Maritime Human Resources Association, 35 per cent of that workforce were women, 52 per cent were men and 13 per cent, unknown. Over 76 per cent of that female workforce have administrative, junior or professional-level occupations. Very few women reach managerial level or above, with just over 10 per cent of those on executive leadership teams being women, and female executives most likely to operate as chief financial officers (Spinnaker Global, 2019).

The Gender, Empowerment and Multi-cultural Crew project (Pike et al., 2017), sponsored by the International Transport Worker's Association Seafarers' Trust, studied welfare and gender issues in three uniquely different maritime nations: China, Nigeria and the United Kingdom. The study found that sexual harassment, abuse and bullying are the key issues faced by women seafarers on board. The mistreatment faced by women, especially in the lower ranks and in the younger age demographic, was similar to that experienced by some vulnerable men and ethnic minorities on board.

Technical skills, education and training

One of the main obstacles relating to the employment of women is their lack of technical skills, particularly in science, technology, engineering and math. A recent study (Microsoft.com, 2018) found that despite the high priority that is placed on such subjects in schools, efforts to expand women's interest and employment in those subject areas, as well as in computer science, are not working as well as intended. This is especially true in technology and engineering. The reasons range from peer pressure to a lack of role models and support from parents and teachers, and a general misperception of careers in science, technology, engineering and math in the real world. But the research also points to ways to better support girls and young women in those subject areas and close this gender gap. These include the following actions: providing teachers with more engaging and relatable curriculum in those subjects, such as three-dimensional and hands-on projects, the kinds of activities that have proven to help retain girls' interest in science, technology, engineering and math in the long term; increasing the number of mentors and role models in those subject areas – including parents – to help build young girls' confidence so that they can succeed in those subjects; and creating inclusive classrooms and workplaces that value their opinions.

As regards maritime education and training, and thanks to efforts by IMO member States, many institutions, including in developing countries, have been increasingly opening their doors to women students. However, such a positive trend would be negated if shipping companies made limited efforts to employ women graduates from such institutions. The biggest challenge for women cadets is often access to ships where they receive onboard training for a total of 12 months to meet the requirements for a certificate of competence based on standards of training, certification and watchkeeping for seafarers. Some women fail to receive a certificate of competence because they are not granted permission to work onboard ships (Kitada and Tansey, 2018).

In one project (Pike et al., 2017), mentoring and training at all levels was considered essential. Throughout the research, lack of training and mentoring were frequently mentioned as contributing to the issues surrounding gender and multicultural crews. The project highlights, inter alia, the importance of raising awareness about the merchant maritime business, particularly to young people of school age, as a vital first step in encouraging more women and men to enter the industry. Providing ship captains and other senior officers with ongoing access to training so that they can adequately respond to any gender-related issues that may arise at sea was also considered important.

Shipping and digitalization

More recently, the board of the International Association of Ports and Harbours announced the allocation of a budgeted fund of $10,000 to develop mentoring programme on women in ports designed to attract, empower and retain female talent in the industry. The programme was launched by the Women's Forum of the Association, which was established in 2012 with the aim to "aspire to advance and empower women in the maritime industry; create a platform for discussing women's issues in the maritime industry, ways to encourage women to join the industry; and to promote training programmes enabling women to better compete for positions at all levels, including those previously not open to women" (www.iaphworldports.org/womens-forum). It will deploy an online system to connect women port professionals with both female and male senior mentors. As the Vice-Chair of the Association stated: "Smart shipping and digitization is set to change the face of port operations. Autonomous vessel operation will require completely different skillsets as well as mindsets. Women port operators such as those remotely managing harbour cargo-handling equipment in Panama have already demonstrated that women have an important contribution to make to the ports of the future" (Safety4sea.com, 2019).

The shipping industry is becoming highly digitalized and automated, with many ship and port systems and components linked on the Internet. Future expansion will require new and higher skills from seafarers, according to the newly redefined roles they will need to assume, both on board and ashore, in order to ensure the safety of vessels and efficiency of operations (Hamburg School of Business Administration, 2018). With less physically strenuous tasks and more information technology skills and knowledge required, there may be increased opportunities for women to actively pursue a career in the maritime sector.

Supporting action at the international level by United Nations agencies and other bodies

The need to promote gender equality has long been recognized within the maritime industry, as evidenced by studies, reports and activities of various relevant bodies, and political action has been taken at various international forums to support women in the industry.

As a specialized body responsible for the safety and security of shipping and the prevention of marine and atmospheric pollution by ships, IMO, through its Technical Cooperation Committee, has approved a number of strategies for the advancement of women in the maritime sector, placing gender as a common agenda topic throughout shipping industry organizations. Since 1988, IMO has developed and implements a gender programme to promote the advancement of women in the maritime industry. Today, the programme, called Women in Maritime, helps put in place an institutional framework to incorporate a gender dimension into IMO policies and procedures, and supports access to maritime training and employment opportunities for women in the maritime sector. Over the years, the programme has helped women reach leadership positions in the maritime sector and bring a much-needed gender balance to the industry by giving them access to high-level technical training (www.imo.org/en/MediaCentre/HotTopics/women/Pages/default.aspx). In addition, the advancement of women is being supported and promoted through the development of human and institutional resources in the maritime sector in the framework of the Integrated Technical Cooperation Programme (www.imo.org/en/OurWork/TechnicalCooperation/ITCP/Pages/Default.aspx), which aims to assist developing countries in building up their human and institutional capacities for uniform and effective compliance with the IMO regulatory framework. An international regulatory measure demonstrating awareness on issues of women seafarers was the adoption in 2010 of the Manila Amendment to the International Convention on Standards of Training, Certification and Watch keeping for Seafarers, 1978, which included a resolution (No. 14) on the promotion of the participation of women in the maritime industry.

For the last two decades, the International Labour Organization has actively promoted the participation of women on board vessels. For instance, according to a 2003 study (International Labour Organization, 2003), a great advantage of having women aboard ships is that it creates a more normal social environment. Seafaring has traditionally not been viewed as a career for women; however, promoting and facilitating their increased participation could address the issue of seafarer shortages. In addition, the responsibilities of shipowners towards women seafarers were reflected in the Maritime Labour Convention, 2006. Flag States that ratify the convention must ensure that separate sleeping rooms and separate sanitary facilities for men and women are available on vessels. Other relevant conventions are the International Labour Organization Maternity Protection Convention, 2000 (No. 183), as well as the Convention on the Elimination of All Forms of Discrimination against Women, 1979.

An International Labour Organization sectoral meeting on the recruitment and retention of seafarers and the promotion of opportunities for women seafarers, held in Geneva, Switzerland, in February 2019, recognized that the sustainability of the shipping sector "depends on the ability to continue to attract a sufficient number of quality new entrants and retain experienced seafarers, including women seafarers and other underrepresented groups. This calls for a creative approach involving the social partners and all relevant stakeholders to achieve both meaningful and viable solutions" (International Labour Organization, 2019c). Encouraging and facilitating a more diverse and inclusive workplace benefits all seafarers. Highlighting the importance of equal opportunities and treatment of seafarers, including women seafarers, the meeting conclusions reiterated that prohibition of discrimination in employment and occupation, one of the fundamental principles and rights at work of the International Labour Organization, should be treated in a holistic manner and address diversity as a whole. All seafarers, regardless of race, colour, sex, religion, political opinion, national extraction or social origin, nationality, gender and sexual orientation, have the right to equal opportunities and treatment.

With regard to women seafarers in particular, it is recognized that a one-size-fits-all approach to combat discrimination is not realistic since there are notable differences in the life at sea of women across different types of ships, cultures and different trading patterns; publications, job advertisements and other information produced by shipowners and others are not always adopted to attract both women and men seafarers; ensuring diversity in the hiring of seafarers is difficult – although in many cases women graduate with excellent results in areas of science, technology, engineering and math subjects, sometimes they see their job applications being turned down systematically; mandatory pregnancy testing as part of the pre-employment medical examination of seafarers is a concern for many women seafarers and may be discriminatory. The issue requires further research and deliberation among interested parties in the maritime industry and medical experts. The meeting recommended that the International Labour Organization conduct a study that would include statistical research and an analysis of the numbers and distribution of women seafarers within the industry, identify the positions and sectors they work in and examine the legislation member States have in place to ensure non-discriminatory access to employment and equal opportunities and to highlight examples of best practice. It also recommended that the Organization carry out a review of the international labour standards related to the maritime sector with the aim of identifying biased language to address and promote diversity and inclusion (International Labour Organization, 2019c).

Other important achievements of the International Labour Organization affecting women seafarers, who often face harassment in the workplace, are the Convention Concerning the Elimination of Violence and Harassment in the World of Work, 2019 and the Recommendation Concerning the Elimination of Violence and Harassment in the World of Work, 2019, adopted by delegates on 21 June 2019, at the conclusion of the Centenary International Labour Conference, in Geneva (www.ilo.org/ilc/ILCSessions/108/media-centre/news/WCMS_711321/lang--en/index.htm). The Convention recognizes that violence and harassment in the world of work "can constitute a human rights violation or abuse… is a threat to equal opportunities, is unacceptable and incompatible with decent work". It defines violence and harassment as behaviours, practices or threats "that aim at, result in, or are likely to result in physical, psychological, sexual or economic harm". It recalls that member States have a responsibility to promote a "general environment of zero tolerance". The Convention will enter into force 12 months after ratification by two member States.

And finally, the global 2019 theme for International Women's Day was "Think equal, build smart, innovate for change" – focusing on innovative ways in which gender equality and the empowerment of women can be advanced in support of Sustainable Development Goal 5, Achieve gender equality and empower all women and girls. In the same vein, IMO in 2019 selected "Empowering women in the maritime community" as the theme of World Maritime Day, providing an opportunity to raise awareness of the importance of gender equality, in line with the Sustainable Development Goals, and to highlight the important contribution of women all over the world to the maritime sector.

Further, IMO has been working with maritime stakeholders towards achieving the Sustainable Development Goals,

particularly Goal 5, to help create an environment in which women are identified and selected for career development opportunities in maritime administrations and in ports and maritime training institutes and to encourage more dialogue for gender equality in the maritime space. IMO supports gender equality and the empowerment of women by granting gender-specific fellowships; by facilitating access to high-level technical training for women in the maritime sector in developing countries; by creating an environment in which women are identified and selected for career development opportunities in maritime administrations, ports and maritime training institutes; and by helping to establish professional women in maritime associations, particularly in developing countries (www.imo.org/en/OurWork/TechnicalCooperation/Pages/WomenInMaritime.aspx). In this context, the need for stronger partnerships and cooperation between the public and private sectors cannot be overemphasized.

Women's empowerment is also promoted by the Women's International Shipping and Trading Association, a networking body established in 1974 that aims to attract and support women at the management level in the maritime, trading and logistics sectors. The Association is currently supported in 45 countries by national embodiments of the Association, striving to empower "women to lead, through their unique perspective and competencies", based on the conviction that "gender diversity is key in providing a sustainable future for the shipping industry internationally" (https://wistainternational.com/).

D. STATUS OF CONVENTIONS

A number of international conventions in the field of maritime transport were prepared or adopted under the auspices of UNCTAD. Table 4.1 provides information on the status of ratification of each of those conventions as at 31 July 2019.

Table 4.1 Contracting States Parties to selected international conventions on maritime transport, as at 31 July 2019

Title of convention	Date of entry into force or conditions for entry into force	Contracting States
Convention on a Code of Conduct for Liner Conferences, 1974	6 October 1983	Algeria, Bangladesh, Barbados, Belgium, Benin, Burkina Faso, Burundi, Cameroon, Cabo Verde, Central African Republic, Chile, China, Congo, Costa Rica, Côte d'Ivoire, Cuba, Czechia, Democratic Republic of the Congo, Egypt, Ethiopia, Finland, France, Gabon, Gambia, Ghana, Guatemala, Guinea, Guyana, Honduras, India, Indonesia, Iraq, Italy, Jamaica, Jordan, Kenya, Kuwait, Lebanon, Liberia, Madagascar, Malaysia, Mali, Mauritania, Mauritius, Mexico, Montenegro, Morocco, Mozambique, Niger, Nigeria, Norway, Pakistan, Peru, Philippines, Portugal, Qatar, Republic of Korea, Romania, Russian Federation, Saudi Arabia, Senegal, Serbia, Sierra Leone, Slovakia, Somalia, Spain, Sri Lanka, Sudan, Sweden, Togo, Trinidad and Tobago, Tunisia, United Republic of Tanzania, Uruguay, Bolivarian Republic of Venezuela, Zambia **(76)**
United Nations Convention on the Carriage of Goods by Sea, 1978	1 November 1992	Albania, Austria, Barbados, Botswana, Burkina Faso, Burundi, Cameroon, Chile, Czechia, Dominican Republic, Egypt, Gambia, Georgia, Guinea, Hungary, Jordan, Kazakhstan, Kenya, Lebanon, Lesotho, Liberia, Malawi, Morocco, Nigeria, Paraguay, Romania, Saint Vincent and the Grenadines, Senegal, Sierra Leone, Syrian Arab Republic, Tunisia, Uganda, United Republic of Tanzania, Zambia **(34)**
International Convention on Maritime Liens and Mortgages, 1993	5 September 2004	Albania, Benin, Congo, Ecuador, Estonia, Honduras, Lithuania, Monaco, Nigeria, Peru, Russian Federation, Spain, Saint Kitts and Nevis, Saint Vincent and the Grenadines, Serbia, Syrian Arab Republic, Tunisia, Ukraine, Vanuatu **(19)**
United Nations Convention on International Multimodal Transport of Goods, 1980	Not yet in force – requires 30 contracting parties	Burundi, Chile, Georgia, Lebanon, Liberia, Malawi, Mexico, Morocco, Rwanda, Senegal, Zambia **(11)**
United Nations Convention on Conditions for Registration of Ships, 1986	Not yet in force – requires 40 Contracting Parties, representing at least 25 per cent of the world's tonnage as per annex III to the Convention	Albania, Bulgaria, Côte d'Ivoire, Egypt, Georgia, Ghana, Haiti, Hungary, Iraq, Liberia, Libya, Mexico, Morocco, Oman, Syrian Arab Republic **(15)**
International Convention on Arrest of Ships, 1999	14 September 2011	Albania, Algeria, Benin, Bulgaria, Congo, Ecuador, Estonia, Latvia, Liberia, Spain, Syrian Arab Republic **(11)**

Note: For additional information, see UNCTAD Transport and Policy Legislation at unctad.org/ttl/legal. For official status information, see the United Nations Treaty Collection, available at https://treaties.un.org.

E. SUMMARY, OUTLOOK AND RELATED POLICY CONSIDERATIONS

Players in the shipping industry are increasingly taking advantage of digitalization and joint collaborative platforms and solutions enabled by new technologies and innovations, including blockchain, thus changing their business and partnership models. These aim to promote efficient and secure trade, including by offering greater supply chain visibility and the use of electronic documents, ultimately benefiting customers who rely on shipping industry services.

Importantly, autonomous ships, or maritime autonomous surface ships – the general term for autonomous ships used at IMO – may soon become a reality, promising to provide enhanced cost savings and safety by removing the human element from certain operations. However, before they start to be fully used in commercial operations, the technology needs to be proven. With regard to the effects on the work of the seafarers, it appears that the further introduction of automation will also create a demand for new types of jobs, such as remote operators, maintenance crews and service providers. As a result, the demand for labour will not completely disappear, but the requirements and skills needed for individual jobs will change, for example, there may be an increase in shore-based jobs and crew reductions on board vessels. Recent international regulatory developments in respect of maritime autonomous surface ships include an ongoing scoping exercise, initiated at the IMO in 2017. The exercise focuses on the review of relevant legal instruments to ensure the safe design, construction and operation of autonomous ships and to guarantee that the legal framework provides the same levels of protection to autonomous ships as for operations with traditional ships. Further, the scoping exercise would benefit from the participation and contribution of all countries, including developing countries.

With respect to environmentally sustainable shipping and the oceans, international regulatory developments at relevant international bodies during the period under review continued to contribute towards the implementation of the 2030 Agenda for Sustainable Development, the Paris Agreement under the United Nations Framework Convention on Climate Change and the Sendai Framework for Disaster Risk Reduction 2015–2030, which collectively provide the foundation for sustainable, low-carbon and resilient development in a changing climate. Important developments worth noting include the Katowice climate package, adopted at the twenty-fourth session of the Conference to the Parties to the United Nations Framework Convention on Climate Change, which aims to promote international cooperation and encourage greater ambition for implementing the Paris Agreement; the Climate Action Summit convened by the Secretary-General of the United Nations in September 2019 to boost political and economic efforts to strengthen climate action and ambition globally; ongoing work at IMO towards setting emissions reduction targets consistent with the Paris Agreement; and the initiation of the fourth IMO study on greenhouse gas.

Various examples concerning the interlinkages between oceans, sustainable development and climate change mitigation and adaptation are worth noting. For example, the call to global climate action made by civil society and industry leaders at the Global Climate Action Summit 2018 suggests that countries increase specific and meaningful ocean-related content in their 2020 submissions of nationally determined contributions and in their adaptation communications. The need to recognize that ocean science will be key in developing effective measures for the purposes of coastal protection and coastal zone management, as well as for climate-risk assessment, adaptation and resilience-building for seaports and other coastal transport infrastructure, will become particularly relevant in the context of the United Nations Decade of Ocean Science for Sustainable Development (2021–2030). This is a matter of concern for developing countries, in particular small island developing States.

A number of important regulatory issues include the following: the required implementation of the new lower 0.50 per cent limit (from 3.50 per cent currently) on sulphur content in ships' fuel oil, applicable globally, as of 1 January 2020 – expected to bring positive results for human health and the environment; and the adoption of an additional amendment to MARPOL 73/78, entering into force on 1 March 2020, which will prohibit not just the use but also the carriage of non-compliant fuel oil for combustion purposes for propulsion or operation on board a ship – unless the ship is fitted with a scrubber. Enforcement, compliance with and monitoring of the new sulphur limit is the responsibility of States party to MARPOL 73/78, annex VI. Ships found not in compliance, may be detained by port State control inspectors, and/or sanctions may be imposed for violations.

As regards other ship-source pollution issues, the Ballast Water Management Convention, 2004 concentrates on its effective and uniform implementation, and on an associated experience-building phase, with emphasis on gathering data on its application. As of July 2019, the International Convention on Liability and Compensation for Damage in Connection with the Carriage of Hazardous and Noxious Substances by Sea, 1996, as amended by its 2010 Protocol, had been ratified by five States, bringing it closer to its entry into force. With the number of ships carrying hazardous and noxious substances cargoes growing steadily, and more than 200 million tons of chemicals traded annually, other countries, including developing countries, are encouraged to consider becoming parties to it as well, thus helping close an important gap in the global liability and compensation framework.

Plastic pollution is a serious environmental concern, directly affecting the sustainable development aspirations of developing countries, in particular small island developing States, which are disproportionately affected by the effects of such pollution. Plastic pollution management is a global transboundary environmental issue that needs to be regulated internationally. Given that there are no existing international legal instruments that are specifically designed to prevent increasing plastic pollution or to comprehensively manage the current pollution levels, a possible way forward may be to strengthen current efforts and focus on each aspect of the lifecycle of plastics, while combining voluntary and binding measures to address the issue.

Marine genetic resources from areas beyond national jurisdiction are also a priority for developing countries, given the economic value that can be generated from their exploitation and the potential development of economic activities in coastal and offshore areas. Therefore, the conservation and sustainable use of marine biodiversity of these areas is important. An intergovernmental conference on an international legally binding instrument on the issue is under way. However, agreement still remains to be reached about a number of important issues. In order for a meaningful consensus to be achieved, it will be important for developing countries, and small island developing States in particular, to actively participate in the international negotiations towards the establishment of a new legal instrument.

Regarding the growing problem of fraudulent ship registration and registries, the IMO Legal Committee in March 2019 agreed on a series of measures to prevent unlawful practices associated with the fraudulent registration and fraudulent registries of ships and approved recommended best practices to assist in combating them. As noted by IMO, UNCTAD and other participants in the Committee's deliberations, addressing fraudulent practices effectively is vital to promoting maritime safety, security and environmental protection.

The attainment of equality between women and men, and the elimination of all forms of discrimination against women are fundamental human rights and United Nations values. While there may be various challenges and barriers in the maritime industry that hinder the ability of women to pursue careers in shipping, the gender gap in the industry also needs to be addressed. Gender equality should be further promoted through political and legal action at the international level, accompanied by corresponding action at the national level.

An important achievement of the International Labour Organization, which is also relevant to women seafarers who often face harassment at the workplace, is the Violence and Harassment Convention, 2019, and its related recommendation, which among others, reminds member States that they have a responsibility to promote a "general environment of zero tolerance".

As the shipping industry embraces digitalization and automation, new and higher skills will be required from seafarers, according to the new redefined roles they will need to assume, both on board and ashore, in order to ensure the safety of vessels and efficiency of operations. Women may enjoy increased opportunities to pursue a maritime career, given that less physically strenuous tasks, combined with the need for more information technology skills and knowledge, are being required in the maritime sector.

REFERENCES

Asariotis R, Benamara H and Mohos-Naray V (2017). Port industry survey on climate change impacts and adaptation. Research Paper No. 18. UNCTAD.

BIMCO (2016). BIMCO/ICS [International Chamber of Shipping] manpower report predicts potential shortage of almost 150,000 officers by 2025. 17 May.

Blasiak R, Jouffray J-G, Wabnitz CCC, Sundström E and Österblom H (2018). Corporate control and global governance of marine genetic resources. Science Advances. 4(6).

Finska L (2018). Did the latest resolution on marine plastic litter and microplastics take us any closer to pollution-free oceans? 10 January. Available at https://site.uit.no/jclos/2018/01/10/did-the-latest-resolution-on-marine-plastic-litter-and-microplastics-take-us-any-closer-to-pollution-free-oceans/ (accessed 23 September 2019).

Fjærli BAB, Nazir S and Øvergård KI (2017). Gender bias in the perception of outstanding leadership in the maritime industry. In: Kantola JI, Barath T, Nazir S and Andre T, eds. Advances in Human Factors, Business Management, Training and Education. Springer International Publishing. Chaim, Switzerland:359–369.

García B, Fang MM and Lin J (2019). All hands on deck: Addressing the global marine plastics pollution crisis in Asia. Working Paper No. 2. Asia–Pacific Centre for Environmental Law.

Hamburg School of Business Administration (2018). *Seafarers and Digital Disruption: The Effect of Autonomous Ships on the Work at Sea, the Role of Seafarers and the Shipping Industry*. International Chamber of Shipping. Hamburg, Germany, and London.

IMO (2014). Report of the Marine Environment Protection Committee on its sixty-fifth session. MEPC 65/22. London. 24 May.

IMO (2016). *Review of the Current State of Knowledge Regarding Marine Litter in Wastes Dumped at Sea under the London Convention and Protocol: Final Report*. London.

IMO (2017a). Report of the first meeting of the Intersessional Working Group on Reduction of GHG[greenhouse gas] emissions from ships. MEPC 71/WP.5. London. 30 June.

IMO (2017b). Report of the second meeting of the Intersessional Working Group on Reduction of GHG[greenhouse gas] emissions from ships. MEPC 72/7. London. 3 November.

IMO (2017c). Guidelines for the implementation of MARPOL Annex V. Resolution MEPC.295(71). London. 7 July.

IMO (2018a). Regulatory scoping exercise for the use of maritime autonomous surface ships: Comments and proposals on the way forward for the regulatory scoping exercise. MSC 99/5/1. London. 22 February.

IMO (2018b). Report of the Maritime Safety Committee on its 100th session. MSC 100/20. London. 10 January.

IMO (2018c). Report of the Working Group on Reduction of greenhouse gas emissions from ships. MEPC 72/WP.7. London.

IMO (2018d). Report of the Marine Environment Protection Committee on its seventy-third session. MEPC 73/19. London. 26 October.

IMO (2019a). Report of the Maritime Safety Committee on its 101st session. MSC 101/24. London. 12 July.

IMO (2019b). Report of the Legal Committee on the work of its 106th session. LEG 106/16. London. 13 May.

IMO (2019c). Regulatory scoping exercise and gap analysis of conventions emanating from the Legal Committee with respect to maritime autonomous surface ships. LEG 106/WP.5. London. 29 March.

IMO (2019d). Draft report of the Marine Environmental Protection Committee on its seventy-fourth session. MEPC 74/WP.1. London. 17 May.

Independent (2018). Cleaner shipping fuels could prevent hundreds of thousands of emissions-related deaths, finds new study. 6 February. Available at https://www.independent.co.uk/environment/cleaner-shipping-fuels-deaths-emissions-related-save-lives-illness-study-asthma-a8197581.html (accessed 4 October 2019).

Intergovernmental Panel on Climate Change (2018). Special report: Global warming of 1.5°C. Available at www.ipcc.ch/sr15/ (accessed 4 October 2019).

International Institute for Sustainable Development Reporting Services (2019a). Summary of the Second Session of the Intergovernmental Conference on an International Legally Binding Instrument under the United Nations

Convention on the Law of the Sea on the Conservation and Sustainable Use of Marine Biodiversity of Areas Beyond National Jurisdiction, 25 March–5 April 2019. Earth Negotiations Bulletin. 25(195).

International Institute for Sustainable Development Reporting Services (2019b). Summary of the Third Session of the Intergovernmental Conference on the Conservation and Sustainable Use of Marine Biodiversity of Areas Beyond National Jurisdiction, 19–30 August 2019. Earth Negotiations Bulletin. 25(218).

International Labour Organization (2003). *Women seafarers: Fighting against the tide? World of Work*. 49:14–16.

International Labour Organization (2017). *World Employment and Social Outlook: Trends for Women 2017*. Geneva.

International Labour Organization (2019a). *World Employment and Social Outlook: Trends 2019*. Geneva.

International Labour Organization (2019b). *Women in Business and Management: The Business Case for Change.* Geneva.

International Labour Organization (2019c). Conclusions on the recruitment and retention of seafarers and the promotion of opportunities for women seafarers. SMSWS/2019/9. Geneva. 1 March.

International Maritime Health Association, International Seafarers' Welfare and Assistance Network, International Transport Workers' Federation and Seafarers Hospital Society (2015). Women seafarers' health and welfare survey. Available at www.seafarerswelfare.org/our-work/women-seafarers-health-and-welfare-survey (accessed 4 October 2019).

International Transport Workers' Federation (2019). *Transport 2040: Automation, Technology, Employment – The Future of Work*. World Maritime University. London.

Kitada M and Tansey P (2018). Impacts of CSR[corporate social responsibility] on women in the maritime sector. In: LL Froholdt, ed. *Corporate Social Responsibility in the Maritime Industry*. Springer International Publishing. Chaim, Switzerland:237–251.

Microsoft.com (2018). Why do girls lose interest in STEM[science, technology, engineering and math]? New research has some answers – and what we can do about it. 13 March. Available at https://news.microsoft.com/features/why-do-girls-lose-interest-in-stem-new-research-has-some-answers-and-what-we-can-do-about-it/ (accessed 4 October 2019).

Monioudi I, Asariotis R, Becker A, Bhat C, Dowding-Gooden D, Esteban M, Feyen L, Mentaschi L, Nikolaou A, Nurse L, Phillips W, Smith D, Satoh M, Trotz U, Velegrakis A, Voukouvalas E, Vousdoukas M and Witkop R (2018). Climate change impacts on critical international transportation assets of Caribbean small island developing States: The case of Jamaica and Saint Lucia. *Regional Environmental Change*. 18:2211–2225.

Norwegian Academy of International Law (2018). The case for a treaty on marine plastic pollution. Available at http://intlaw.no/en/nail-policy-papers/the-case-for-a-treaty-on-marine-plastic-pollution/ (accessed 4 October 2019).

Ostry JD, Alvarez J, Espinoza RA and Papageorgiou C (2018). Economic gains from gender inclusion: New mechanisms, new evidence. Staff Discussion Note No. 6. International Monetary Fund.

Pike K, Broadhurst E, Zhao M, Zhang P, Kuje A and Oluoha N (2017). The gender empowerment and multi-cultural crew project summary, 2015–2016 for the ITF[International Transport Workers' Federation] seafarers' trust. Southampton Solent University.

Port Technology (2019). Digital association of major carriers officially formed. 16 April. Available at www.porttechnology.org/news/digital_association_of_major_carriers_officially_formed (accessed 4 October 2019).

Safety4sea.com (2019). IAPH[International Association of Ports and Harbours] launches women in ports mentoring programme. 5 April. Available at https://safety4sea.com/iaph-launches-women-in-ports-mentoring-program/ (accessed 4 October 2019).

Spinnaker Global (2019). Gender diversity in maritime. 20 February. Available at https://spinnaker-global.com/Blog/Details/0_20-Feb-2019_gender-diversity-in-maritime (accessed 4 October 2019).

Splash 247 (2019). Digital Container Shipping Association welcomes five more carriers. 14 May. Available at https://splash247.com/digital-container-shipping-association-welcomes-five-more-carriers/ (accessed 4 October 2019).

The Guardian (2018). "Window is narrowing": Scientists urge action at UN[United Nations] climate talks. 11 December.

The National Academies Press (2010). *Ocean Acidification: A National Strategy to Meet the Challenges of a Changing Ocean*. National Academy of Sciences. Washington, D.C. Available at www.nap.edu/read/12904/chapter/1 (accessed 4 October 2019).

The Pew Charitable Trusts (2018). The push to safeguard 30 per cent of the ocean: Marine protected areas are essential to achieve full sustainability. 31 October.

UNCTAD (2011a). *Review of Maritime Transport 2011* (United Nations publication. Sales No. E.11.II.D.4. New York and Geneva).

UNCTAD (2011b). The 2004 Ballast Water Management Convention – with international acceptance growing, the Convention may soon enter into force. In: Transport Newsletter No. 50.

UNCTAD (2012a). *Review of Maritime Transport 2012* (United Nations publication. Sales No. E.12.II.D.17. New York and Geneva).

UNCTAD (2012b). *Liability and Compensation for Ship-source Oil Pollution: An Overview of the International Legal Framework for Oil Pollution Damage from Tankers* (United Nations publication. New York and Geneva).

UNCTAD (2013). *Review of Maritime Transport 2013* (United Nations publication. Sales No. E.13.II.D.9. New York and Geneva).

UNCTAD (2014). Closing the Distance: Partnerships for Sustainable and Resilient Transport Systems in SIDS[small island developing States].

UNCTAD (2015). The International Ballast Water Management Convention 2004 is set to enter into force in 2016. In: Transport and Trade Facilitation Newsletter No. 68.

UNCTAD (2018a). *Review of Maritime Transport 2018* (United Nations publication. Sales No. E.18.II.D.5. New York and Geneva.

UNCTAD (2018b). Risk to trade if ports not climate change proofed. 7 December. Available at https://unctad.org/en/pages/newsdetails.aspx?OriginalVersionID=1949 (accessed 4 October 2019).

UNCTAD (2018c). 2018 demonstrates extreme weather's impact on development. 31 August. Available at https://unctad.org/en/pages/newsdetails.aspx?OriginalVersionID=1840 (accessed 4 October 2019).

UNCTAD (2018d). Economic challenges lie ahead as climate change wreaks havoc. 17 October. Available at https://unctad.org/en/pages/newsdetails.aspx?OriginalVersionID=1882 (accessed 4 October 2019).

UNCTAD (2018e). Conservation and sustainable use of marine biodiversity of areas beyond national jurisdiction: Recent legal developments. 29 October. Available at https://unctad.org/en/pages/newsdetails.aspx?OriginalVersionID=1905 (accessed 4 October 2019).

UNCTAD (2019). Making digital platforms work for development. Policy Brief No. 73.

United Nations (2019a). *World Economic Situation and Prospects* (Sales No. E.19.II.C.1. New York).

United Nations (2019b). *World Population Prospects 2019: Highlights* (Sales No. E.19.XIII.4. New York).

United Nations (2019c). Draft text of an agreement under the United Nations Convention on the Law of the Sea on the conservation and sustainable use of marine biological diversity of areas beyond national jurisdiction. A/CONF.232/2019/6. New York. 17 May.

United Nations (2019d). New oceans treaty must be robust, practical in application, delegates stress, closing third round of marine biodiversity negotiations. 30 August. Available at www.un.org/press/en/2019/sea2118.doc.htm (accessed 4 October 2019).

UNEP (2016a). The first global integrated marine assessment: World ocean assessment. Available at www.unenvironment.org/resources/report/first-global-integrated-marine-assessment-world-ocean-assessment-i (accessed 4 October 2019).

UNEP (2016b). Decision adopted by the Conference of the Parties to the Convention on Biological diversity: Addressing impacts of marine debris and anthropogenic underwater noise on marine and coastal biodiversity. CBD/COP/DEC/XIII/10. Cancun, Mexico. 10 December

UNEP (2017). Combating marine plastic litter and microplastics: An assessment of the effectiveness of relevant international, regional and subregional governance strategies and approaches. UNEP/EA.3/INF/5. Nairobi. 15 February.

UNEP (2018a). Possible options under the Basel Convention to further address marine plastic litter and microplastics. UNEP/AHEG/2018/1/INF/5. Nairobi. 22 May.

UNEP (2018b). Barriers to combating marine litter and microplastics, including challenges related to resources in developing countries. UNEP/AHEG/2018/1/2. Nairobi.

United Nations Framework Convention on Climate Change (2016). Report of the Conference of the Parties on its twenty-first session, held in Paris from 30 November to 13 December 2015, addendum part two: Action taken by the Conference of the Parties at its twenty-first session. FCCC/CP/2015/10/Add.1. Paris. 29 January.

United Nations Framework Convention on Climate Change (2018). New era of global climate action to begin under Paris climate change agreement. Press Release. 15 December. Available at https://unfccc.int/news/new-era-of-global-climate-action-to-begin-under-paris-climate-change-agreement-0 (accessed 4 October 2019).

World Bank (2018a). World Bank Group announces $200 billion over five years for climate action. 3 December. Available at www.worldbank.org/en/news/press-release/2018/12/03/world-bank-group-announces-200-billion-over-five-years-for-climate-action (accessed 4 October 2019).

World Bank (2018b). Multilateral development banks announced a joint framework for aligning their activities with the goals of the Paris Agreement. 3 December. Available at www.worldbank.org/en/news/press-release/2018/12/03/multilateral-development-banks-mdbs-announced-a-joint-framework-for-aligning-their-activities-with-the-goals-of-the-paris-agreement (accessed 4 October 2019).

World Economic Forum (2017). *The Global Gender Gap Report 2017*. Geneva.